A Second Look
Native Americans in Children's Books

by
Andie Peterson

Andie Peterson

authorHOUSE®

AuthorHouse™
1663 Liberty Drive, Suite 200
Bloomington, IN 47403
www.authorhouse.com
Phone: 1-800-839-8640

© *2007 Andie Peterson. All rights reserved.*

No part of this book may be reproduced, stored in a retrieval system, or transmitted by any means without the written permission of the author.

First published by AuthorHouse 10/11/2007

ISBN: 978-1-4343-3663-7 (sc)

Library of Congress Control Number: 2007907215

Printed in the United States of America
Bloomington, Indiana

This book is printed on acid-free paper.

To the memory of my parents Christian and Icel Anderson and in memory of my daughter, Colleen.

Acknowledgements

I am grateful to the following people for sharing their wisdom with me. Any errors are completely mine and mine alone.

A Second Look was built upon the contributions of the Grand Portage Band of Lake Superior Chippewa. Their willingness to share was phenomenal. Over the years, many people have contributed their ideas, thoughts, and judgments concerning children's literature and its effect on Native children as well as the impact on the non-Native child.

I am especially indebted to Dr. Robert Powless, Ruth Myers, and Nora Hakala. Their patience in sharing their experiences, opinions, and questions was extraordinary.

How do I say thanks to all the staff and students at the Grand Portage Elementary School and the Grand Portage Tribal Council? I am so grateful to all of you who shared feelings about life and books. To the students who wrote letters to various entities asking questions I offer my heartfelt gratitude.

Others who helped this project are the tribal leaders, historical societies, librarians, and staff of state and national parks who responded to my personal visits, letters of inquiry, and phone calls regarding customs, language, and culture of the specific Nation. They were all so kind and helpful. It was extraordinary.

I'd also like to thank the authors of the books that are true treasures for Native children.

And always - thank you to my family.

Miigwech.

A Second Look

Being young is never uncomplicated. On a daily basis, children must face the hidden curriculum that lets them know where they fit in, whether they can achieve their goals, whether they even dare to dream. An overwhelming part of that hidden curriculum begins with books that are more than narrative and illustrations; they are books that carry a message of politics and values.

At times, there is a collective denial that allows damaging books to remain on the shelves. Censorship becomes an issue when trying to remove hurtful books from schools and public libraries. No one wants to be the censor. It must be noted, however, that anyone who orders books for an institution is already in the role of censor. Someone decides which books will be on the shelves and which books will be denied readership simply with the marks on the order form.

Putting more books on the shelves about Native people is not an antidote if those books are toxic. Whenever an order goes in for a Lynn Reid Banks book or a Virginia Grossman/Sylvia Long book and the books by Paul Goble and Joseph Bruchac are overlooked, that is censorship of an institutional kind.

Some people have asked why I chose to review books that have old copyright dates. One reason is that many of those books are still on library shelves and available through book stores and Internet sources.

It also helps to view older books to understand how adults have formed ideas about Native people. When a child continually reads negative passages regarding Native people, it sets in motion attitudes of prejudice that persists for years.

A conscious decision was made by many elementary schools in Minnesota to not use the state textbook, **Minnesota, Star of the North,** by Ford and Johnson. I have included the review of that text in this book.

Four-hundred-twenty-five books have been reviewed in **A Second Look.** I chose to review a number of books from different time periods because at various workshops I've taught people asked for examples. Participants in the workshops wanted something concrete that they could take back to their school districts or public libraries. If you want to remove a book from circulation and have to explain the rationale, it helps to have an opinion in writing.

Should books be removed from circulation? Absolutely. What good was served by the textbook, **Minnesota, Star of the North**? How will reading **Ten Little Rabbits** give a child anything, but a distorted view of Native life? Removing the books doesn't mean they have to be banished. Some of the books can be dispatched to the reference section of a library to be available for analysis.

It is the intent of this bibliography to give teachers, librarians, administrators, and parents a guide to use in selecting books for children. I have read the books at least twice, some of them I've read many times.

Assigning a grade level to each book is somewhat arbitrary. Children may read on one level, but comprehend on a different level. Books that appear to be simple reading may actually be appropriate for all ages. Conversely, many of the books that would seem too difficult for certain ages are quite useful when read aloud.

The impact of negative images in books on all children is substantial. It's time to disturb the peace and end the ritual of damage.

A Lesson from the Elders of the Hopi Nation

The Story of the Children's Fire was left in my mailbox at school. The only author noted was the Elders of the Hopi Nation.

"The whole community sits around a circle called A Medicine Wheel. Around the wheel are represented all the different aspects of the community. In the east, there's the fool. In the west, there's the wizard. In the south, there's a hunter. In the north, there's the creator. There's also the shaman, the politician, and so on, all the way around the circle and in the center, there's the children's fire. Next to the children's fire, there's the Grandfather and Grandmother. If you want to build a condominium on Spirit Lake, you have to enter the medicine wheel in the place of the east, the fool. The question is, may I build a condo on Spirit Lake? Then the fool takes your question, turns it around backwards and asks, what would Spirit Lake say about such a condo? You have to take the question the fool gives you all the way around the medicine wheel and ask each position. Each will respond to you according to their position. And then the last people you must ask the question of are the Grandmother and the Grandfather who guard the children's fire. If these two decide that it's not good for the children's fire, then the answer is no. They are the only ones in the circle who have veto power. The concept of the ultimate question is simple: does it hurt or help the children's fire. If it is not good for the children, for the future, then it cannot be done."

First, Let's Examine a Minnesota Textbook

Minnesota, Star of the North was the textbook approved for teaching Minnesota history to sixth graders. It was written by Antoinette E. Ford and Neoma Johnson and published by Lyons and Carnahan in 1963. It was used in Minnesota schools for many years.

Attitudes of a whole generation of students was filled with the stereotypes and negativity in this textbook. Sixth grade students in the 1960s and early 1970s are now in their forties and fifties. Measuring the impact of this textbook on adult attitudes is not quantifiable. I will let the book speak for itself. All quotes are directly taken from the text.

"The Sioux called themselves Dakotas, which meant allies; but the Chippewas called them by a long name, which they also applied to a snake or to anything they hated greatly. The last part of this long name was "sioux"; and the French traders, to avoid exciting the attention of the Indians while talking before them, used names which were not recognized."

"The Sioux were expert horsemen, living largely on the prairies. They were taller and were quicker in their movements; but the Chippewas, living in the forests, were wonderful woodsmen and had greater strength and endurance."

"There are many reminders of the red men still with us, the most common being the many beautiful Indian names." Red men is a term used throughout the book in reference to the Native people of Minnesota.

In reference to the hunting of the buffalo by Native people: "Since such numbers were killed, it is no wonder that the buffalo is no longer found roaming our plains." There is no mention that the buffalo were almost lost because they were slaughtered for sport by Europeans.

In reference to the treading of the wild rice hulls: "Stange to say, this was always done by a man; and some say that this is the only kind of work which a male Indian was ever known to do."

"With game and fish, together with wild rice, corn and berries, there was quite an attractive as well as a healthful variety in the red man's food."

"As the harvest time for the wild rice draws near, one may see an Indian family bound for the rice marshes in an old wagon drawn by a hungry looking horse. The picture is stranger yet when a battered old Ford is substituted for the horse and wagon."

In regard to Pipestone in the southwestern corner of the state, "To the Indians of North America this spot was the center of the world, as they believed their race started here."

In response to Radisson and Groseillier attempting to get the "Indians" to go with them to transport beaver skins, the Indians "refused to go." "The two Frenchmen used all their eloquence, begging and threatening the Indians. Finally Radisson pulled a beaver skin from the shoulders of one of the Indians and beat him with it. He called him a coward and said that if they would not come with him, he and Groseilliers would go alone. The brave young Frenchman so impressed the Indians that he gained his point."

"Father Hennepin gave Lake Pepin the name of 'Lake of Tears' because here the Indians who wished to kill him and his friends wept all night, to induce the others to consent to their death."

Later, when Father Hennepin was involved in a situation, he was told that "it was a striking blow to France, to suffer such an insult from a savage people."

"Sometimes he hunted with the red men."

Throughtout the text, Native people are referred to as red men, savages, or Indians and rarely with tribal identity.

"This reminds one of Captain Miles Standish, who with an equally small army, had awed the savages in a similar manner nearly two hundred years before in the old town of Plymouth, Massachusetts."

"From the time of his arrival at Fort Snelling, Taliaferro fought the whisky traffic among the Indians just as Duluth had done years before."

In reference to the traders who continually broke the law concerning selling liquor to the Indians, it is said: "They claimed that they had to furnish the Indian with 'firewater' or lose their trade."

"As the boat approached the Indians stood in speechless crowds on the shore, placing their hands over their mouths. This was their usual way of expressing astonishment. As the huge monster advanced against the current, they thought it some enormous water god, puffing out its hot breath and spouting water in every direction. A salute was fired from the fort. When the boat began to blow off steam, it was like the unbottling of an earthquake. Squaws forgot their children and with streaming hair ran for safety. Even the stoutest braves, contrary to their usual quiet habits, shook with terror and scampered away like frightened deer. In a twinkling every redskin had vanished into the woods, screaming and shouting."

"Near the lake they saw fine cornfields which had been cultivated by Indian squaws."

In reference to Yellow Head Point, it was "named for Schoolcraft's trusty Indian guide."

"The post also marks the warpath of the Sioux and Ojibways or Chippewa in the seventeenth century. The mounds which we see were made by the Sioux before they were driven out by the war-like Chippewas."

No one had settled the land "except for Indians."

"The Indians were glad to give four muskrat skins, valued at eighty cents, for little mirrors, which cost four cents."

In visiting the Sibley house, "The steep stairs led down from the kitchen; many an Indian had used them." Still in the Sibley house, "We see a real Indian canoe and many other reminders of Indian life. And here is a portrait of that good Indian, John Other Day, who saved the lives of many white people during the dreadful Sioux Massacre."

"Unfortunately, the little Indians, most of whom attended school wrapped in their blankets, were not very eager to learn."

Minnesota needed a seal and motto. "The first seal was not entirely satisfactory; so after Minnesota became a state, the design was changed to the one now in use. Examine the seal carefully, for it tells its story in very positive language. You can see a white man plowing the land where he now has made his home. Near him lie a powder horn and gun. An Indian is riding at full speed toward the setting sun; this means that the white man and civilization are here to stay and that the savage must go."

In 1850, Governor Ramsey gave a speech at an Indian council "for the purpose of settling the troubles between the Sioux and the Chippewas. He began his speech by telling the Indians…to settle their difficulties and bury the hatchet. Then he told them to leave off war and to learn that a bushel of potatoes was worth more to one who is hungry than a pile of eagle plumes. The white people, he said, had long before had the Indian notion about labor, but they now had changed."

When land was sold, trickery on the part of the whites was apparent, but the documents were signed. "The next day, $30,000, which had been set apart by a previous treaty, was given to the Lower Sioux. In the week following they crowded the streets of St. Paul with their sacks of money, spending it for anything they pleased. About $10,000 went for horses, many of which were good for nothing."

In speaking of the reservations that the "Sioux Indians…were supposed to live on…" "When you remember that for many years these savages had roamed the woods and plains wherever they wished, it is little wonder that the restraint of life on the reservations was very hard on them."

"Always lazy, the Indians depended on the food and clothing, as well as money, supplied by the government according to the terms of the treaties."

"Some of the Indians had become farmers and lived in houses like the whites, but many of the so-called 'blanket Indians' were as wild as ever and greatly discontented with their lot."

Regarding the "War with the Sioux" as one chapter is called: "On Sunday, August 17 a party of Sioux hunters stopped at a settler's cabin and without cause murdered five white people in cold blood."

"At heart Little Crow was a heathen Indian."

"The cannon proved too much for the savages, however, and after three hours of fighting, Little Crow called off his men."

Later, "The savages were again repulsed, discouraged by the fire from the barricade."

"Thirty-eight Indians were hanged at Mankato on December 26, 1862. Many people criticized the President for pardoning so many of the Sioux."

"On the morning of the execution the condemned men broke into a weird death song."

There is a workbook to accompany the textbook.

In one section of the workbook there are twenty words with a blank before each one. The students are instructed to "Write the letter S for Sioux and the letter C for Chippewa in front of the word or group of words, which apply to the correct Indian tribe.

Some of the words include: "expert horsemen, quicker in their movements, graceful, stronger, skilled woodsmen" and so on through the list.

One of the sections deals with "the Indian" before and after "the white men came among them."

There is also a part where the students must underline the correct answer. "Gardens were cared for by the (squaws, braves). The Indians' gardens were (large, small)."

Parts of the workbook ask for inferences to be made. "Explain clearly the following points. Explain why famines were quite common among the Indians. Explain several ways by which famines might have been prevented."

Suggestion of things to do include: "Teach an Indian dance to the class. Learn an Indian chant and sing it to the class."

One of the assignments is to explain the meaning of the words of Governor Ramsey when he said "…well-earned eagle feathers, showing the foes he had killed." " Now try to explain what Governor Ramsey meant when he told the Indians to stop war and to learn 'that a bushel of potatoes was worth more to one who is hungry than a pile of eagle plumes.' " The assignment clairfies, "Remember that Indians thought working with the hands was only fit for squaws. Remember, too, how common famines were among Indians."

Toward the end of the workbook there is this instruction for the student: "After each nationality listed below, write an outstanding contribution it has made to Minnesota. German. Swedish. Danish. Swiss. Finnish. Norwegian." No mention is made of the significant contributions of Native people.

Ruth Myers, an enrolled member of the Grand Portage Band of Lake Superior Chippewa, worked diligently to have the book removed from schools.

Criteria for Judging Books About Native People

I wish to express my appreciation for the suggestions, contributions, questions, and encouragement from the many people who played a part in forming this criteria: in particular, Nora Hakala, Ruth Myers, Dr. Robert Powless, and the students and parents at Grand Portage.

Always remember the lesson from the Hopi Nation. Does the book hurt or help the children?

1. Is the book free of derisive words that are offensive? Are there degrading descriptions or stereotypical words such as: "savage", "scalping", "bloodthirsty", "massacre" or other hurtful words? Are stereotypes reinforced that describe Native people as pagan, childlike, dirty, lazy, warlike, cruel, or unintelligent?

   Does the narrative contain insulting overtones? Note the use of adjectives, adverbs and descriptive phrases. Used in a negative context, they can be terribly destructive to a child's perception of Native people.

   Watch for the writer's manipulation of vocabulary that may cause harm to both the Native and non-Native child. The impact of negativism fostered by stereotypes is not measureable, but it is damaging.

Betty Baker's ***Do Not Annoy the Indians*** uses a number of ruinous images. The people are "half-naked, painted" "savages" who lick off their plates and dribble food down their chins. The ceremonies of the people are described as disappointing with lots of shuffling and the singers and dancers having "no connection with the thud of the drums".

In ***Indian Fighter: The Story of Nelson A. Miles*** by Ralph Edgar Bailey, the author chooses to use a one-sided narrative throughout the text. There is talk about the "Lonely homesteads and wagon trains" being "victims of their sudden massacres". The Sioux are called "cutthroats" and the Native people are repeatedly called "hostiles" or "savages".

2. Do the characters speak in vocabulary that is realistic or is it some Grade B movie broken English? Does the syntax reinforce the concept that Native people had a sub-standard language pattern? On the other hand, be wary of books in which the speech of Native people is overly poetic and romanticized.

Lynn Reid Banks has written a series of books about ***The Indian in the Cupboard.*** This is how Little Bear talks: "I help...I go...Big hole...Want fire."

By contrast, ***Knots on a Counting Rope,*** by Bill Martin, Jr. and John Archambault uses dialogue that is overly poetic and constitutes a highly romanticized language pattern for the people.

3. Is the book offensive in dealing with Native religion? Does the book present a confused or distorted view of religion or does it respect the spirituality of the people? Is the religion "magic" or "superstitious" or belittled in any way?

Victor Barnouw inappropriately deals with the curing ceremony of the Anishinabe (Chippewa/Ojibwe) in ***Dream of the Blue Heron.*** There's lots of chanting, swallowing of bones, shuddering and writhing. "With a final terrifying groan Wolf Claw spewed out the two bones, all slimy with spittle, into his shaking hands". After the spitting and shaking there's more quivering and shuddering and terrible silences.

Barbara Beck's books on the Aztec and Maya people describes in detail the human sacrifices that was a part of the history of these groups of Native people. They "set about the task of slashing open the captured victims' chests, snatching out their hearts, and offering them to the gods. Needless to say, the ceremony went on for days, and lesser lords in turn took over the grisly task".

Children do not have the necessary experience and sophistication to handle the stories of human sacrifice. The stories reinforce misconceptions.

4. Is the book culturally accurate? Are the skills and contributions of Native people realistically discussed? The contributions should be specific and go beyond the "corn" and "squash" mentality. If discussing foods of the Western Hemisphere, of course those vegetables will be discussed, but books seem to focus on corn and

squash and negate the numerous inventions of Native people.

Does the book adequately reflect the beauty of the culture and the complexity of the social structure? Are the Native people described as being all the same, generic, or are they characterized as separate Nations with their own language, religion, culture, and lifestyles? Are they shown as individuals within the framework of their own unique Nation?

Peggy Parish, Margaret Friskey and Betty Baker are authors who standardize the culture of Native people in books. On the plus side are the books by Paul Goble and Joseph Bruchac, which are sensitive, honest and insightful.

5. Does the text correctly portray the history of the Native people? How does the book deal with the discovery of the North and South American continents? Does the book show that Native people were the first people in the Western Hemisphere? Does it realistically portray the impact the European invasion had on Native people? How does it handle treaty rights? Does it rightfully acknowledge that Native people were fighting in defense of their land? Does the text give the correct name to the Nation being discussed?

A powerful book dealing simply and intelligently about the epic story of Native people is ***The People Shall Continue*** by Simon Ortiz.

6. If the book is dealing with modern times, does it give a realistic, honest portrayal of life in contemporary society?

Does it seem as though there are no Native people anymore; that they just sort of "vanished"; relegated to a quaint history? Children need to recognize that Native people continue to exist in all parts of modern-day society and in all geographic areas. They did not disappear. Children need to read materials about present-day Native people and read books by Native authors and illustrators.

7. Are Native people in the book presented as natural and real or are the characters presented from a distorted point of view? Is the role of Elder respected? Are Native women inaccurately portrayed as doing all the work and the men characterized as sitting around waiting to go to war?

    In Elizabeth George Speare's **Sign of the Beaver**, the young girl is referred to as a "squaw" and has a demeaning role. "Me Marie, sister of Attean...Me go with...Attean think squaw girl not good for much..." Throughout the book, Native people are referred to as performing "savage rites"; they "strutted and pranced in ridiculous contortions, for all the world like a clown in a village fair".

    "Squaw" is a controversial word with considerable debate about its etymology. The bottom line is that it is insulting to many Native women.

8. Does the book present a superior view of the non-Native world? Is it the "white" person who must come to the aid of Native people in order for things to "work out all right"? What is the measure used for success? Are

non-Native standards the rule by which other things are gauged?

In ***The Double Life of Pocahontas*** by Jean Fritz, Powhatan is intrigued by the "power of guns" and by the other inventions he observes the Europeans using. He is made to appear tiresome and naive rather than being a man of intelligence and curiosity who recognizes and accepts a new invention.

The Europeans in turn must have been amazed at the agronomy and technology of the various Native tribes they encountered. This side of the story is rarely told.

9. Does the book use a double standard in dealing with behavior? From Meadowcroft's ***The First Year*** : "We paid them for the grain we took. They returned the tools they stole". Note that the "Indians" are referred to as having stolen, but the colonists merely "took" something.

10. Is the human body drawn in a sensitive and realistic manner? Is the head drawn with normal proportions? Be watchful for drawings with distortions of the nose and other facial parts. Are the illustrations caricatures ridiculing the group represented? Are they cartoon-like? Is the clothing accurate to the Nation and time frame being discussed in the text? Do the drawings correctly depict the housing, furnishings and other aspects of every day living?

11. Is it formula non-fiction? The majority of these books tend to be encyclopedic in nature. Many authors have devised a formula that is commercially successful.

Matthew Grant, Ben Hunt, Robert Hofsinde and Sonia Bleeker are some of the authors who have written extensively about Native people using a standard formula. Overall, they have attempted to be accurate about the material presented.

These are the kinds of books kids check out of libraries when doing a research project or report for a school assignment. Students need to be aware that there is more depth than is available in these books and should be encouraged to look beyond the formula-type texts. That's not to negate the value of an encyclopedic narrative; it's simply that it is the beginning of research, not the end.

12. A look at the copyright date is an indicator of vocabulary. Words like "redman" are used more in books dating from earlier times. Often, the author did not intend to show disrespect, but was using the language of the day. It is essential that adults explain the history of these words and to encourage students to look at copyright dates.

13. What place in the narrative does the term "Indian" have? Many Native people refer to themselves as "Indian", "American Indian", "First Americans", "First Nations", and "Native American". The term "Indian" is used extensively in our society. Three examples are the Bureau of Indian Affairs, The National Museum of the American Indian that opened in Washington, D. C. in September of 2004, and the North American Indian Traveling College. The word Indian is incorporated into the names of many museums and schools across the country. The Denver Art Museum has an "American

Indian Gallery". At one time, T-shirts saying "Indian and proud" were quite popular. Many Native people call themselves "Indians" or "American Indians".

Many non-Native people are perplexed about the tribal names used to identify various groups. Native people usually refer to themselves by their traditional names. The Anishinabe/Anishinaabe/Anishinawbe, which means "original people", are also referred to as the Ojibwe, Ojibwa, Ojibway, and Chippewa which adds to the dilemma. In Minnesota, the legal name is Chippewa; hence, The Minnesota Chippewa Tribe. All of this occurred because of the corruption of original Anishinabe words by early Europeans.

It should be noted that Native Americans describes anyone born in America.

14. Is it an alphabet or picture book for young children? Is it a beginning reader or a controlled vocabulary text? Many of these books use "Indians" in a generic, superficial sense with illustrations that are cartoon-like caricatures. "I" is for "Indian" or "Igloo". "E" is for "Eskimo". Often, the books use Native people as the humorous objects of the narrative, such as the **Indian Two Feet** books by Margaret Friskey or **Let's Be Indians** by Peggy Parish. In these instances, the results are unacceptable. **What Eddie Can Do** by Wilfried Gebhard is an example of the "warrior" concept that many picture books use.

15. Is it a book about Pocahontas or Squanto? Pocahontas and Squanto are popular subjects for books because these individuals helped the European colonization of the

Western Hemisphere. In reality, most of the books are generalizations that add nothing to the understanding of who these people were.

How are the people characterized who helped their own Nation protect themselves against the European invasion?

Is the book correct when describing Black Hawk, Joseph, Osceola, Cochise and others who fought to protect their homeland and families? When their stories are told, it is often in the negative vein. They are "murderous", "attacking peaceful settlers", when in truth, men such as Joseph, Tecumseh and the others were men of peace with a strong sense of spirituality.

16. Is there a juxtaposition of Native people and animals? In too many books, Native people are compared to wild animals. They have "eyes like a baby fox", they pick up their food and "gnawed it as if it were a dog with a bone", or they are compared to a "tame wolf, it was a gentleness never to be trusted". In *The American Indian*, it is said: "They were lazy, insolent, and thievish as monkeys".

Virginia Grossman and Sylvia Long take the same approach in *Ten Little Rabbits*. Rabbits are dressed in the Native costumes of the Sioux, Tewa, Ute, Menominee, Blackfoot, Hopi, Arapaho, Nez Perce, Kwakiutl, and Navajo. Each page is devoted to one number and one tribe; such as "Seven merry mischief-makers playing hide-and-seek". The "mischief-makers" are supposed to represent the Arapaho. The result is a depersonalization, superficial, damaging, dehumanizing, and demeaning image of Native people.

The continued juxtaposition of Native people and animals in literature is unacceptable. Don't fall for the "cuteness" angle or any other excuse offered for such images.

17. Is it a book about the white child captured by "Indians"? These can be overly sensationalized and can cause much damage to the child reader. Frequently, the Indian parents adopt the white child and a mutual bond of love develops. In writing about actual events, which happened on the frontier to children, many authors manipulate the plot in order to heighten the excitement for the reader.

    Often, the books abound with negative stereotypes with the Native people being presented as cruel and naive. These books can be especially harmful to children, both Native and non-Native, who are adopted.

18. Is it an adventure book? Lots of books have "Indian" in the title even though the book isn't about Native people at all. Publishers have learned that "Indian" in the title increases sales.

19. Are there errors by omission? Books on the "First Thanksgiving" or Christopher Columbus marginally mention the fact that there were people living in the Western Hemisphere when the Europeans arrived. It's the Nobody Lives Here - Let's Take the Land Mentality. Don't fall for it.

20. What psychological effect will the book have on a child? It's crucial to make sure that children are not shaped by the negativisms in books. Racism is insidious and dangerous, but people unwittingly perpetuate bigotry and intolerance through the selection of books available for children.

    How can the self-esteem of a Native child fail to be injured when repeatedly confronted with the negative images about Native people available through books?

    When the non-Native child continually reads negative passages about Native people, how can they help but develop unhealthy attitudes and distorted images of Native people?

21. Are "Indians" used to sell something - either an idea or a product?

    Susan Jeffers book **Brother Eagle, Sister Sky** is concerned with selling environmental concerns to children. In so doing, a fabricated speech attributed to Chief Seattle is used and romanticized versions of Native people illustrate the text. Native people do not need fables created for them or speeches written for the dead chiefs. It is not acceptable to use "Indians" to sell a cause - no matter how worthy that case may be.

Abisch, Roz; *'Twas in the Moon of Wintertime: The First American Christmas Carol;* illustrated by Boche Koplan; Prentice-Hall, 1969; Grades K – 3

Father Jean de Brebeuf established the first Jesuit mission for the Huron people. In the early 1640s, Father de Brebeuf wrote a hymn celebrating the birth of Christ. It is believed to be the first Christmas carol written in the "New World". The song related the birth of Christ in terms of the Huron culture and language. The tune is from an old French folk song.

The book is a retelling of the carol with color illustrations on every page. At the end of the book, the musical accompaniment is written along with the words in English, with one verse given in Huron.

If this book is used, as it often is at Christmas time, explain the part about the "charms" - "To keep them safe from harm and evil the Hurons made charms out of beavers' teeth and fish bones, out of odd shaped pebbles and splinters of wood...Into this new land of hunters and warriors, into this place of strange spirits and charms..." You should talk about the illustrations also. The pictures are stylized and attempt to complement the text, but the "Indian" angels aren't really a part of the carol as written by Father de Brebeuf.

This book can't be ignored - it seems to be on every library shelf and the song is used by many schools for their "winter, multicultural" music programs.

Aliki; ***Corn is Maize;*** illustrated by the author. Crowell, 1976 Grades K - 3

> A simple description of how corn was discovered and used by Native people is the focus of the book. A brief history of how corn became a significant food throughout the world and a simple scientific description of the evolution of corn into the plant we know today is also discussed and illustrated. The final page shows how to make a corn husk wreath.
>
> Bright, colorful illustrations add meaning to the text. No tribal indentify is given to the Native people; they are Indians and tribes. Students who reviewed the book wondered why one boy in a picture is not wearing a shirt. Other students wondered why no modern techniques were shown with the "Indian farmers" of today.
>
> Aliki is "Greek and American".

→✣←

Amon, Aline; ***Talking Hands;*** illustrated by the author; Doubleday, 1968; Grades 3 - 6

> Many people through the ages have used sign language as a means of communication. A type of universal sign language is explained and illustrated throughout the book. The book is simply written and may appeal to younger children as well.
>
> The illustrations are simple - a young "Indian" complete with a single feather demonstrates the gesture or technique used for each word. At the end of the book, there are non-Native children pretending to be "Indians"; dressed in buckskin and ceremonial headdress. The book deals in such a superficial manner it is spiritless. There are words for telephone, motion

picture, airplane and bicycle. The "sign" for motion picture is to make the sign for owl and "pretend to turn the crank of an old-fashioned movie camera".

Some sample sentences: "I called Red. I stay town in United States. I see friend come...We play Indians? We live tepee. We hunt buffalo...I have clothes like chief. I have bow with many arrows. I chief."

The book totally lacks insight, sensitivity and knowledge of the culture of Native people.

>*<

Armer, Laura, **Waterless Mountain;** illustrated by Sidney Armer and Laura Armer. Mckay, 1931. Grades 6 – up

Awarded the Newberry medal in 1932, the book is a poetically descriptive story of a young Navajo boy born in the early 1900's. The setting is Northern Arizona and a traditional Navajo family. Younger Brother gains much wisdom in the wonders of nature and in the beauty of the Native culture. Navajo legends are used effectively throughout the book.

The black and white illustrations are sensitively drawn and enhance the mood of the text. It is a well-written, story that captures the warmth and reality of the Navajo Nation.

>*<

Ashabranner, Brent; **Children of the Maya: A Guatemalan Indian Odyssey;** Photographs by Paul Conklin; Dodd, Mead and Co., 1986; Grades 6 – up

More than 150,000 Mayan people in Guatemala have been forced to flee their traditional highland villages and move to refugee camps in Mexico. A small number of the people found a new home in Indiantown, Florida, where the residents helped them begin a new life.

The story raises disturbing questions, both political and military, about the abuse of power. The author begins by telling about the Florida town, then about Guatemala, and finally about the people themselves. As in Ashabrenner's other books, the strength of the text lies in the people being allowed to speak for themselves.

Ashabranner's tone is calm; the overall impact is powerful. Some of the photographs are of drawings made by Mayan children. One of them shows a village being bombed by army planes. "They just do it", the boy said. "I don't know why". Another shows people praying in front of church with an army helicopter firing bullets at them. "I saw it all", said the girl.

A sample of the dialogue: "One of the boys had seen soldiers decapitate a guerrilla. When he told the psychologist about it, he spoke in a whisper and his face was sweaty." "I saw it all", he said, "but they didn't see me".

Ashabranner and Conklin have successfully collaborated on a book that is well documented, objective and acutely honest.

Mr. Ashabranner had successful careers with the Peace Corps and the Ford Foundation before turning to writing. He sometimes collaborates with his daughter, a photographer.

Ashabranner, Brent; ***Morning Star, Black Star;*** Photographs by Paul Conklin, Dodd, 1982; Grades 6 - up

>   ***Morning Star, Black Star*** tells the touching history of the Northern Cheyenne and discusses the confrontations between the energy companies and the Native people.

A serious challenge to tribal life has arisen because of the vast quantities of natural resources, especially coal, on the reservation land. The book deals with the issues that are seen as an economic opportunity, but present a significant threat to the preservation of the Northern Cheyenne culture and beliefs.

Joe Little Coyote closes the book with these words: "Every generation of Northern Cheyenne must have strength to fight for survival or we will disappear. Sweet Medicine told us we must not forget who we are. Well, we do not intend to forget".

It is a superb book and the poignant photographs by Paul Conklin add to its overall success.

Mr. Ashabranner worked in Ethiopia, Libya, Nigeria, India, the Philippines, and Indonesia. He worked for the Peace Corps and the Ford Foundation. He has written a number of books about different cultures and has done a series on American memorials.

>―<

Ashabranner, Brent; ***To Live in Two Worlds;*** Photographs by Paul Conklin; Dodd, 1984; Grades 6 - up

>   Through the words of young Native men and women, Ashabranner documents the story of individuals striving to save

their heritages, while at the same time trying to be successful in the dominant culture they come in contact with. It is the story of the young people who have shared a part of their lives with the reader.

The narratives are honest and optimistic and the overall strength of the book comes from dealing with real people and situations. Critics may view it as too sugarcoated, but it is a pleasant change from the negative image of most books dealing with Native people.

Paul Conklin's photographs add a meaningful dimension to the book.

→←

Awiakta, Marilou; ***Rising Fawn and the Fire Mystery;*** illustrated by Beverly Bringle; St. Lukes Press, 1983; Grades 4 - 6

Rising Fawn is based on actual events that happened on the frontier to Native children. It is a poignant story of a small Choctaw girl, the removal by the government of the Native people, brutal soldiers, and of a childless white couple who adopt the child. During her ordeal, she is sustained by the final words of her Grandmother, "A voice like the embrace of wind in the pines: 'Be like the seed...live deep in your spirit' ".

Rising Fawn is cared for and loved by the couple, but she never speaks. It is not until Christmas and the lighting of the Christ Candle that Rising Fawn "felt a new confidence, and a deep belief that there was to be a time for her to come forth like the flame within the seed had come forth".

The "Woman" uses words like "pagan" and "heathen" and the child is transformed during Christmas. A reader may, therefore, conclude that the book is unacceptable. Not so. It is a profoundly moving story of a child who is so secure in the love, culture and history of her birth family that she is able to endure the painful experience and move into a new life.

Marilou Awiakta has given us a story that is honest and perceptive. The illustrations by Beverly Bringle are lovely.

Awiakta, Cherokee, has received many awards. In 1972, she received the Jesse Hill Ford Award for poetry. She received an Honorary Doctorate of Humane Letters from Albion College, Albion, Michigan, in 1999 and the Appalachian Heritage Writer's Award from Shepherd College in 2000, plus many other awards.

→←

Bailey, Ralph Edgar; *Indian Fighter: The Story of Nelson A. Miles;* William Morrow and Co., 1965; Grades 5 - 6

The career of Nelson A. Miles is chronicled from the Civil War through the early 1890s. General Miles is the commander, who, according to the book's jacket, "drove Sitting Bull out of the country and forced Crazy Horse to surrender. Miles was also the general who received the moving surrender from Chief Joseph... and who captured Geronimo." It is an absorbing, emotion filled story that children will find thoroughly engrossing.

Because of the story's intensity, the child reader may find it difficult to be objective about the contents of the novel. Throughout the text, the Native people are referred to as "savages" or "hostiles" and seldom given a tribal identity. The women are called "squaws", youthful males are "young bucks" and the people are "Indians".

It is a one-sided narrative: "Lonely homesteads and wagon trains were victims of their sudden massacres." "Already the fleeing savages were killing and burning". "The fierce Sioux Indians, the cutthroats..." "The Sioux called themselves the Dakota Nation, but they were not truly a nation..." In reference to Sitting Bull: "...wild eyed...an enraged savage...like a wild beast..." The warriors: "...burst into wild yells..." used "...old Indian tricks...yelling and whooping..." and are "fierce", "lurking" and "skulking". Their dance was "...a wild, defiant war dance".

Though Miles is described as sympathetic and fair, the author's continued manipulations of adjectives and descriptions are heavy-handed. War is not an easy subject to write about, but in the end, children will feel that it was the "only answer". That can not be acceptable.

➸✦

Baker, Betty; ***Do Not Annoy the Indians;*** illustrated by Harold Goodwin; Macmillan, 1968; Grades 3 - 6

The book appears to be a light-hearted, amusing tale of the Old West. The story centers on the Barnes family and their contract with the Butterfield Overland Mail Company. Thirteen year old Jeff is newly arrived on the Arizona frontier and must contend with a bossy older sister, a stubborn younger brother and a "band of Yuma Indians". It is a humorous book which makes it especially insidious.

Most of the humor stems from the antics of the "Indians" who are portrayed in a stereotyped, childish manner. The Native people appear foolish and the dialogue is in broken English.

Some examples from the text: "A half-naked, painted savage crept from the stairs to the upper deck. With a shriek that raised the hair on Jeff's neck, the Indian scooped up the yelling, kicking Benjie and disappeared around the corner of the deckhouse."

In reference to their appearance: "Two Indians sat with their backs against the sunny wall...The old one...had a long bone stuck through a hole in the center of his nose. Long strings of black hair half hid his leathery face." The younger one is described thusly: "His eyes were circled in yellow, his cheeks streaked with blue, and his whole nose painted bright red. Just looking at the savages dried Jeff's mouth and gave his knees the wobbles."

Descriptions of their eating: "He handed the Indian a biscuit. Tebarro crammed it all in his mouth, dribbling crumbs as he chewed...Tebarro licked his own plate and reached for Kwanami's... Tebarro was licking the grease from his uncle's plate."

This is how the people talk: "I go to Fort Yuma. Big Feast. Many gifts from White Father. My people hear boat toot-toot. They come Fort Yuma. Your people hear boat?"

As far as the ceremonies of the people "The Indians shuffled around a fire, their steps showing no connection with the thud of the drums. The singers didn't seem to pay attention to anyone. One would start up, shaking a rattle as he sang, for no reason that Jeff could see. Just when the chant was well started, singer and rattle would stop. But the drums and shuffling continued...The feast Tebarro had bragged about proved just as disappointing."

"The way the overgrown Indian spent the rest of the morning playing with Benjie and the wagon, Jeff figured Tebarro hadn't the ordinary sense folks were born with."

Unfortunately, these are not occasional instances of offensive prose. The book is filled with negative images.

The absolute tragedy of a book like this is that children today are reading it. It's still on library shelves, available through Internet sources, and is considered a "popular" book.

This book is damaging to Native people.

―※―

Baker, Betty; ***Three Fools and a Horse;*** illustrated by Glen Rounds; Macmillan, 1975, Grades 1 – 2.

The book is an attempt to tell some of the amusing stories of Apache folklore. It fails miserably. The main characters are Little Fool, Fat Fool, and Fool About and they are some of the Foolish People who live on Two Dog Mountain. In one story, they mistake a bug for a buffalo and are confused when confronted by a horse. Is it a deer, a dog or good to eat?

Little Fool wins a horse from a flatlander by the name of Big Nose - by outrunning it. As the story continues, Fool About learns to stay on the horse by gluing himself to it with pine sap.

Instead of telling tales with wit and sensitivity, the author and illustrator have devised a tale that is embarrassing and completely unacceptable. The book is a shame.

※

Baker, Laura Nelson; ***O Children of the Wind and Pines;*** illustrated by Inez Storer; Lippincott, 1967; Grades 3 - 6

Poor motherless Atatase. She thought her voice was like a crow and her feet were ugly. The young Huron girl yearned for beauty and love. The book presents Father Jean de Brebeuf as the one who is patient and understanding and helps Atatase find love and beauty at Christmas time.

The background of the story is based on the writing of the first Christmas carol on the North American continent. Father de Brebeuf composed the song for the Huron People over three hundred years ago. Atatase is a fictional character based on the early diaries kept by the Jesuit missionaries.

Though it would appear the author has tried to deal sympathetically with the story, there are some flaws that must be noted. The priests are referred to as having "magic", while the Native religion is something ineffectual having a "witch doctor". The Native people pray to a "beaver bone" while the priests pray to God. In this purely fictionalized account, Atatase is caught "stealing" a picture of the "Mother Mary". Why include a scene of a young child stealing? The whole stealing concept simply causes misconceptions and underscores stereotypes.

Father Jean de Brebeuf had a reputation for dealing sympathetically with the Huron people. Any book about him should reflect the concern he had for the people.

Baker, Olaf; ***Where the Buffaloes Begin;*** illustrated by Stephen Gammell; Warne, 1981; Grades 3 - 5

"Over the blazing camp-fires, when the wind moaned eerily through the thickets of juniper and fir, they spoke of it in the Indian tongue…And Nawa, the wise man,…declared that if you arrived at the right time, on the right night, you would see the buffaloes rise out of the middle of the lake…"

Thus begins the story of Little Wolf. The young boy begins an adventure that ends with a spectacular ride through the night. It is a beautifully written, powerful book that can be used with children. However, it would be important to inform the children that the book was written in 1915 which may explain some of the language that mars an otherwise remarkable book.

Some of the unacceptable references to the Assiniboin warriors - "On moccasins noiseless as the padded feet of the wolves, as intent, and almost more cruel, these painted warriors…" and "his people's enemies, the Assiniboins," who would "kill and scalp you as neatly as could be."

The book's authenticity, lovely pictures and dynamic story telling make it a book that could be used in a discussion of time, place and changing concepts.

Bales, Carol Ann; ***Kevin Cloud: A Chippewa Boy in the City;*** Photographs by the author. Reilly & Lee; 1972; Grades 3 - 6

A photo-essay in which the author lets Kevin tell his own story. Kevin Cloud, ten years old, lives in the Up-town area of Chicago. In simple language, Kevin tells the story of his life in the city, of school and family, and visits to the reservation with his grandmother.

The photographs and text make a worthwhile book. Because of the 1972 publication, it would be useful in social studies classes or literature studies for historical reference.

→←

Bamman, Henry, Leonard Kennedy and Robert Whitehead; *Mystery Adventure of the Indian Burial Ground;* illustrated by George Rohrer; Benefic Press, 1969; Grades 3 - 6

Thad, Jeanine and Bev find themselves in the midst of an exciting adventure revolving around an Indian burial ground, a golden statue of an Indian, and the bad guys who are trying to steal the statue. Lightfoot, an Indian, is the owner of the statue and the only Indian left in that area.

"At one time, a tribe of Indians had lived in the forest, but that was many, many years ago. Now, Lightfoot was the only Indian left in the forest." Regarding the burial ground, Lightfoot says: "Come back tomorrow...and help us dig in the burial ground of my people. Perhaps you will find something there that you will want to keep."

Lightfoot is portrayed as constantly attempting to please the young people he has come in contact with. He is the "only Indian left", the Tonto image of some Grade B Movie and is eager to let the youth dig around in the burial ground for something for themselves – all of which is totally wrong. The book puts "Indians" comfortably in the background, subservient and solicitous. And, yes, this book is still available. What a shame.

⋈

Banks, Lynne Reid; *The Indian in the Cupboard;* illustrated by Brock Cole; Doubleday, 1980; Grades 4 - 6

Nine-year old Omri receives a plastic Indian, a small white cupboard and a key for his birthday. When he puts the tiny Indian into the cupboard, the figure comes to life and a series of adventures begin. Omri's life becomes centered on "his Indian" whom he names Little Bear. Little Bear is Iroquois, although no attempt is made to give him any legitimacy as a Native person.

It is an enchanting, well-written, adventurous story that will delight children. That's too bad, because an inventive cast of characters and lively action obscures a book filled with negative stereotypes and dreadful cliches. Can you imagine a book title with any other cultural group "in a cupboard?"

This is how Little Bear talks: "Day come! Why you still sleep? Time eat - hunt- fight- make pictures!" and "I help...I go...Big hole...Want fire. Want make dance." Then there's the chapter - "Thirty Scalps". The book is filled with images that are hurtful to Native people.

The New York Times selected this as "The Best Novel of the Year" and it has received many literary awards. How sad. The flaws in the book are serious and contribute to the "white superiority" and "simple Natives" concept that abounds in far too many books. This book joins a host of other texts that are damaging to the Native people they attempt to portray.

Mrs. Banks lives in England.

>+<

Banks, Lynne Reid; *The Return of the Indian;* illustrated by William Geldart; Doubleday, 1986; Grades 4 - 6

"Their headdresses...even their movements...were alien. Their faces, too - their faces! They were wild, distorted, terrifying masks of hatred and rage..."

"He saw an Indian making straight for him. His face, in the torchlight, was twisted with fury. For a second, Omri saw, under the shaven scalp lock, the mindless destructive face of a skinhead just before he lashed out...The Algonquin licked his lips, snarling like a dog...the whole pack of Algonquin began to run, howling and yelling...their monstrous shadows sliding along the ground..."

Taken as a whole, the book is insensitive and children will be unaware of its negative impact. The "Indians" are portrayed as barbarous, the battle scenes are brutally graphic and the underlying theme is one of "white" superiority and bloodthirsty Indians. The book is demeaning to Native people, but popular with children and parents - that's the worst part of all.

Mrs. Banks lives in England.

>+<

Banks, Lynne Reid; ***The Secret of the Indian;*** illustrated by Ted Lewin; Avon, 1989; Grades 4 - 6

> Lynne Reid Banks has written her third book about the adventures of Omri and "his Indian." Though she has created an appealing literary device, no attempt has been made to deal sensitively with Native people. She also allows Omri's father to refer to his son as a "little-HALF-WIT" and "daft". Much of the conversation is sprinkled with "Oh, God" and Little Bear's speech patterns continue to be inarticulate.
>
> Mrs. Banks books have won critical praise and continue to seep children's literature with toxins.
>
> Omri eventually comes up with a solution "born of a deep, long, strong fear…and the pain of knowing that they had meddled where they shouldn't and had done a lot of harm." Exactly.

→←

Bannon, Laura; ***When the Moon is New;*** illustrated by the author, Whitman; 1953; Grades 3 - 6

> Rainbow Jumper is a seven-year-old Seminole girl who lives in the Florida Everglades. She sensed a mystery in camp, but was told to wait. While waiting, she sews herself a lovely new skirt on Grandmother's sewing machine. She also visits her cousins at Gopher Camp. At the Gopher Camp she takes care of her newest cousin and makes dolls to sell at the store. With the arrival of the new moon, the promised happening occurs and presents a surprise ending.
>
> The story is simply told. The illustrations, in water-colors, catch the mood of the Everglades.

Barnouw, Victor; ***Dream of the Blue Heron;*** illustrated by Lynd Ward; Delacorte, 1966; Grades 6 - Up

Wabus is a young Chippewa boy growing up in Northern Wisconsin in 1905 and 1906. His beloved grandparents follow the traditional life of the Chippewa. The grandparents are the focal point of his life, but his tranquil life is interrupted when his father appears on the scene. Conflicts arise in the world in which Wabus lives, both personal and cultural.

The author has described Chippewa life and culture with an ominous tone of desperation. The life of the people is not shown with any joy or laughter or hope. Everything seems destitute unless the "white men" are there to help them find a better life. There's lots of coughing and feebleness and irritation.

Native medicine is reduced to a couple of chants and some old bones. Nothing is described of the various medicines that were employed for curing people; everything is "magic" and is made to look ridiculously simple.

A chapter on the curing ceremony portrays the medicine man as "weaving from side to side...brandishing a rattle...giving a strangled sob". Later, "He had warned them all not to make a sound when he swallowed the bones...Then he brought it up to his mouth and gulped it down, making a grimace of swallowing as he did so...After a tense pause Wolf Claw ominously held up the second bone. This too was popped into his mouth and bolted down with a shake of the head and shudder of the body. Then the old man, hunched forward, began to gag and choke so violently that his whirling head grazed his patient's ribs...the strangling sounds that escaped from the wizard's throat were terrible to hear...Twisting and writhing..."

Unfortunately, this chapter is rather long: "With a final terrifying groan Wolf Claw spewed out the two bones, all slimy with spittle, into his shaking hands." There's more quivering and shuddering and terrible silences and finally "...the old man hobbled off..."

In the end, Wabus learns who his guardian spirit is - it's the disciplinarian from the school that whipped him so horribly. Oh, yes. There's also a killing and some jail scenes.

Mr. Barnouw is a non-Indian anthropologist.

Barth, Edna; ***Turkeys, Pilgrims, and Indian Corn: The Story of the Thanksgiving Symbols;*** illustrated by Ursula Arndt; Clarion Books, 1975; Grades 3 - 6

The book traces the history of the celebration of Thanksgiving and the development of the various symbols and legends regarding the custom surrounding harvest time. Included are chapters on "The Pilgrims", "The Mayflower", "The Pilgrim Fathers", "The Pilgrim Mothers", "Pilgrim Children", "Pilgrim Faces", "Pilgrim Clothes", "Pilgrim Animals", "Pilgrims Houses", "Pilgrim Rock", etcetera.

The illustrations suit the text, with its abundant emphasis on the Pilgrims and an occasional picture of "Indians" looking in wonder at the newcomers. To be fair, there is one chapter devoted to "Indian Neighbors" and the expected chapter on "Indian Corn".

The problem with the book is its general feeling of European superiority with the Native people relegated to a substandard role. There are hostile Indians, the Pilgrims must fence in their village and lock it, the Indians are puzzled about selling land, and it was "too bad, he wrote, that they had not made the Indians into Christians before killing them".

In discussing religion: "The Pilgrims had done their best to impose their religion on all the Indians they knew. They wanted to 'help' them. But the Indians had their own religion and tribal customs...Robbed of these, they lose self-respect and become confused".

Actually, what's confused is the attitude toward Native people shown throughout the text. The treatment of the customs, spirituality, and beliefs of the Native people are dealt with inappropriately. Ethnocentric bias is evident throughout the book and translated into stereotypical images. Don't buy into the "Thanksgiving Symbols" story line.

→←

Baylor, Byrd; A ***God on Every Mountain Top;*** illustrated by Carol Brown; Charles Scribner's Sons, 1981; Grades 3 - 6

"In the southwest, each tribe has a homeland marked off by sacred mountains and each mountain has a story. Call them myths - or call them truth. It doesn't matter...What is written here is what the people tell about their mountains...To tell them is to honor sacred mountains."

Byrd Baylor has collected a small number of the many stories that Southwest tribes tell about their mountains. They are told simply and with respect. The illustrations by Carol Brown retain the authenticity of the tales.

Byrd Baylor lives in Arizona. ***The Way to Start the Day*** written by Ms. Baylor and illustrated by Peter Parnall was named a Caldecott Honor Book in 1979. The original work is at the Kerlan Collection at the University of Minnesota. Two other Caldecott Honor Books by Ms. Baylor and Mr. Parnall are: ***The Desert is Theirs,*** 1976, and ***Hawk I'm Your Brother,*** 1979.

A God On Every Mountain Top has been reissued as ***The Way to Make Perfect Mountains: Native American Legends of Sacred Mountains,*** 1997, Cinco Puntos Press.

➤✦

Baylor, Byrd; ***And it is Still That Way;*** Charles Scribner, 1976; Grades 3 - 6

A collection of forty-one stories as told by Native children in Arizona, the stories are as old as the tribes, some go back to the oldest memories of the community. The book speaks of times when animals talked like people, the world was new and the first humans needed to learn many things. The book is categorized into topics such as Brother Coyote or Why Our World Is Like It Is. When the storytellers are finished, they never end with the feeling that the tale is from the past. Instead, they will probably say, "And it is still that way."

Ms. Baylor has received many awards, including the Texas Bluebonnet Award and the Caldecott Award. She lives in Arizona.

➤✦

Baylor, Byrd; ***Before You Came This Way;*** illustrated by Tom Bahti, E.P. Dutton, 1969; Grades 3 - 6

The scope of the book is best stated in the dedication, "To the ancient unknown artists whose drawings on stone inspired this book."

Prehistoric Indian petroglyphs on a canyon wall set a child's imagination in full swing as an effort is made to grasp the feeling of what life was like in those ancient times when the drawings were made. Ms. Baylor has set those feelings into print in an original and poetic evocation of the past. We also see the beginnings of art in one of its earliest and simplest forms.

The illustrations were done on amatl paper, "a rough, handmade bark paper made by the Otomi Indians of Puebla, Mexico."

Adults with questions about the petroglyphs may want to check out two books that can be helpful. ***Sinagua Sunwatchers*** by Kenneth J. Zoll and ***A Field Guide to Rock Art Symbols of the Greater Southwest*** by Alex Patterson are a start. Sometimes, the more you know, the more you realize that trying to interpret things for children may not be wise. Petroglyphs and pictographs hold strong, sacred traditions for Native people.

>‹

Baylor, Byrd; ***Coyote Cry;*** illustrated by Symeon Shimin; Lothrop, Lee & Shepard; 1972; Grades 3 - 6

Antonio and Grandfather tend the flocks of sheep and listen to the coyotes cry. Antonio and Coyote are enemies until something happens and Antonio learns the coyote song. Antonio is one of the people who can tell what things Coyote is saying.

The author has created a beautifully written story about the southwest. It is a sensitive and poetic tale. The illustrations add warmth and life to the text.

⇥⇤

Baylor, Byrd; ***The Desert is Theirs;*** illustrated by Peter Parnall, Charles Scribner's sons, 1975; Grades K - 3

The Papagos are "strong, brown Desert People who call the earth their mother." The Papagos share the land with their animal brothers. Byrd Baylor speaks simply and poetically about the closeness of people and land. She has the gift of making you a partner in the world she writes so powerfully about. She writes, "Talk to Papago Indians. They're Desert People. They know desert secrets that no one else knows, --- They sing it's songs. They never hurt it. And the land knows." Through the skill of her writing, we too learn about the desert and its people. We are invited to share and what a magnificent experience! Artistic and colorful paintings add to the spirit of the text. The words and pictures convey the mood of the desert and quality of Papago life in this rhythmic story. It is a lovely story suitable for reading aloud.

Today, the Papago are known as Tohono O'Odham.

The Desert is Theirs was a Caldecott Honor book in 1976 and an ALA Notable Children's Book. Ms. Baylor and Mr. Parnall were awarded Caldecott Honors for ***Hawk I'm Your Brother*** in 1977 and ***The Way to Start a Day*** in 1979.

Baylor, Byrd; ***They Put on Masks;*** illustrated by Jerry Ingram, Charles Scribner's Sons; 1974; Grades 3 - 6

"Yes and they made them of magic and dreams and the oldest dark secrets of life."

Thus begins the special magic of Byrd Baylor's sensitive book. Brilliant writing and great depth of feeling add to the high quality of the book.

Flowing designs create an aura of color to the authentic recreations of the masks. The children and adults who reviewed this book thoroughly enjoyed it.

However. There were some concerns about recreating the masks that are still used as part of religious ceremonies. Ms. Baylor writes that some of the masks "are worn in ceremonies today." The very fact that the book is high quality and appears sensitive leads to a sense of questioning about the very nature of writing about Native religion. Should this have been done? Children grasped the understanding of the sacredness of the masks and that this was a persons spiritual life being discussed. Adults said they enjoyed the book, but wondered if permission had been granted for writing about the masks that are still used as part of religious ceremonies.

The book is available through libraries and Internet sites and book stores. Intervene with this book.

Baylor, Byrd; ***When Clay Sings;*** illustrated by Tom Bahti, Charles Scribner's Sons; 1979; Grades 3 - 6

> The author has created a picture of the past that sings poetically and eloquently of Indian life in an earlier time. "The Indians say that every piece of clay is a piece of someone's life," writes Ms. Baylor. "They even say it has its own small voice and sings in its own way."
>
> The author and illustrator have been sensitive to that small voice and have shared the song with us.
>
> Designs used in the book are all derived from prehistoric Indian pottery of the American Southwest.

>→←<

Bealer, Alex W.; ***Only the Names Remain: The Cherokees and the Trail of Tears;*** illustrated by William Sauts Bock; Little, Brown and Co., 1972; Grades 3 - 6

> The Cherokee were an independent nation with their own government, language and alphabet. The book chronicles the history of the Cherokee from their days before Columbus through the times of contact with early European settlers. Leaders such as Sequoyah and John Ross are introduced in the text. The tragic story of the Cherokee Removal and infamous Trail of Tears is presented realistically and with respect.
>
> Some parts of the book contain negative images. "They saw that the white man could not be defeated because he knew many things the Indians had never learned. The Cherokees decided to follow the white man's path, share his vast knowledge..." and "They wished to learn how to farm and raise cattle." Sequoyah's

mother is termed a "Cherokee princess". These passages have a European superiority undertone.

The Native people are presented in the past tense; they are "gone like the buffalo". For example: "Now, in all of Georgia and Alabama, there is nothing left of the nation that had lived there for a thousand years before the white man came...They are gone like the buffalo and the elk which once roamed the mountain valleys. They have disappeared like the passenger pigeons...Now only the names remain..."

On the other hand, the last part of the book can have tremendous impact on students. It discusses the Cherokee Removal in such a way that children can begin to comprehend the horror that resulted from such governmental action. Said one soldier: "I fought through the Civil War and have seen men shot to pieces and slaughtered by the thousands. But the Cherokee Removal was the cruelest work I ever knew".

The overall impression is of a book written with sensitivity and accurate research, but with some flaws that children must be made aware of. As children become involved in critiquing texts, they will have a better understanding of unacceptable terminology. This book will enable children to find both the positive and the negative points in the text.

→←

Beals, Frank Lee; ***Chief Black Hawk;*** illustrated by Jack Merryweather; Harper, Row; 1963; Grades 4 - 6

1943 is the original copyright on this book about Black Hawk. The story records the life of Black Hawk from his youth to the

"Black Hawk War" and his eventual imprisonment. Freedom was finally gained for Black Hawk who was a chief, leader and protector of his people.

Though the author does use terms such as "squaw", "brave" and "Indian" throughout the text, it is more a sign of the language of the day than any intent to be demeaning. For example: "The ten white families had taken over most of the three thousand acres of fertile land near Saukenuk. They had built fences around the old Sauk cornfields and the Indians could not use them. The squaws planted their corn where the land was not fenced. When the corn which the squaws planted was high the white men plowed most of it under. The squaws who protested were beaten. Several young braves were beaten to death when they tried to help their squaws."

Frank Beals has attempted to write the story of Black Hawk sympathetically and accurately. Some of the black and white illustrations are all right, but the ones of the "Indians" doing their "war dance" are standard stereotypes. Some of the other pictures are unacceptable as well. Children who reviewed the text noted that the author did not use typical words such as savage, wild, dirty, or other such adjectives but the word "squaw" was used. The dialogue spoken by Native people is not fractured English. The students wondered what kind of a book he would have written today.

Overall, comparing this book to others written in the same time period, the children thought that by 1943 standards, the author had done quite well. Sadly, some of the books being published today are much worse.

There is much controversy over the use of the word squaw; it is hurtful to many Native women.

Unless a book is needed to show how stereotypes are acquired, leave this one alone.

→←

Beck, Barbara L.; ***The First Book of the Aztecs;*** illustrated by Page Cary; Watts, 1966; Grades 3 – 6

The history, culture and religion of the Aztecs is chronicled in the book. It also discusses the education and social classes of this great civilization. The achievements of the Aztecs are presented and a final chapter discusses the effect of the Spanish conquistadores on the Aztec culture. Brown and white illustrations accompany the text.

Also discussed throughout the text is the human sacrifices made by the Aztecs. "Upon winning the war, the Culhuan chief rewarded the Aztecs by giving his daughter to their chief. The Aztecs promptly sacrificed the girl. This, they thought, was the highest honor they could pay her." Because of this, the Culhuan chief "massacares" a number of Aztecs.

Then there's the tale of what happens to captives: "The two victorious kings set about the task of slashing open the captured victims' chests, snatching out their hearts, and offering them to the gods. Needless to say, the ceremony went on for days, and lesser lords in turn took over the grisly task."

One illustration presents a picture as "a priest plucks out the heart of a victim and sacrifices it to the sun." What about drunkenness? "…and the punishments for public drunkenness ranged from having one's head shaved to being beaten or strangled to death."

Do you know what children think of all this? The negative impact is horrific. The whole aspect of the religion of the Aztecs is handled in a way to reinforce misconceptions.

※

Beck, Barbara L.; ***The First Book of the Maya;*** illustrated by Page Cary; Watts; 1965; Grades 3 - 6

The book discusses the history, arts, communication, and religion of the Maya civilization. The great cities of the Maya are described. Black and white drawings and photographs illustrate the text.

The religion of the Maya is handled inappropriately. "Sacrifice played an important part in Mayan religion…Then blood was essential to the gods…Priests and commoners alike pierced their tongues and ears, smearing their blood on the idols…" And: "Generally the human sacrifices were made either by cutting the heart out of the victims, by throwing short spears at a painted area on the victim's chest, or by flinging the victim into a cenote, or sacred well." Etcetera. Etcetera.

※

Behn, Harry; ***The Painted Cave;*** Harcourt, Brace & World; 1957

Great Hunter was a small Indian boy with a name taller than a pine tree. He lived in a cave beside a river at the bottom of the

Grand Canyon. He wanted to know why his name was Great Hunter and went in search of the answer among the animals and gods of his country. In the process, he discovers the true values of life.

The marvelous shapes and designs of Mr. Behn's illustrations capture the mood of the Southwest. It is an unusual story with underlying values quietly told in a simple text.

Many children reviewed this book and the concensus was that it was acceptable.

→←

Belting, Natalia; *The Earth is on a Fish's Back: Tales of Beginnings;* illustrated by Esta Nesbitt; Holt, Rinehart and Winston; 1965; Grades 3 - 6

There are stories from around the world in this collection telling how various people perceived "beginning". Simply told, each legend is about two to three pages in length. Accompanying pictures in black and white are lucent additions to the text.

Of the twenty-one tales included in the book, eleven are from Native people of the Western Hemisphere. Some of the stories include: "How Spider Taught Women to Weave" as told by the Chaco Indians of Argentina, "How It Came About That There Is A Sun And A Moon" by the Kutenai Indians of the United States, "Why The Sun Is Brighter Than The Moon" from the Lilloet Indians of British Columbia and "Why There Are Four Seasons in the Year" as told by the Chippewayan Indians.

This collection can be used with children of all ages and is wonderful for reading aloud. Overall, the book seems to work, both for Native and non-Native readers. Teachers will find it appropriate for the classroom.

The Sun is a Golden Earring written by Ms. Belting and illustrated by Bernarda Bryson was a Caldecott Medal honor book in 1962.

⁂

Belting, Natalia; ***The Stars are Silver Reindeer;*** illustrated by Esta Nesbitt. Holt, Rinehart & Winston; 1966; Grades 3 - 6

The book is a poetic translation of how people all over the world have viewed the heavens. In Australia, the stars are pink and blue water lilies floating in the pale river of the Milky Way. The Milky Way is a river to the Aleutian Indians, too, but the stars are floating Kayaks. People have gazed at the stars since the beginning of time and have seen in them beautiful pictures and entrancing stories. The text presents fourteen poetic interpretions of these stories by various cultural groups.

It is an unusual book that could be used to stimulate creative expression in the classroom. The poem translations and the unique drawings captivate the imagination. Some students may find it difficult to understand at first, so it would be a useful book to read aloud and discuss.

⁂

Benchley, Nathaniel; ***Red Fox and his Canoe;*** illustrated by Arnold Lobel; Harper, Row; 1964; Grades K - 3

"Like all Indian boys, Red Fox had a canoe to go fishing in. But he wanted a bigger one." When he gets one, he welcomes aboard some talking bears, a talking raccoon and other animals. After much confusion, the canoe sinks and he returns home in a smaller canoe.

The book is intended as a humorous tale. Guess who provides the laughs? The drawings of the "Indians" are cartoon-like. The fanciful characters along with the preposterous illustrations depersonalize Native people and create an impression of absurdity. There is a juxtaposition of animals and child that reinforces negative images.

Nathaniel Benchley's father was the well-known writer and humorist Robert Benchley. Nathaniel's son is Peter Benchley author of *Jaws*.

Nathaniel Benchley was a witty and gifted writer. Arnold Lobel was a talented, funny and accomplished artist. Their involvement in this book is puzzling.

→←

Benchley, Nathaniel; ***Small Wolf;*** illustrated by Joan Sandin; Harper, Row; 1972; Grades K - 3

Small Wolf is a young boy who lives on the island of Manhattan. When he first encounters Europeans, he is surprised by their appearance. Small Wolf and his father try to make friends with the new people but the settlers are unfriendly and shoot their guns at them. Small Wolf's father does not accept selling the sky or sea. Small Wolf and his family find they must move from their homeland. The move is repeated again and again and again.

The story attempts to present the "Indian" concept of land as opposed to the European concept. The idea left with the reader is that the original inhabitants had no abstract thought of land ownership. This is a myth that has been perpetuated far too long by the publishing industry - probably to explain how people from another continent justified claiming the land for themselves. In reality, Native people did claim sovereignty over certain areas of land. Specific tribes had well-established boundaries for hunting, farming, fishing and living.

The ending leaves the impression that the people vanished and does not deal with the presence of Native people today.

In spite of the weaknesses in the text, the author shows a genuine desire to counteract the negative images in other books. Children should learn the truth about the conquest of the American continents and an adult can use this book to help them. Read this book, then follow it with **_The People Shall Continue_** by Simon J. Ortiz. The first is a simply told tale, the latter is a masterpiece.

→←

Benton-Benai, Edward; *The Mishomis Book: The Voice of the Ojibway*; illustrated by Joe Liles; Indian Country Press; 1979; Grades 4 and up

Edward Benton-Benai "is a full-blood Ojibway of the Turtle Clan of the Wisconsin Lac Court Orielles Band...The stories ...are in fact a reflection of the life he lived as a youth in the company of tribal elders."

The Mishomis Book is history and spirituality. It begins with the Ojibway creation story and continues to inform the reader of how original man walked the earth, the search for his grandmother, the story of the great flood, and continues with stories of Waynaboozhoo and the migration of the Anishinabe.

The book is a combination of beauty, richness and truth, and a delightful read. An introduction states: "This book is only a glimpse into the magnitude and depth of the spiritual history and heritage of the people from whom it came - the Ojibway Anishinabe". It is a wonderful glimpse, an amazing book.

The book is available through Internet sites and has been found at used book stores and library sales. ***The Mishnomis Book*** would be a significant gift to a teacher, a library, or a family. Highly recommended.

>‹

Bernstein, Margery and Janet Kobrin; ***The Summer Maker: An Ojibway Indian Myth;*** illustrated by Anne Burgess; Charles Scribner's Sons; 1977; Grades 1 - 4

The Ojibway Indians (the Anishinabe), told this story of how Summer first came to the world. Ojeeg, the fisher, wanted to help his son who was always cold. He sets out with Beaver, Wolverine, Otter and Lynx to find Summer. They must seek the help of a powerful spirit - a manitou.

In a daring adventure, the animals bravely succeed in bringing Summer into the cold world. Ojeeg, however, was unable to return to earth. "He dashed up a tree and scrambled all the way to the top of the sky. There, he clung to the stars…He could never reach the earth again." Every year Ojeeg watched as Summer came. "He was content."

The story is well handled and nicely adapted for readers in the primary grades. It will appeal to all ages as a faithful retelling of an Ojibway tale.

⇻⇺

Bierhorst, John; *The Dancing Fox, Arctic Folktales;* illustrated by Mary K. Okheena; William Morrow and Company; 1997; Grades 3 – 6

Inuit stories are rich, powerful, filled with realism, and sometimes touched with magic. In collecting the eighteen folktales, Bierhorst has been careful to retain the distinctive characteristics of the original stories. The introduction is a critical component of the book, explaining the depth and breath of storytelling for the Inuit.

"A Giant and Her Little Son" (Canada and Greenland), "The Dancing Fox" (Alaska), "The Great Giant Kinak" (Alaska), and "The Soul Wanderer" (Alaska, Canada, and Greenland), are some of the stories included in the collection. Inuit stories are living tales, filled with giants, strong women, tricksters, and heroes.

Inuit artist Mary K. Okheena has enriched the book with illustrations that are imbued with reverant expression and quiet energy that bring out the drama of the stories.

⇻⇺

Bierhorst, John; ***Doctor Coyote;*** illustrated by Wendy Watson; Macmillan; 1967; Grades 1 - 3

The stories included in **Doctor Coyote** bring together the Old World fables of Aesop and the trickster tales of the Native people of America. A sixteenth-century Indian scribe used the stories of Aesop and made Coyote the principal character. Trickster stories played a significant role in many cultures around the world. The trickster figure is complex, changing and growing with the various cultures. The trickster could be selfish or generous, hero or villain, foolish or wise.

In this tale, Coyote is seen wearing denim jeans, sitting in an aluminum chair, riding in a blue pickup truck, and visiting a sculptor. There are twenty stories with a moral on each page. A picture, on the opposite page, accompanies each tale.

The author's note is an essential part of the book. In it, Bierhorst gives information about the stories: "Entitled **Nican ompehua y cacan-illatoli**, (Here begin fable-stories), the Aztec collection is preserved in the manuscript known as 1628-bis in the National Library of Mexico."

Trickster stories are important to Native people. The question regarding this book lies mostly in the illustrations. Should Coyote be wearing a squash blossom necklace? Why are the female coyotes wearing silver-and-turquoise bracelets? A concern is also raised as to why Aesop is mixed up in the trickster tales of Native people. What purpose did the "Indian scribe" have in mind when he composed the stories?

Bierhorst, John, Ed; ***The Fire Plume: Legends of the American Indian;*** illustrated by Alan E. Cober; The Dial Press; 1969; Grades 3 - 6

A collection of American Indian tales, the legends were gathered by Henry Rowe Schoolcraft. During his travels through the upper Mississippi Valley and Great Lakes Region, Schoolcraft gathered the tales as he heard them. They are stories from the Chippewa, Shawnee, Ottawa and Menominee. There are tales of adventure and romance, refreshingly different from anything recorded in the present time.

The striking illustrations are hauntingly beautiful and heighten the element of mystery in the tales. The tales are not strict interpretations but the editors have preserved the spirit of the original tale.

→✦←

Bierhorst, John Ed. & Curtis, Edward S.; ***The Girl Who Married a Ghost and Other Tales from the North American Indians;*** illustrated with photographs by Edward S. Curtis; Four Winds; 1978; Grades 6 - Up

Edward S. Curtis was a photographer-writer-explorer during the early 1900's. Curtis collected a massive number of narratives from the masterpieces of American Indian folklore. His completed work filled twenty volumes and included the major tribes west of the Mississippi.

Included in the book are nine of the tales collected by Curtis. The tales represent the geographical range of the tribes Curtis studied. There is a ghost story from the Northwest Coast, from the Northwoods is the story of a woman who dressed like a man, and a sacred origin myth from the Southwest. The tribes represented are the Nisqualli, Kwakiutl, Gros Ventre, Comanche, Navajo, Hopi and Cree.

Editor Bierhorst has selected thirty mythic photographs to accompany the text.

⇥⇤

Bierhorst, John, Editor; ***The Ring in the Prairie: A Shawnee Legend;*** illustrated by Leo and Diane Dillon; Dial; 1970; Grades K - 3

The book is a retelling of a Shawnee tale first recorded by Henry Schoolcraft in the early 1800's. Worn into the tall prairie grasses is a strange circle that intrigues a young hunter. He discovers the circle was created by the dancing of twelve beautiful sisters who came from the sky. Waupee marries the youngest and most beautiful of the sisters, the daughter of a star. She eventually leaves him and takes their child home to the sky. Waupee follows and they are reunited in the heavens and return to earth as white hawks.

The beauty of the story is enhanced by the flowing illustrations in full color.

⇥⇤

Bierhorst, John Ed; ***Songs of the Chippewa;*** illustrated by Joe Servello; Farrar, Straus & Giroux; 1974; Grades 3 - 6

The songs are adapted from the collections of Frances Densmore and Henry Rowe Schoolcraft. They were collected near the western shores of the Great Lakes in the early 1900's by Densmore and in the mid 1800's by Schoolcraft. Some of the songs are in English and a few retain their original Chippewa words. Dream songs, lullabies, medicine charms and ritual chants are included. The simple arrangements are for piano or guitar.

The hauntingly beautiful illustrations create an aura of color that flow with the spirit of the text.

→←

Big Crow, Moses Nelson (Eyo Hiktepi); *A Legend from Crazy Horse Clan;* illustrated by Daniel Long Soldier; Tipi Press; 1967; Grades 4 - 6

When a midnight buffalo stampede catches a sleeping village by surprise, the people are scattered. Tashia Gnupa (Meadowlark) and her baby raccoon, Mesu (Little Brother), are left behind in the confusion. They "waited many days by their buffalo robe, but no one found them." Thus begins an odyssey as Tashia joins the Buffalo Nation and becomes a legend.

The editor's note has this to say about the book: "When he was a child, Moses Nelson Big Crow spent many winter evenings listening to his grandfather tell stories of Lakota life before and after the coming of the white man...Indian oral narration is spoken American literature in its finest form. When Lakota children of the 1980s become grandparents themselves, they will tell the legends again. Thanks to Moses Big Crow, one of those legends may well be A *Legend from Crazy Horse Clan.*"

There is a wondrous power and life to this story that comes from the author's family and people. The illustrations by Daniel Long Soldier add brilliance and vitality to the superb book.

➤⬅

Blades, Ann; *A Boy of Tache;* illustrated by the author; Tundra; 1973; Grades K - 3

Young Charlie eagerly awaits the signs of spring that tell him it is time to go north with his grandparents to trap beaver. At last, they are on their way and reach the cabin where they will spend their time while beaver trapping. When Grandfather becomes ill, Charlie and his grandmother care for him. When Grandfather gets sicker, Charlie makes the lonely trip back to get help.

The book portrays the essence of the people and their environment. Soft-tone watercolors illustrate the text.

In 1986, Ann Blades was the first recipient of the Elizabeth Mrazik-Cleaver Award. She received the Book-of-the-Year Medal in 1972 from the Canadian Association of Children's Librarians for the book *Mary of Mile 18.*

➤⬅

Blassingame, Wyatt; *Sacajawea, Indian Guide;* illustrated by Edward Shenton; Garrard; 1965; Grades 3 - 6

Sacajawea was twelve years old when she was captured by Minnetaree warriors and became their slave. She was later sold to Charbonneau, a French trapper, who made her his wife. The story tells the adventure of the search for the Northwest passage as Sacajawea, Charbonneau and their infant son lead Lewis and Clark on the famous journey through the Rocky Mountains to the Pacific coast.

As the story opens: "The girl ate the buffalo meat raw. There was no time to cook it. She was too hungry. She held the raw meat in her hands and tore it with her teeth. All the other Indians, standing around the dead buffalo, ate in the same way."

Even though Sacajawea is credited with getting the men through difficult times, she is portrayed as being simple and naive.

When Charbonneau and Sacajawea move to St. Louis, "...she grew restless. She was an Indian." When her son returns from Europe, he returns to the West. "...the Indian blood was strong in him."

The illustrations are preposterous and stereotypical. The opening picture matches the text and shows the people eating the raw meat and drinking the blood, though the buffalo isn't even skinned yet. It's an outrageous representation. There is no new material here, instead just another oversimplified, generalized account of a remarkable woman.

→←

Bleeker, Sonia; *The Apache Indian: Raiders of the Southwest;* illustrated by Althea Karr; Morrow; 1951; Grades 3 - 6

Sonia Bleeker has written a series on various American Indian Tribes. The book is presented in simple and direct language and tells the historical aspects of everyday life, seasonal activities and a glimpse of the tribe today. Raiders is an unfortunate choice in the title.

Simple drawings in black and white accompany the text.

Note: The Sonia Bleeker books are formula non-fiction that have been highly successful. For the most part, they are well researched and present an encylopedic type narrative. At times in the books, there is some reference to "scalping" and "women doing the work". Children need to be aware of the negative aspects of some of the vocabulary and should be able to look at the texts objectively using the Criteria for Judging Books about Native people. The books can be the beginning of analytical research for students. Ms. Bleeker said she began writing children's books about Native people when her sons were young because she could not find any books for their age level.

Many contemporary books have listed Sonia Bleeker as a source.

Ms. Bleeker has written many books about Native people. Her husband was Herbert Spencer Zim who was the author of many pocket-size books on nature.

→←

Bleeker, Sonia; *The Aztec: Indians of Mexico;* Morrow; 1963; Grades 3 - 6

Sonia Bleeker describes the Aztecan way of life, their food and clothing, their ceremonies and the end of their civilization.

Simple drawings in black and white accompany the text.

See note above.

>><<

Bleeker, Sonia; *The Cherokee: Indians of the Mountains;* illustrated by Althea Karr; Morrow; 1952; Grades 3 - 6

Details of daily life are interwoven with legend and history in a lively manner. Various chapters deal with marriage customs, hunting, shamans and an enthusiastic ball game.

Drawings are in black and white.

See note with *The Apache Indian.*

>><<

Bleeker, Sonia; *The Chippewa Indians: Rice Gatherers of the Great Lakes;* illustrated by Patricia Boodell; Morrow; 1955; Grades 3 - 6

The Chippewa followed a life of seasonal travel. The fascinating life of the Chippewa through the Crane family's activities is a focus of the book. It deals with the Chippewa historically and includes a final chapter on the Chippewa of the fifties. (Note the copyright date.)

The lively, detailed drawings in black and white match the text.

See note with *The Apache Indian.*

Bleeker, Sonia; ***The Crow Indians: Hunters of the Northern Plains;*** illustrated by Althea Karr; Morrow; 1963; Grades 3-6

The Crow Indians depended on the great herds of buffalo for sustenance. They followed the herds and their culture was interwoven with the buffalo. The book describes the hunts, organization of camps, dress, customs, legends and history.

The black and white illustrations match the text.

See note with ***The Apache Indian.***

Bleeker, Sonia; ***The Delaware Indians: Eastern Fishermen and Farmers;*** illustrated by Patricia Boodell; Morrow; 1953; Grades 3-6

The hunting practices, fishing, clamming and customs of the Delaware are presented in the story of one family's daily life. Also included are some legends and ceremonies of the tribe.

It is a well-researched and, to the children that read the book, "it was full of information." Black and white illustrations accompany the text.

See note with ***The Apache Indian.***

➤⬅

Bleeker, Sonia; *The Eskimo: Arctic Hunters and Trappers;* illustrated by Patricia Boodell; Morrow; 1959; Grades 3 - 6

> An informative account of the resourcefulness of the Eskimo, the book describes the Eskimo people, their customs and culture as well as giving a report of the land and climate. A final chapter summarizes Arctic exploration. The copyright date gives a clue to the use of Eskimo instead of Inuit.
>
> Accompanying drawings in black and white are carefully accurate yet expressive.
>
> The note with *The Apache Indian* gives additonal information.

➤⬅

Bleeker, Sonia; **Horsemen of the Western Plateaus: The Nez Perce Indians;** illustrated by Patricia Boodell; Morrow; 1957; Grades 3 - 6

> This is a highly informative book which describes in factual style the life of the Nez Perce Indians. The history of the tribe is given from the coming of the white man to life on a reservation. Spotted Salmon, an experienced hunter, fisherman and horseman, is the guide to the customs and culture of his tribe.
>
> The illustrations are imaginative and reasonable.
>
> The note with *The Apache Indian* gives additional information.

Bleeker, Sonia; ***The Inca: Indians of the Andes;*** illustrated by Patricia Boodell; Morrow; 1960; Grades 3 -6

Sonia Bleeker describes the achievements of the Inca, relates the history of their conquests and of their eventual, tragic destruction by the Spaniards.

The illustrations are carefully researched. For additional information on this formula style book, see ***The Apache Indian***.

Bleeker, Sonia; ***Indians of the Longhouse: The Story of the Iroquois;*** illustrated by Althea Karr; Morrow; 1950; Grades 3 -6

The book precisely relates the daily life of the Iroquois before the invasion on their land by white people.

It is written authoritatively in an encyclopedic manner. Black and white illustrations accompany the text.

See note with ***The Apache Indians.***

Bleeker, Sonia; ***Mission Indians of California;*** illustrated by Althea Karr; Morrow; 1956; Grades 3 - 6

The book introduces the ceremonies, legends, customs and food as vividly portrayed through the activities of Little Singer. Little

Singer is a young 18th century California Indian. Descriptions of an old way of life are intimately detailed.

The black and white drawings illustrate the text.

See note with *The Apache Indians.*

→←

Bleeker, Sonia; *The Navajo: Herders, Weavers and Silversmiths;* illustrated by Patricia Boodell; Morrow; 1958; Grades 3 - 6

Slim Runner, a thirteen year old Navajo boy, learns to draw while spending months in the hospital. The text describes Navajo life and culture and the conflicts in the life of Slim Runner. A final chapter tells the history of the Navajo.

Effective drawings by Patricia Boodell add interest and vitality to the story.

See note with *The Apache Indians.*

→←

Bleeker, Sonia; *The Pueblo Indians: Farmers of the Rio Grande;* illustrated by Patricia Boodell; Morrow; 1955; Grades 3 - 6

With forthright simplicity the book tells the culture, customs and history of the Pueblo people. Young Hawk, living in the time before the white people came, is the son of a chief. The daily activities of the Pueblo unfold as we follow Young Hawk and meet his people. The last chapter deals with Pueblo life in the fifties.

The text presents a realistic description of an old way of life. Black and white drawings illustrate the text.

See note with ***The Apache Indians.***

>←

Bleeker, Sonia; ***The Sea Hunters: Indians of the Northwestern Coast;*** illustrated by Althea Karr; Morrow; 1951; Grades 3 - 6

The Indians of the Northwest Coast had great respect for the creatures they hunted. Ceremonies which pay tribute to the hunted are described. Sonia Bleeker brings to life with excellent narration the activities of the Northwest Coast People.

Illustrations in black and white add clarity to the text.

See note with ***The Apache Indians.***

>←

Bleeker, Sonia; ***The Seminole Indians;*** illustrated by Althea Karr; Morrow; 1954; Grades 3 - 6

The Seminole Creek Indians of Alabama and Georgia were forced to move to Florida. The author chronicles their struggles, wars and adaptation to a new home. A concluding chapter details the Seminole living in Florida in the fifties.

Illustrations complement the easily read text. The note with ***The Apache Indians*** gives additonal information on this formula style book.

❧❦

Bleeker, Sonia; ***The Sioux Indians: Hunters and Warriors of the Plains;*** illustrated by Kisa N. Sasaki; Morrow; 1962; Grades 3 - 6

The book chronicles the life of the Sioux from their glorious days while the buffalo were abundant until settlers invaded their land. The Sun Dance is discussed. Life in the early sixties is also covered.

The book's clear and simple writing style along with explanatory illustrations add to its appeal. Sioux was the standard word used in 1962 publishing. The book is formula style in nature. There are some instances of stereotypical reporting. See note with ***The Apache Indians.***

❧❦

Blood, Charles, and Martin Link; ***The Goat in the Rug;*** illustrated by Nancy Winslow Parker; Four Winds Press; 1076; Grades 1 - 3

Okay. The scenario in the book is a place near Window Rock with the heroine being a goat. (Yes - a goat) In fact the goat - Geraldine, tells the story. It seems that Geraldine's Navajo owner, Glenmae, was observed sharpening a pair of scissors.

Glenmae is a weaver and Geraldine provides the raw material from whence to weave a rug. Geraldine is not about to take a back seat, however, and describes for the reader the step by step procedure of clipping, carding, dyeing and weaving the final product.

It is a charming story that the child reader will find amusing. Geraldine weaves her special magic in the form of a very unique, humorous tale. The illustrations contribute to the overall humor and enjoyment of the informative text.

※

Brewer, Linda Skinner; ***O Wakaga: Activities for Learning About the Plains Indians;*** illustrated by Roger Fernandes and Pat Klink; Daybreak Star Press; 1981; Grades 1 - 6

O Wakaga - I made it! - is a book designed to give children meaningful ways to learn about Lakota people. A wealth of information is included with some remarkable activities for children to actually do and make. There are directions for making a parfleche, an eagle art project, a shield, a trail language story and a Lakota moon calendar. Some recipes are included that are simple to make and quite good.

Along with activities, there is accurate commentary contrasting the history of the people with the scene as it is today. Teachers and parents who want to teach understanding and respect for Native cultures will find this book extremely valuable. The library should be able to assist in locating a copy for loan. Buying the book through various Internet outlets would be a way of owning this wonderful book. It's worth it.

※

Brewster, Benjamin (pseud. - Mary Elting); ***The First Book of Indians;*** illustrated by Ursula Koering; Watts; 1950; Grades 3 - 6

The book gives an overview of North American Indian life in historical perspective. It gives a brief introduction to a few specific tribes. It details early living conditions of some tribes, their beliefs, contributions to civilization and their meeting with non-Indian settlers.

There are illustrations on every page.

Overall, this book deals with issues of Native people on an extremely superficial level. It's an "Everything you wanted to know about" Indians in sixty-nine pages. There is too much material presented and little information. It will give children the idea that there really isn't all that much to be learned about Native people.

The author has tried to deal sensitively with the material, but sometimes simplification can mean trivializing the subject matter. It's exactly the kind of text that kids look for when they need to write a report on "Indians". Children need to know there is no in-depth look at tribal life in the pages of this book.

→←

Brink, Carol Ryrie; ***Caddie Woodlawn;*** illustrated by Trina Schart Hyman; Macmillan; 1935; Grades 4 - 6

Caddie Woodlawn was awarded the John Newberry Medal for the most distinguished contribution to American literature for children.

The pranks and adventures of redheaded Caddie captivate children everywhere. The book takes place on the Wisconsin

A Second Look, Native Americans in Children's Books

frontier in the 1860s when Caddie is eleven years old. An "Indian" village is near Caddie's home. The settlers worry about an Indian massacre, patronize the Indians and don't trust them.

Throughout the narrative there is a lot of talk about massacres; in fact, one chapter is entitled "Massacree!". Another chapter called "Scalp Belt" uses the word "scalp" or "scalp belt" nineteen times. The ten pages of this chapter are references to how the Indians obtained scalps.

Also in the chapter "Scalp Belt", Mrs. Woodlawn tells Caddie, "You do have a way with savages, Caroline..." " 'Ooh! ooh!' said Hetty. 'Is it real hair off people's heads?' " There's lots of Oohing as the older brother pretends to scalp Hetty and says: "Where's the butcher knife, Warren?" But as the dialogue continues, they decide that it's "not white folks' scalp locks anyway..."

There's talk about the Indians "bright black eyes" and "tangled hair". One of the chapters describes how an Indian woman leaves her three children because her husband is embarrassed "now" to have married an Indian. (Seems there's lots of white folks around and the Indian woman needs to go.) She says her good-byes to her crying children in the schoolroom in front of all the students and the teacher.

In the evening, the family discusses the mother leaving her children and that "father would never do that." Because... " 'Father marry an Indian?' cried Tom. 'He never would' ".

" 'Perhaps not,' said Mrs. Woodlawn, smiling a little and tossing her head, remembering how pretty she had been as a girl in Boston. 'But, if he had...' "

In reference to the Woodlawn family it says that the Indians had never "...got used to seeing them. White men and their children they had seen often enough, but never such as these, who wore, above their pale faces, hair the color of flame and sunset. During the first year...the Indians had come from all the country around to look at them...touching the children's hair and staring. Poor Mrs. Woodlawn, frightened nearly out of her wits..."

Mrs. Woodlawn says "those frightful savages will eat us out of house and home"... "...the way they look at the children's hair frightens me. They might want a red scalp to hang on their belts." Page after page of this type of dialogue and narrative flows through the text.

Put your mind at ease though for the settlers have found one "good Indian" in the group, "You needn't be afraid, Caddie. He's a good Indian." (It's - Indian John!)

Caddie lets out an occasional "Indian war whoop", and helps the abandoned Indian children with "their half-savages eyes". When Caddie talks to "Indian John", he always speaks in Grade B Movie "Indian" dialogue. Such as: " 'John go, too,' said the Indian." "Him hurt", says John in reference to a dog. Later when giving the scalp belt to Caddie: "Him very old..." He calls the scalp belt "him", too.

It could be said that the book is merely presenting the settlers' point of view. That is an understandable assumption. It steps over the line, however, with the author's use of adjectives, dialogue, plot twists and characterization of Native people. The author manipulates the narrative in such a manner to be demeaning to the "Indian" people being represented.

This book continues to be popular in libraries and is in paperback form in many bookstores. Children will not understand the negative impact of such a book. It's only purpose will be to show children how negative stereotypes are formed and preserved.

Carol Ryrie Brink won the Newberry Award in 1936 for ***Caddie Woodlawn.*** She also won the Friends of American Writers Award in 1956 for ***The Headland*** and the Irvin Kerlan Award in 1978 for ***Four Girls on a Homestead.***

When books like ***Caddie Woodlawn*** receive awards, it merely spawns decades of similar stories that perpetuate stereotypes and harmful images with chilling regularity.

→←

Brown, Dee; ***Tepee Tales of the American Indian: Retold for Our Times;*** illustrated by Louis Mofsie; Holt, Rinehart and Winston; 1979; Grades 4 - 6

Tale spinners have captivated their audiences down through the centuries, whether it is around campfires, in tepees or wherever groups gathered to hear the tales. Thirty-six stories from more than two dozen tribes are part of the collection.

The book is arranged according to category – When Animals Lived as Equals with People; Allegories; Tricksters and Magicians; Heroes and Heroines; and so forth. Brown gives a brief lead-in to each section giving background information that could be helpful to the storyteller.

These stories could be useful for modern-day talespinners who have the gift of captivating audiences and who follow the oral tradition.

One of the disturbing aspects of the book is in the introduction where credit is given to a few "far-sighted anthropologists, ethnologists, folklorists, and non-professional lovers of good stories" who saw the value of these stories and wrote them down. Otherwise, "...we would now have almost no legends of these people". It's a shame Brown does not give credit to the Native people for preserving their own stories.

Louis Mofsie is of Hopi and Winnebago ancestry.

→><←

Bruchac, Joseph; ***The Earth Under Sky Bear's Feet: Native American Poems of the Land;*** illustrated by Thomas Locker; Philomel Books; 1995; All ages

The girl asked if Sky Bear could see everything from the sky. "Hen, Granddaughter, as she travels the sky this whole earth is stretched beneath her feet. Listen, and I will share with you some of the stories our old people tell about what Sky Bear sees and hears through the night."

Thus begins the wonderful collection of poems by Joseph Bruchac. The tales of many Nations are reflected in the pages of this book: "Song to the Firefly" Anishinabe, Great Lakes. "Flute Song" Pima, Southwest. "The Scattered Stars" Cochiti

Pueblo, Southwest. Twelve exceptional poems are told from the viewpoint of Sky Bear.

Mr. Bruchac lovingly connects Native American storytelling with the essence of the natural world in which it is based. As Bruchac relates in the author's note: "I wanted to remind readers that, as Native children have always been taught, there can be as much to see in the living night, as in the more famliar light of day."

Thomas Locker has shared remarkable paintings to accompany the collection of poems. Life has been breathed into the stories through the power and mystery apparent in the striking illustrations. Thomas Locker is an internationally known artist.

Joseph Bruchac is a well-known writer and storyteller. He is the recipient of many awards, including the PEN Syndicated Fiction Award and an American Book Award. Mr. Bruchac is of Abenaki, Slovak, and English ancestry.

→←

Bruchac, Joseph; *The First Strawberries, A Cherokee Story;* illustrated by Anna Vojtech; Dial Books for Young Readers; 1993; Grades 1 – 4

"Long ago when the world was new, the Creator made a man and a woman....They married, and for a long time they lived together and were happy." One afternoon a quarrel came between them, they were both angry and the woman said she could no longer live with the man. The woman walked toward the sun; her husband followed, but he could not catch up with her.

The Sun watched the husband and saw that the man was sorry. "…I will help you said the Sun." The Sun shone and raspberries grew up, but the woman paid no attention. Sun grew blueberries and blackberries, but the woman's anger was so great that she did not see them. Finally, Sun caused strawberries to grow. "They glowed like fire in the grass, and the woman had to stop when she saw them in front of her." The sweetness of the strawberries reminded the woman of how happy she had been with her husband before their quarrel. It was the gift of the strawberries that had the power to reunite the couple. Even today, when "the Cherokee people eat strawberries, they are reminded…that friendship and respect are as sweet as the taste of ripe, red berries."

Watercolors by Anna Vojtech glow with the spirit of the story. Every page dances with brightly colored pictures that breathe with life.

Joseph Bruchac is an award winning author and storyteller. He is of Abnenaki, Slovak, and English ancestry.

※

Bruchac, Joseph; *Iroquois Stories: Heroes and Heroines, Monsters and Magic;* illustrated by Daniel Burgevin; The Crossing Press; 1985; Grades 4 - 6

This is an excellent book; the stories live.

In the introduction of the book, Joseph Bruchac sets the tone for all the wonderful stories he tells. He gives background information in "Telling the Stories" while "The People of the Longhouse" gives a history of the people. Part III of the introduction is "The Storytellers" and presents helpful information about traditional settings as well as a perspective on the storytellers.

It is an impressive collection of stories that "entertain, instruct and empower". As it states at the beginning "...a wise leader of the Senecas said, 'Our religion is not a thing of paint and feathers, but of the heart.' So it is true of the stories of the Hotinonsonni, the longhouse people. These stories do not need longhouses, or central fires, or fur robes, or ceremonial garments to come alive."

Mr. Bruchac is of Abenaki, Slovak, and English ancestry. He is the recipient of many awards including the PEN Sydicated Fiction Award, an American Book Award, the Hope S. Dean Memorial Award from the Foundation for Children's Books, the Cherokee Nation Prose Award, and the NEA Creative Writing Fellowship.

→←

Bruchac, Joseph; ***Seeing the Circle;*** photographs by Joseph Bruchac; photographs by John Christopher Fine; Richard C. Owen Publisher, Inc.; 1999; All grades

Fans of Joseph Bruchac will delight in this simply told story of how Mr. Bruchac became a writer and how he spends his days. A compelling part of the narrative tells how the author learned about his Abenaki background.

"When I was very young, I lived with my mother's parents, and they would never mention our Indian blood. Why? Back then it was shameful or even dangerous to be identified as Indian."

The photographs add immeasureably to this glimpse into the author's life.

➜✛

Bruchac, Joseph, ed.; ***Songs from this Earth on Turtle's Back: Contemporary American Indian Poetry;*** Greenfield Review Press; 1983; Adaptable for all ages.

The quality of writing in this collection is marvelous. In his introduction, Joseph Bruchac says: "It is a collection of contemporary writers, not a compilation of chants or songs put together in the 19th century by a non-Indian ethnologist or 'retranslated' by a contemporary non-Indian writer."

There are selections from fifty-two Native American poets in this anthology. Though the target audience is adults, this anthology can be used with elementary children as well. Sixth graders who read the text selected certain subjects that appealed to them, and they all expressed delight in the photos of the poets and the autobiographical information about each person. Younger children enjoyed having the poetry read to them.

Joseph Bruchac, of Abenaki, Slovak, and English ancestry, has received nurmerous awards, including the Cherokee Nation Prose Award.

Bruchac, Joseph, and Jonathan London; ***Thirteen Moons on Turtles Back: A Native American Year of Moons;*** illustrated by Thomas Locker; Philomel Books; 1992; Grades 1 – 6

Bruchac and London convey the depth and lyrical feeling of the thirteen moons of the year. In this clear, flowing collection of poems, the voice of the natural world reaches out and envelops the reader in wonder and awe.

Beginning with the Northern Cheyenne Moon of Popping Trees to the Anishinabe Maple Sugar Moon and the Seneca Strawberry Moon, the book continues through to the Thirteenth Moon – the Big Moon of the Abenaki.

In reference to the scales on turtles back, Grandfather explains that "There are always thirteen on Old Turtle's back and there are always thirteen moons in each year. Many people do not know this. They do not know, as we Abenaki know, that each moon has its own name and every moon has its own stories."

A celebration of the traditions of Native people, the authors remind us "that all things are connected and we must try to live in balance."

Dramatic, striking paintings by Thomas Locker accompany each poem. Joseph Bruchac, of Abenaki and European heritage, is an award winning-author. Jonathan London, a poet and author, has work in many publications.

Bruchac, Joseph; ***The Wind Eagle and Other Abenaki Stories;*** illustrated by Kahionhes; Bowman Books, 1985; Grades 4 - 6

> ***Wind Eagle*** is one of the best collections available of Gluskabi stories. In a preface, John Moody gives a brief history of the Abenaki people. He says: "Listen, then, give the gift of your attention to the spirit, the meaning, the depth of ancient knowledge breathing here. These are the stories and songs, the people of this place, the Dawn Land. Listen. Listen well, an ancient voice is speaking."
>
> Included in the anthology are stories of "The Coming of Gluskabi", "Gluskabi and the Game Animals", "Gluskabi and the Wind Eagle", "How Gluskabi Stole Tobacco", "Gluskabi and the Water Monster", and "How Gluskabi Brought the Summer".
>
> Joseph Bruchac, of Abenaki, Slovak, and English ancestry, is an outstanding storyteller who has retold a number of Iroquois and Abenaki stories available in other collections. Kahionhes, whose illustrations add immeasurably to the spirit of the text, is a member of the Turtle Clan of the Mohawk Nation.

→✦←

Bryant, Kathleen; ***Kokopelli's Gift;*** illustrated by Michelle Tsosie Sisneros, Kiva Publishing; 2002, Grades K – 3

> Kokopelli is known throughout the Southwest as a trickster, a trader, and sometimes he is considered a priest or god. People speak of Kokopelli in terms of growth, music, magic, hunting, rain and fertililty. ***Kokopelli's Gift*** is one of the many stories

of the trickster known to the Pueblo, Navajo, Hohokam, and Apache.

In this story, Kokopelli arrives at "an ancient pueblo during a time of drought". People of the village are engaged in their regular day-to-day activities when young Nali sees a traveler "coming up the path…" He was "…carrying a pack on his back. He was tired and dirty and thin."

Because of the drought and the small amount of food for the village, the elders tell Kokopelli he can rest in the shade, but then he must go away. While Kokopelli rested in the shade of the cliffs, he played his flute and the children went to listen. Soon others came to listen to the fluteplayer.

Kokopelli offered the people more than music and happy sounds; he gave them seeds. "Inside the pot were hundreds of seeds, of all different colors, like a rainbow." The people brought him gifts and he taught them to do the dance that would bring rain.

Imbued with energy and merriment, the illustrations by Michelle Tsosie Sisneros dance with the music of the text. Sisneros has won many awards for her paintings. She is Navajo, Laguna, Santa Clara, and Mission Indian.

Kathleen Bryant is the author of five novels and numerous magazine articles.

Buff, Mary and Conrad; *Dancing Cloud;* illustrated by Conrad Buff; Viking; 1957; Grades 3 - 6

> A colorful picture is created of the life of the Navajo people. Dancing Cloud and his sister live with their family in a hogan at the foot of Pottery Butte. The reader is included in their everyday life as they tend the flocks, shear sheep, weave blankets, have adventures in the buttes, visit the trading post and listen to the talk of their elders as they sit around the fire.
>
> Throughout the text, the people are called Navajo and Dineh. Sometimes, though, there is reference to the Indian. "An Indian told him…" "…the Indian saw a very high red cliff…" "The Indian had happened upon a band of wild horses."
>
> Note the copyright date of 1957. The book very much reflects the fifties. The book jacket states: "For this new and revised edition, Mrs. Buff has made slight changes in the story and Mr. Buff has drawn new pictures in black and white for the whole book. This brings back into print one of the favorite books about the Indians." Children enjoyed the historical aspect of the book. For the child reviewer, the 1950s was a "long time ago."

>―<

Buff, Mary and Conrad; *Hah-Nee of the Cliff Dwellers;* Houghton Mifflin; 1965; Grades 3 - 6

> Hah-Nee is a cliff dweller who lives during the time of the "Great Drought", Hah-Nee and his family set forth to begin life anew in the distant land of the Great River. The setting is the southwestern United States during the 13th century.

A well-researched book, the text gives a correct picture of the devastation the Great Drought had upon the culture and lives of the cliff dwellers. It is beautifully written and illustrated with sensitivity, warmth and understanding.

Buff, Mary and Conrad; **Kemi-An Indian Boy: Before the White Man Came;** Ward Ritchie Press; 1966; Grades 3 - 6

The setting is the Indian Stone Age in California. Kemi breaks a treasured stone cooking pot belonging to his mother. He accompanies his father on a long journey to the sea. He hopes to trade with the island people to obtain a new pot to replace the one he accidently broke.

It is a well-written adventure story with artistic pencil drawings that add to the spirit of the text.

Buff, Mary and Conrad; **Magic Maize;** Houghton Mifflin; 1953; Grades 3 - 6

The story reveals the ancient Mayan culture and presents an intimate view of the strong family unit and the deep spirituality of the people. Fabian secretly plants twenty kernels of corn and uncovers a rare jade earplug of the ancients. The maize and earplug lead to interesting adventures that convince Fabian's father that old traditions and new ways can blend to bring good fortune.

The illustrations are realistic and the text in large print and simple language make this an interesting, attractive book.

Bulla, Clyde Robert; ***Eagle Feather;*** illustrated by Tom Two Arrows; Crowell; 1953; Grades 1 -4

Eagle Feather is a young Navajo boy whose daily tasks involve caring for the sheep and goats for his family. One day Eagle Feather and his brother and sister carelessly cause a truck to be damaged. The mistake forces Eagle Feather to leave his home and go to work for a cruel cousin. After summer is over, there is a plot to escape from his cousin, and he is reunited with his family.

Though the story revolves around Native people, there is no in-depth look at Navajo culture. Instead, the cruelty of "his cousin" is emphasized. They have names like "Crook Nose", "Round Woman" and "Teasing Boy". Eagle Feather received his name because he once found an eagle feather when he was a baby and he finds another one in the story and "put it in his headband". And no, that is not how Native people become entitled to wear an eagle feather.

Clyde Robert Bulla began his career as a reluctant writer, but went on to publish more than eighty books.

Tom Two Arrows, the illustrator, is "a pure-blood Iroquois, born and educated on the Onondaga reservation in New York".

Bulla, Clyde R.; *John Billington, Friend of Squanto;* Crowell; 1956; Grades 3 - 6

> John Billington was among the passengers of the Mayflower when it sailed for Plymouth. Life was difficult that first year, but with the help of Squanto the colonists survived the winter. Young John was always getting into trouble and one day while lost in the woods, he was taken by a group of Indians to their village. Squanto found him and returned him to his home. When Thanksgiving was observed, Chief Massasoit's "Indians" were invited. However, the Indians who had captured John also came as friends to see John. John Billington came to be known as the boy who brought peace between the Indians and white men.
>
> The book contains larger than average print, an easy vocabulary and action which make it one enjoyed by children. The book adds to the continuing mystique about Squanto and perpetuates the myth.

Bulla, Clyde Robert; *Pocahontas and the Strangers;* illustrated by Peter Burchard; Scholastic Books; 1971; Grades 3 - 6

> Sometimes, when a book is based on real events and is well written, the flaws can be overlooked. In this retelling of the Pocahontas story, the deficiencies serve to reinforce the myths that surround a whole nation of people.

In this version of John Smith and Pocahontas, she is constantly referred to as a "princess" and her father is a "king". Once again it must be pointed out that there is no such thing as "Indian" kings or princesses. The culture of the English is made to seem superior since the Native people are fascinated with the possessions of the "palefaces". The "firesticks are stronger than bows and arrows" and John Smith made "marks on the paper" - "She seemed puzzled". When two young women help Pocahontas into some dresses they said: " 'Something is wrong,' said Betsy." " 'Her hair,' said Mary."

Pocahontas is made to appear simple and naive, both in her own land and when she accompanies her husband to England. In London she is enthralled with everything. Referring to the Tower of London, she says: "So tall." When she sees London Bridge for the first time: "How can it be? How could they build it all the way across the river?" Her naivete is referred to throughout the book.

The eternal story of Pocahontas saving the life of John Smith is an integral part of the narrative. Children need to know that historians generally agree that John Smith was a dishonest teller of tales and more than likely he made up the myth of Pocahontas coming to his rescue. As a whole, the book presents nothing new, but instead further reinforces a fantasy.

➻➻

Bulla, Clyde R.; *Squanto, Friend of the Pilgrims;* Crowell; 1954; Grades 3 - 6

Squanto is the well-known "Indian" who saved the colonists of Plymouth from starvation their first winter in the colony. Mr. Bulla goes more deeply into the story of Squanto and tells of his adventures in England, his stay in London and his kidnapping by a greedy ship captain when Squanto returns to his homeland. The story continues through his escape and finally tells of his lasting friendship with the Plymouth colonists.

The book is formula storytelling, but the truth of the various Squanto stories must be questioned. The myth is so ingrained that it is difficult to challenge. It is important that the child reader is aware that there may be "fiction" in these tales.

Caduto, Michael J. and Joseph Bruchac; ***Keepers of the Animals: Native American Stories and Wildlife Activities for Children;*** illustrated by John Kahionhes Fadden; Fulcrum, Publishing; 1991; All ages

Vine Deloria, Jr. has written a foreward for this book.

Keepers of the Animals speaks eloquently and reverently of the relationship humans have with all the earth's creatures. The book provides a comprehensive study of ecology, natural history, stewardship, and a reverence for all life. The authors and illustrators provide a rich look at Native American stories, combined with hands-on activities for students. There is a section that gives "Tips and Techniques for Bringing This Book to Life."

The goals of the book are clearly defined as shown in the beginning of the book: "Foster Aesthetic Appreciation", "Include Moral Issues: Environmental and Social Ethics", "Respect Spiritual and Religious Beliefs", and "Conducting the Field Trip (With Special Tips for Larger Groups)". Many more tips are included throughout the narrative of the book that will be especially helpful to adults and group leaders.

The stories are wonderful and the tribal group is recognized for each story. "How the Spider Symbol Came to the People (Osage-Plains)" "Eagle Boy (Zuni - Southwest)" "Turtle Races With Beaver (Seneca – Eastern Woodland)" There are twenty-four stories in all with activities accompanying each story.

Michael J. Caduto is a storyteller, educator, and has received the New England Award for Excellence in Environmental Education.

Joseph Bruchac is the recipient of many awards for writing, including the PEN Syndicated Fiction Award, an American Book Award, and the Hope S. Dean Memorial Award from the Foundation for Children's Books. Mr. Bruchac is of Abenaki, Slovak and English ancestry.

John Kahionhes Fadden has illustrated more than twenty books about Native people. A member of the Turtle Clan of the Mohawk Nation, he has illustrated other books written by Mr. Caduto and Mr. Bruchac.

Every book written by this team of authors/illustrator should be in every library and available for every teacher. The books are treasures.

Caduto, Michael J. and Joseph Bruchac; ***Keepers of the Earth: Native American Stories and Environmental Activities for Children;*** illustrated by John Kahionhes Fadden and Carol Wood; Fulcrum, Inc.; 1988; All ages

N. Scott Momaday has written the foreward for this book.

Keepers of the Earth is a wonderful combination of Native American Stories with social studies, science and environmental activities accompanying each story. It is participatory learning at its finest; with hands-on activities, clearly defined goals, an interdisciplinary approach to teaching and legitimate tales from Native people.

It is exactly the kind of book needed by classroom teachers who feel overwhelmed by the multitude of requirements of a present-day curriculum. The stories are brief, usually two or three pages, and the activities are open-ended to enable the teacher to determine the amount of time that will be spent on each lesson. The lesson plans are detailed, materials needed are listed and there are ideas for extending the lesson.

To further aid the teacher, the authors have devoted a chapter on "Tips and Techniques for Bringing This Book to Life" and have included a Glossary to the Native American words that appear in the book. Twenty-five stories from twenty different tribes have been selected for the text.

Joseph Bruchac is of Abenaki, Slovak, and English ancestry. He has received many awards for writing, including the NEA Creative Writing Fellowship. Michael J. Caduto is a storyteller, an author, and an ecologist. John Kahionhes Fadden is a member of the Turtle Clan of the Mohawk Nation. Carol Wood's pen and ink drawings have appeared in numerous articles.

It is an absolutely marvelous book that should be in every school and library. This extraordinary book is not for teachers only - it's for everyone.

⇢⇠

Caduto, Michael J. and Joseph Bruchac; *Keepers of Life: Discovering Plants Through Native American Stories and Earth Activities for Children;* Story illustrations by John Kahionhes Fadden and David Kanietakeron Fadden; Chapter illustrations by Marjorie C. Leggit and Carol Wood; Fulcrum Publishing, 1994, All ages.

Marilou Awiakta, Cherokee, has written the forward for this book.

Keepers of Life includes an extraordinary collection of stories and hands-on activities that will promote curiosity and environmental awareness in children. The book presents an interdisciplinary and experiential approach to the connectiveness of all living things. Students are encouraged to become totally involved in the lessons by using all their senses. Children will be invited to touch a seed, taste a berry, listen as the wind blows through the trees, smell the flowers, and look at the natural world.

Some of the stories included in the book are: "The Sky Tree (Huron – Eastern Woodland)", "Fallen Star's Ears (Cheyenne

– Plains)", "Koluskap and Malsom (Passamaquoddy – Eastern Woodland)" and "Why Some Trees Are Always Green (Cherokee – Southeast)". The activities following each story are clearly defined, with goals, procedures, appropriate ages for the activities, and materials needed.

Emphasis is placed on creative thinking, sensory awareness, responsibility to the natural world, and the interconnectedness of the environment. Questions following the activities help the leader and student come to an understanding of what was learned. A synthesis of knowledge and experience is an expected outcome.

Michael J. Caduto, who is of Italian ancestry, is a storyteller, an author, and an ecologist. He received the New England Award for Excellence in Environmental Education.

Joseph Bruchac has received numerous awards for his writing, including the NEA Creative Writing Fellowhip, a PEN syndicted Fiction Award, and an American Book Award. Mr. Brubac is of Abenaki, Slovak, and English ancestry.

John Kahionhes Fadden is a member of the Turtle Clan of the Mohawk Nation. He has illustrated more than twenty books about Native people.

David Kanietakeron Fadden is a Museum Educator at the Iroquois Indian Museum in Howes Cave, New York. He is a member of the Wolf Clan from the Mohawk Community of Akwesasne.

Carol Wood's pen and ink drawings have appeared in many publications and in other books with Caduto and Bruchac.

Marjorie Leggit is an illustrator in numerous publications and has been a contract artist for the Denver Museum of Natural History.

※

Campbell, Camilla; *Star Mountain and Other Legends of Mexico;* illustrated by Ena McKinney; McGraw-Hill; 1946; Grades 3 - 6

The legends of Native people are mingled with the history of Mexico. The legends tell of gods and beginnings. It includes the stories surrounding the reasons things are as they are.

It is a good collection that captures the feeling of Mexico and the people. A bibliography and glossary are included at the end of the book.

※

Campbell, Karel; *Blue Jay and the Monster;* illustrated by Birte Seir; Lerner Publications; 1967; Grades K - 3

"Little Big Man was the only son of Chief Red Cloud and his wife, Eagle Woman. They lived in a tepee village called "At the Woods." Thus begins the story of a "very unusual boy" who grew with no hair on his head. Because his father thought he was "possessed by evil spirits", he banished the boy to live alone in a tepee on the edge of the village. Eventually his mother glues a blue feather "on top of his head with balsam glue" so he won't be so unhappy.

The preposterous tale doesn't improve as the story continues. Native people as illustrated in this book are cartoon-like images who are made to look simple and ridiculous. The entire book is outrageous.

Cedar, Georgiana Dorcas; ***Little Thunder;*** illustrated by Robert L. Jefferson; Abingdon Press; 1966; Grades 3 - 6

Cricket, a young Shawnee boy, was skilled in the crafts expected of children his age. He must make the long trek with his people from Indiana territory to the shores of Lake Huron to aid the British in a war that they thought would restore their land to them. The story of the War of 1812 is presented from Cricket's viewpoint. It is while he is in battle that he earns the name Little Thunder.

A well-researched story, ***Little Thunder*** carefully deals with the war and presents Native culture in a realistic manner. The culture is described in terms of Native attitudes and values. There are a few times when the women are referred to as "squaws" and the work of the Prophet is called "magic", but the overall integrity of the book is not compromised. Explain to children why the words squaw and magic are inappropriate in this narrative. Taken as a whole the book is sensitive and honest.

The brown and white line drawings at the beginning of each chapter are well done with "notes on the chapter and endpaper decorations" explained on the book jacket.

In the end there is no repatriation and Little Thunder feels he must "go to school…" so he can "learn what the pale ones teach". Regrettably, it is a realistic ending.

⇥⇤

Chandler, Edna; ***Buffalo Boy;*** Benefic Press; 1968; Grades K - 3

A controlled vocabulary reader, ***Buffalo Boy*** was written for children with limited reading ability.

It is the story of a "Sioux" Indian living on the plains long ago. The story gives a glimpse into the culture, customs and daily life of the tribe. The glimpse is very superficial as usually happens with controlled vocabulary books.

The people call themselves Dakota, Lakota, Nakota, or Ocheti Shakowin.

Mrs. Chandler and her husband spent severals years working for the Indian Service in the United States. She is also the author of the ***Cowboy Sam*** series.

⇥⇤

Chandler, Edna; ***Little Wolf and the Thunder Stick;*** illustrated by Jack Merryweather; Benefic; 1956; Grades K – 3

Little Wolf is a member of the Iroquois Nation. The daily life of the people of the forest is presented through the adventures of Little Wolf. At the conclusion of the book, there is a brief explanation of the Iroquois League and added information about forest Indians. The book is a controlled vocabulary reader for the third grade. The book is an attempt to motivate children to read. The resulting narrative is stilted and some of the images are stereotypical.

Mrs. Chandler is the author of the ***Cowboy Sam*** series.

Chandler, Edna; ***Taka and his Dog;*** illustrated by Jack Merryweather; Benefic; 1962; Grades K - 3

Taka and his Dog is a controlled vocabulary reader for first grade, the story is about the relationship between a young Eskimo boy and his dog. A limited view of Eskimo life is presented in the book.

Chandler, Edna; ***Tall Boy and the Coyote;*** Benefic; 1968; Grades K - 3

The text is a controlled vocabulary reader intended for use in the first or second grades. The story revolves around Tall Boy, a young Navajo, as he tends his father's sheep. He proves himself brave when he protects the sheep from a hungry coyote. Some of the images are stereotypical.

Chandler, Edna; ***Young Hawk;*** illustrated by Jack Merryweather; Benefic; 1957; Grades K - 3

> Young Hawk is a young Indian boy living in the southwest. The setting is historical and takes place in what is now California. Through the daily adventures of Young Hawk we learn about the life of the early California Indians. The book is a controlled vocabulary reader at the third grade level. The very essence of the controlled vocabulary produces a stilted narrative and some of the illustrations present a stereotyped view of Native life.

→←

Charging Eagle, Tom, and Ron Zeilinger; ***Black Hills: Sacred Hills;*** Tipi Press; 1984; Grades 1 - 6

> Full-page black and white photographs are accompanied by text on the opposite page. The book deals clearly and effectively with the meaning of the Black Hills for the Lakota People. An introduction by Frank Fools Crow gives a brief summary of the history of the Black Hills and their acquisition by the United States government. He also speaks eloquently of the spiritual significance these hills hold for the Latoka.
>
> The introduction alone would be helpful in explaining to children some of the dishonorable appropriation of lands by the government. The text and photographs make it accessible to young children and could be used as a source of discussion. The deeper issues involved make this appropriate for all ages.

→←

Chief Joseph; ***Chief Joseph's Own Story;*** photos courtesy of Nez Perce Tribe; Montana Indian Publications; 1972; Grades 4 - 6

In 1879, Chief Joseph delivered an oration on his trip to Washington, D.C. In this eloquent speech, In-mut-too-yah-lat-lat (Thunder-traveling-over-the-mountains) tells the history of the Nez Perce from the time they first encounter non-Native people through their exile to Oklahoma Territory.

The text includes several of the more familiar quotes of Chief Joseph and historical photographs illustrate his story. Known as a brilliant leader and honorable statesman, Joseph was "asked to show my heart". The speech is written as Chief Joseph spoke it, no editorializing or commentary. It is powerful and moving.

Clark, Ann Nolan; ***Blue Canyon Horse;*** illustrated by Allan Houser; Viking; 1954; Grades 3 - 6

Blue Canyon Horse is a gentle, poetic story of a young mare who desires freedom and joins a herd of wild horses. It is also the story of a young Navajo boy who feeds and cares for the mare, but is left behnd when the mare leaves the safety of the canyon. The boy searches for his missing mare and rescues her when she is attacked by a mountain lion. Sensing a deeper longing, the mare returns with a colt to the shelter and safety of the boy's village.

Dynamic gouache paintings by Allan Houser, Chiricahua Apache, artist, and teacher, capture the mood of this fine tale. Houser uses space and color to correspond with the rhythm of the story. Fields of corn and squash, towering canyon walls and striking red-rock formations depict scenes of Navajo life. Houser effectively uses pen-and-ink drawings to highlight certain aspects of the story. The shift between the pen-and-ink drawings and the gouache paintings unveils the power of the Navajo nation.

Though the setting is not identified, many people in the southwest feel the story is set in Canyon de Chelly in northeastern Arizona. The site holds particular significance to the Navajo nation because it was in this canyon that nine-thousand Navajos were gathered and forced to march to Bosque Redondo in New Mexico.

><

Clark, Ann Nolan; *Circle of Seasons;* illustrated by W. T. Mars; Farrar, Straus & Giroux; 1970; Grades 6 - Up

The life of the Pueblo Indians revolves around the seasons. Each day is important as it flows into the time span of the season. The seasons circle, bringing times of ceremony, prayer, laughter, fiesta and work. The culture of the Pueblos is described in the time span of a full year.

The book is a poetic translation of the modern day Pueblo, blending the old with the new.

Mrs. Clark was encouraged by the Bureau of Indian Affairs to write reading texts for Native children. The children illustrated the text and the books were published by "Indian" schools where printing was taught.

Clark, Ann Nolan; *The Desert People;* illustrated by Allan Houser; The Viking Press; 1962; Grades 2 – 4

Ann Nolan Clark has extreme reverence for the people she portrays in her books. In *The Desert People*, she describes the Papago who live in southwestern Arizona. A young boy tells of his home, his village, the houses, and the ramada. He says: "I live in a village/in the desert country,/the flat sand country,/the hot dry country." Later he explains, "We have ways/of doing things/that have been given/to us/by Desert People/who have gone/before us." "They are the footsteps/of our Ancients."

The book's clear, rhythmic text mirrors traditional Native poetry. Mrs. Clark's work appeals to children because of its honesty and realism. *The Desert People* was written as a companion book to *In My Mother's House.*

Gouache paintings by Allan Houser, Chiricahua Apache, are poetic and perceptive in detailing the narrative. He uses pen-and-ink drawings throughout the text to match the movement of the story so that the child reader will understand the life of the Papago people. The gouache paintings effectively capture the feel of the houses of the village, the Rain House, the purple mountains, and the old Spanish Mission.

The Desert People is a great book to read aloud to allow a child to experience the cadence of the oral storytelling tradition that is basic to the Papago/Tohono O'Odham. Some people worry about the 1962 copyright date; instead, delight in the history that is shared in this exceptional book.

Both author and artist are true to the "footsteps of our Ancients."

※

Clark, Ann Nolan; ***In My Mother's House;*** illustrated by Velino Herrera; The Viking Press; 1941; Grades K – 3

The book is a poetic metaphor of life for the Pueblo people. Ann Nolan Clark wrote the book for her third grade class in the Tewa Indian village of Tesuque, New Mexico, so they would have a book to read about their own life. The text is simple, yet conveys the message of a complex culture. Written in the first-person, the voice is that of a young Pueblo child.

"My Mother's house,/It does not stand alone;/ Its sister houses/ Are all around it." The book ends as the child's voice details life in the Tewa community and says: "The pueblo, /the people,/ And fire,/And fields,/And water,/And land,/And animals - I string them together/Like beads./They make a chain,/A strong chain,/To hold me close/To home,/Where I live/In my Mother's house."

Mrs. Clark learned that "home" was the most important word to the children in her class and so she had her students write about home at the end of each day. ***In My Mother's House*** broke new ground for children's literature about Native people. Working for the Bureau of Indian Affairs, Mrs. Clark learned very quickly that there were no books which Native children could read that related to their life in the pueblo. The children in her class each illustrated her text and bound the book with calico. The book builds on the oral tradition of Native people and should be read aloud.

Valina Herrera's illustrations for the book are extraordinary. Pages of black and white line drawings capture daily life of building a house, planting corn, and cutting wood, showing great respect for the every day tasks of the people. Color illustrations stand out in bold simplicity and emphasize the dignity of the community. Herrera, Ma-Pe-Wi, of Zia Pueblo, had studio space at the Museum of New Mexico. Some historical documents spell Herrera as Herrerra.

In 1945, the *Horn Book Magazine* stated that **In My Mother's House** was "probably the most distinguished book on the Indian way of life...which tells in singing prose how the Indians work together, play and rest, raise their crops, tell their stories, and dream their dreams."

Ann Nolan Clark was an exceptional teacher who continued to write books for children while working in schools for the Bureau of Indian Affairs. Part of her career was spent in Washington, D. C., where she was the principal writer for the department. Speaking of writing children's books, she said that "children need children's books that have been written with honesty, accuracy, and reality. They need books that develop deeper understandings and broader acceptances, that enrich imagination. Their need is my challenge."

In My Mother's House was a Caldecott Honor Book in 1942. It also received the New York Herald Tribune Children's Spring Book Festival Award.

Clark, Ann Nolan; ***Medicine Man's Daughter;*** illustrated by Don Bolognese; Farrar, Straus & Giroux; 1963; Grades 6 - Up

>Tall Girl is a fifteen year old Navajo. She is the daughter of Chanter, a respected medicine man. Some day Tall Girl will be a medicine woman to her own people. Tall Girl's hopes are shattered when she is sent away to school and faces a culture conflicting with her Navajo beliefs. Finding the medical training she needs to help her people is part of this sensitively written book.

>The book deals with the Navajo past in relationship to the cultural present.

Clark, Ann Nolan; ***Secret of the Andes;*** illustrated by Jean Charlot; Viking; 1952; Grades 6 - Up

>Ann Nolan Clark has proven her mastery of storytelling in the tale of Cusi, a young Indian boy and Chuto, the old llama herder. It is a poetic story of Cusi as he tends the llamas; feeding, training and shearing them. The llama corral is part of a ruined temple from the days when Peru was ruled by the Incas. Misti is Cusi's special black llama with whom he shares many happy times. Cusi loved the Andean mountain tops that were his home, but he had one longing. He wanted to feel the warmth and security of family life.

From high in the mountain, Cusi could see people down a zigzag trail. "I have not seen people before, not that I remember. Isn't it wonderful that I can come here and see them every day...Isn't it wonderful?" When Cusi leaves the mountain and travels into the valley to the world of people, he is told: "Grieve not if your searching circles." Chuto helps him find the family that had been in Cusi's heart. The reader journeys with Cusi back to the mountaintops and listens as he makes the ultimate decision to keep the ancient secret.

The book is alive with vivid descriptions of majestic mountains with canyons and gorges, wildflowers, pastures, and lovely pools. The richness of the Incan culture is treated with dignity and honor. Superb.

Secret of the Andes won the Newberry Award in 1953.

→←

Clark, Ann Nolan; *The Little Indian Basket Maker;* illustrated by Harrison Begay; Melmont; 1957; Grades K - 3

The Little Indian Basket Maker is a well-written story of a young Papago girl who accompanies her grandmother into the desert to collect plants for basket making. Through the love of her grandmother, the girl learns that the weaving must come from her heart as well as her hands. Grandmother tells her, "Baskets and mats are made by plaiting yucca leaves. Meal bowls and water baskets are made by coiling bear grass and sewing the coils with willow or yucca." One of the awls is "a cactus thorn in a lump of pinon gum." The story tells in simple step by step form how the young girl makes a mat and when it is finished "it is strong and good. Its pattern is plain. Its edges are straight. My hands rest, my heart sings."

An introductory page tells about the Papago Indians of Arizona, the country where they live, and the need for baskets. Information about the author and artist is given at the end of the book. Children will grasp the nuances and motion of the oral tradition if the story is read aloud.

The colorful illustrations by Harrison Begay, a Navajo artist, are faithful to the culture. The drawings, filled with warmth and vitality, eloquently record the ways of the Papago people. (The Papago are known today as Tohono O'Odham.)

⇥⇤

Clark, Ann Nolan; *The Little Indian Pottery Maker;* illustrated by Don Perceval; Melmont; 1955; Grades K - 3

The story of a Pueblo Indian girl, the book tells how the girl makes a bowl out of clay as well as telling in simple form the story of the Pueblo and its people. It is a well-written book with a few explanatory illustrations.

Ann Nolan Clark had a distinguished career teaching and writing. She worked for the Bureau of Indian Affairs and said that "she quickly realized that there were no textbooks which Indian children could relate to – vocabulary, background, and values in the books then available were foreign to them and could not be understood."

Mrs. Clark effectively captures the mood and setting of her stories. Her books speak eloquently of the life of Native people.

During her career, Ann Nolan Clark worked to develop reading materials that were appropriate for Native children.

→←

Clark, Ann Nolan; *This for That;* illustrated by Don Freeman; Golden Gate; 1965; Grades K - 3

A young Papago boy living in the southwest has three names and everyone is worried about him because he is forgetful. "The boy who lives/in the Indian house/inside the fence/that grows around it/has three names,/not one name,/not two names,/but three names./Can you believe it?/This boy who is half/as high as high/has three long names." One of the boy's names is Put-it-Pick-it because he is always putting something down then picking something up. "White Shell is his Indian name…Joe-John is for school." Put-it-Pick-it learns a lesson in responsibility from his grandfather. In the end, the boy says: "I think I have learned something. I think I won't forget something. I think I would like to be called Brings-it-Back."

The author has written a sensitive account of a young boy and presents a solution that demonstrates the wisdom of the Papago way. Sensitive, colorful illustrations add warmth to the text, creating an artistic whole.

Ann Nolan Clark has said that schoolbooks need to reflect the lives of the children for whom they are written. Her books resonate with the cadence and rhythm of the storytellers of the Papago. Reading the story aloud for children helps them experience the oral tradition.

Today the Papago are known as Tohono O'Odham.

>*<

Clark, Ian Christie; ***Indian and Eskimo Art of Canada;*** Photography by Dominique Darbois; Ryerson; 1970; Grades 3 - 6

A remarkable collection of superb photographs offers a unique opportunity to view the highlights from an exhibition of Canadian aboriginal art. The photographs are full page in both black and white and color. Featured in the book are one hundred twenty objects including ceremonial robes, sculptures, masks, woodcarvings, a miniature shaman's charm and an elaborately carved house post. It is a handsome and magnificent record of a widely acclaimed exhibition that was viewed throughout Canada and Europe.

The book is a visual delight and the introductory text sketches the background of aboriginal art.

>*<

Clutesi, George C.; ***Son of Raven, Son of Deer;*** illustrated by the author; Gray; 1967; Grades 3 - 6

The author shares twelve tales of the Tse-Shaht people from the northwest coast. The introduction to the book is especially noteworthy for teachers, parents and anyone interested in the culture of Native people. In the introduction, the author provides significant insight into the differences between fairy tales and the stories of Native people.

The author retells the legends that were told to him by his parents. According to one librarian in Canada, Mr. Clutesi's book is the "first book of legends by an Indian." She did not specify if his was the first Canadian book or "first book" of legends written by an Indian.

This impressive collection of tales centers on the adventures of Ko-ishinomit, Son of Raven and Ah-tush-mit, Son of Deer. The stories are beautifully recorded and opens the mind to a rich and cultured people; a people whose intellect was brilliant, imaginative and resourceful.

These authentic stories are not only fascinating, but will provide background for an increased understanding of the West Coast People. Strong illustrations in black and white are faithful to the culture presented.

Mr. Clutesi is a member of the Tse-Shaht band on Vancouver Island.

→←

Clymer, Eleanor; *Chipmunk in the Forest;* illustrated by Ingrid Fetz; Atheneum; 1965; Grades 3 - 6

Chipmunk is afraid of the forest and because of this he feels he is a disappointment to his family. One day his uncle sends him home from a hunting expedition because of Chipmunk's fear in the wilderness. Chipmunk's little brother goes hunting alone in the deep woods and becomes lost. When Chipmunk searches alone for him and then returns him safely to their village, Chipmunk overcomes his fear of the forest.

Though the book does not deal with a specific tribe, it does give a glimpse of the Woodland Indians. The story is simply told with understanding and could provide recreational reading for a child. Black and white drawings illustrate the text.

The Anishinabe children who read the book felt it was okay and provided a reasonable story. One caveat – they felt the tribal identity should have been given.

※

Clymer, Eleanor; ***The Spider, The Cave and The Pottery Bowl;*** illustrated by Ingrid Fetz; Atheneum; 1971; Grades 3 - 6

Johnny and Kate went to the mesa to help their grandmother for the summer. Grandmother was not well and she slept much of the time. There was no pottery making either, for Grandmother's clay was all gone. When Johnny gets into trouble, Kate discovers a way to give Grandmother what she needs to help her get well again.

Interwoven into the story are short legends of the people of the mesa. It is a well-written story set in 1971 that captures the spirit of the mesa country. Fine line drawings complement the mood of the text. Several children reviewed this book and found nothing offensive.

Clymer, Theodore; *Four Corners of the Sky;* illustrated by Marc Brown; Little, Brown and Co.; 1975; All grades

>Theodore Clymer represents many tribal groups in the selections in the book. There are medicine chants, lullabies, ceremonial songs, game songs, chants for hunting and playing, as well as expressions of love and hope.

>*Four Corners of the Sky* is a celebration of life, a collection of songs, chants, and oratory of the American Indian. "These poems were originally recorded from various tribes over a broad span of time and from a number of places." - From an introduction by Theodore Clymer. He also has provided commentaries along with sources that add to the sense of wholeness that this book provides.

>The bold, colorful illustrations by Marc Brown capture the mood of the text with great respect. This is a delightful book that children thoroughly enjoyed.

Coatsworth, Elizabeth; *The Cave;* illustrated by Allan Houser; Viking; 1958; Grades 3 - 6

>Jim Boy-Who-Loves-Sheep, a young Navajo, must take the sheep to summer pastures. Fernando, a Basque from across the sea, accompanies him on the difficult journey. Jim conquers his fear of the Canyon of the Dead and wins the friendship of Fernando.

It is a sensitively written story set in the culture of 1958. In prose that is poetry, the author has created a lovely and unusual story with the hauntingly beautiful qualities of a modern legend. Allan Houser, Chiricahua Apache, displays the artistry and feeling of the Southwest through his exquisite drawings. Mr. Houser's Granduncle was Geronimo.

Coatsworth received the Newberry Medal in 1931 for her book ***The Cat Who Went to Heaven.***

→←

Cohlene, Terri; ***Clamshell Boy: A Makah Legend;*** illustrated by Charles Reasoner; Watermill Press; 1990; All grades

A young Makah girl named Salmonberry "was playing with her friends on the beach. It was during the month of the sparkling moon, and each day the sun spirit smiled longer on the People of the Cape". When Salmonberry's mother warns the children that Basket Woman would be coming soon, she makes the children promise to be home "before the sun sleeps". Salmonberry, however, scoffs at the idea of such a one as Basket Woman and it is then that the dreaded woman captures the children. It is Clamshell Boy, newly born from the tears of the mother, who sets forth to rescue the children and secure their freedom. Gifts and celebrations begin, for "It was Clamshell Boy who brought potlatch to the People of the Cape".

A concluding chapter provides information on the customs and lifestyles of the Makah People. Historical photographs, drawings and bold color pictures add clarity and understanding to the text. A glossary, map and "Important Dates" help put things in perspective. It's too bad the first date to be included is "1492 - Columbus discovers the New World", but it in no way negates the strength of the tale.

Coleman, Sister Bernard; *Eagle Wing;* illustrated by Ruth Maney; Greenwich; 1956; Grades 3 - 6

Sister Coleman spent many years among the Chippewa. Eagle Wing is a Chippewa boy living in the 1880's in Minnesota. The reader accompanies Eagle Wing as he participates in the daily and seasonal activities of his people. Children who read the book were interested in Eagle Wing's family and the tales of his grandfather as he recounts the traditions of the Chippewa.

Accompanying illustrations enhance the tale. It is very much a book of the Fifties, but that need not detract from its usefulness. Children connected to the historical aspect of the book and they gained insights into 1950s perceptions of history.

Collura, Mary-Ellen Lang; *Winners;* Dial Press; 1984; Grades 4 - 6

At fifteen, Jordy Threebears had lived in "eleven foster homes in eight years, and was moving again." He is returning to Ash Creek Reserve to live with a Grandfather he vaguely remembers. It is not a happily-ever-after reunion. The Grandfather lives on the lonely prairie in a cabin with no phone or electricity and he doesn't know exactly what to do with Jordy.

The Grandfather's gift of a wild mare begins to make Jordy's life appear to be "agreeably simple", but the intense, relentless hatred of one white man threatens Jordy's happiness.

In the end, Jordy wins a much-publicized horse race in a sensational climax. There's the excitement of camera crews, people and of course Siksika. When the camera crew wants to know the name of the mare, Jordy tells them it's not "Horse" but Siksika.

"What's that?"

"Blackfoot," said the chief and his eyes shone brightly. "The name means Blackfoot!"

Kids will like this book a lot.

Cooper, Amy Jo; **Dream Quest;** Annick Press, Ltd.; 1987; Grades 4 - 6

There are two stories in this book - "The Big Save" and "Hack's Choice". Both of them are based on films of the same title produced by Spirit Bay Productions. Bernard Mide of Spirit Bay introduces both stories and says: "So you listen to both stories, listen carefully. Then maybe you can figure out what the real story is".

In the first story, "The Big Save", the story is told twice. Rabbit and Rose take turns telling their version of what happened; which includes broomball, a blizzard, an accident with the school bus and the action they take to save the children on the bus.

"Hack's Choice", the second story, describes the dilemmas of young Native people and the choices they must make about what they must give up and what is to keep. The Elder, Bernard Mide, tells Rabbit: "Dreams are no jokes. What is real will not trick you...They are a gift from the moon...They enlighten us..."

Dream Quest is a book of real people, elders who are valued, and genuine, warm relationships. The language is the way people actually talk and the kid's arguments are reasonable.

" ' Are you mentally dewormed, Rabbit?' Marvis said...

'Stuff it, Marvis' - oh, he was mad.

'Take off, Rabbit.'

'Make me.'

'I don't make garbage. I burn it.'

Rabbit just shut up then; pretended we weren't there."

Anyone who has worked with children will recognize that this is the way kids talk. No gloss, just real kids and a remarkable story.

Black and white photographs illustrate this excellent book.

Creekmore, Raymond; ***Lokoshi Learns to Hunt Seals;*** illustrated by the author; Macmillan; 1951; Grades K - 3

>Lokoshi, an Eskimo boy, is going on his first seal hunt. The story tells everything about the seal hunt, including the outfitting of the hunters and other details. The text also describes the building of an igloo.
>
>It is a well-written story with an accurate picture of Eskimo life. Sensitive lithographs add to the visual appeal of the text. An excellent book for young children.
>
>Explain to children that Inuit is the name for the people sometimes called Eskimo. Note the 1951 copyright date.

※

Dalgliesh, Alice; ***The Courage of Sarah Noble;*** illustrated by Leonard Weisgard; Scribners; 1954; Grades 3 - 6

>Based on a true account, Sarah was eight years old when she accompanied her father into the "wild" frontier in 1707. She was to cook for him while he built a new house for his family in what is now New Milford, Connecticut. When the house is finished, Father returns to his former home to bring the rest of the family to their new homestead. Since Father feels the trip would be a hardship on her, Sarah is left behind with an "Indian" family while he makes the journey.
>
>The story continues with Sarah living with the "Indians", her experiences in their culture and her reunion with her own family. For the most part, it is sensitively written and the writer shows respect and consideration for the people involved. There

A Second Look, Native Americans in Children's Books

are some passages that are troubling, however. The author slips in the "white superiority" concept even though it may have been unintentional.

Part of the narrative includes children teasing Sarah and trying to frighten her as she prepares to leave for the new territory. "The Indians will eat you...They will chop off your head...They will skin you alive..." Later, when Sarah meets the "Indian" children she is shocked "that they were not wearing clothes - unless you could call that one piece of cloth 'clothing'. Sarah, secure in dress and cloak and petticoats, felt very well dressed indeed." Mother refers to the people as "those heathen savages".

It has the possibilities of being a lovely story, but the inclusion of the negative passages is regrettable. Sarah at least has some sense: " 'But they are not savages,' Sarah said. 'They are our friends and Tall John's wife takes good care of her children.' "

There are ample illustrations to accompany the text. The book received Newberry Honors. Didn't anyone notice the negative language?

>*<

Dalgliesh, Alice; *The Thanksgiving Story;* illustrated by Helen Sewell; Charles Scribner's Sons; 1954; Grades 3 - 5

The opening of the book states: "This is the story of the first Thanksgiving in America, it happened more than three hundred years ago." The people aboard the Mayflower brought with them "bright-colored cloth...beads and knives and little mirrors - all things that they had heard the Indians like to have".

Upon arrival in the new land, the Pilgrims wanted to "see if it was safe. There would be Indians. The settlers had heard all kinds of stories about Indians. So the men carried their guns."

The Pilgrims must search for corn or they might die of starvation. "They looked everywhere. Once they saw some Indians and a dog, but these ran away into the woods." Concerning the people who owned the land: "This was a good place for homes. Indians had lived here, and there were fields where corn had been grown."

Corn was found, "…there was a little old basket filled with corn! Now they had corn to plant…They found other baskets. These were big baskets, and it took two men to carry one. They filled their pockets with corn." It is acknowledged that "Some day they would find the Indians and pay them for it."

Following this passage, the text says that "One day they did see some more Indians. These Indians were not friendly. They shot at the settlers with their bows and arrows."

Explain to children that the Native people lived on this land, grew the corn, and cleared the fields where plants grew. Make the book relevant to how any of us would feel if someone took our land and crops.

The book goes on to relate that the land was "a good place for homes. Indians had lived here, and there were fields where corn had grown. There was rich black earth for planting and plenty of fresh water."

"The people of Plymouth were surprised to see that the Indians wore so few clothes. It was still cold weather...They gave him an old coat." And, of course, there is "Squanto, the friendly Indian..."

The final page at least recognizes that the "Indians may have understood about the prayer, for their people had a Thanksgiving of their own. They gave thanks to their God, who made 'the trees grow, the corn grow, and all kinds of fruits.'"

The book is the typical "First Thanksgiving" story, replete with the various stereotypes, distortions and confused look at Native people. Inform children that Native cultures throughout the world had celebrations of thanksgiving.

And yes – children are still reading this book.

→←

D'Amato, Janet and Alex; ***Indian Crafts;*** Lyon Press; 1968; Grades 3 - 6

A well-organized book, the text classifies "Indian" crafts into areas: transportation, dwellings, weapons, clothing, household items, and ceremonial items. The introduction describes the distinct craft styles of different tribes, the specific meaning of decorative design and the symbolism of color. Illustrations show building procedures step by step. A brief introduction to some tribes is also included.

The book is standard fare, with the usual acknowledgements made to everyday life of Native people. Because it is easy to use, children will find it a convenient reference. The material presented is quite often what students need for classroom assignments. It would be more appropriate for the traditional research required for a class project to include more depth than is found in this book.

⸻

d'Aulaire, Ingri and Edgar Parin; ***Buffalo Bill;*** Doubleday & Company, Inc.; 1952; Grades 2 – 4

The d'Aulaire's have written and illustrated a number of books that are considered classics. Many of them date from the 1930s through the 1950s and are based on the prevailing attitude of white superiority. Most of these books are still available through public and school libraries and at the usual retail outlets. Somewhere along the way, people failed to recognize the blatant racist content of the text and illustrations.

"Bill's playmates were Kickapoo Indian children…He traded his brand-new buckskin suit for a little wild Indian pony, and so he had a horse of his own. Sometimes he rode Indian fashion…" "Buffalo country was Indian country, too…One moonlit night Bill spied an Indian aiming his arrow at one of the bullwhackers. Quick as a flash he raised his gun and shot the Indian first."

The illustrations match the text with Indians attacking the wagons or looking on at Buffalo Bill doing his mighty acts. At one point, he found a relay station in ashes, "…the men killed by Indians."

Another time, the text abandons the "Indian" issues and shows the glorification of Buffalo Bill killing as many buffalo as he could. "Bill had shot almost half again as many as his rival." In the background of the picture is a train load of people waving as Bill destroys the buffalo.

But the Indians were growing "in fury" at losing their land and the pictures show the "Indians" in "full fury." "Buffalo Bill was sorry for the Indians. But he knew that, vast as the plains were, there wasn't room for Indians and white men both." "Soon the last hostile Indian was forced to move toward the setting sun."

And then Buffalo Bill "…hit gold." He rounded up some rough-riding friends and some Indians and started his Wild West Show. The pictures continue in their stereotypical fashion and Buffalo Bill continues with his show for forty years.

George Washington by the d'Aulaire's follows the pattern of the other books. Men came from England and "chased the Indians away." George "thought their war dance was very funny." And so it continues through the pages.

It is disheartening that after fifty years, these books are still considered classics. Is anyone paying attention?

>*<

d'Aulaire, Ingri and Edgar Parin; ***Pocohontas;*** Doubleday; 1946; Grades 2 - 4

"In the dark woods of Virginia, where dusky owls hooted over the treetops…there lived a stern old Indian chief named Powhatan…He had a little daughter…She was as sweet and pretty as he was ugly and cruel." So begins this picture book about an "Indian princess", the "squaws" and men with "magic sticks that spat fire..." There are medicine men who juggle and conjure and talk with grunts while the Indians "worried and wondered".

Throughout the book, Native people are either silly or naive, depicted as cruel, and are entranced by the European culture that is presented as being superior to Native life. The common denominator of both text and illustrations is to make the Native people appear fatuous.

In spite of this, the book has been "approved" by the National Council of Teachers of English and The Association for Childhood Education International. In 1946, when the book was first published, the stereotypes in the book were the norm. Is it any wonder whole generations of children grew up with negative images of Native people? The book continues to be on recommended reading lists for use with children. Since this book is still on the shelves in schools and libraries throughout the country, children must be taught that these are indeed stereotypes and the information is false and misleading.

→←

dePaola, Tomie; ***The Legend of the Bluebonnet;*** illustrated by the author; G.P. Putnam's Sons; 1983; Grades 1 - 3

The book is a retelling of a Comanche story of how a young child's sacrifice results in the creation of a lovely flower. A great drought is upon the land and the people "called Comanche" are wondering how they have offended the Great Spirit. The shaman tells them they "must make a burnt offering of the most valued possession among us." No one believes that so much will be required except for one small child.

The author's note explains: "...for me it is more a tale of courage and sacrifice of a young person. She-Who-Is-Alone's act of thrusting her beloved doll into the fire to save her people represents the decisive sort of action that many young people are capable of, the kind of selfless action that creates miracles."

In the night, the child burns her beloved doll and scatters the ashes in the four directions. When she awakens, she is surrounded by a luscious green earth and exquisite blue flowers. The rains return and the girl is thereafter known as "One-Who-Dearly-Loved-Her-People."

The one pitfall that is somewhat unsettling is the young child's complete aloneness. In spite of this, it is a skillful retelling of an "old tale of Texas."

DePaola's illustration are respectful and lovely. He has legendary author/illustrator status.

Dolch, Edward and Marguerite; ***Lodge Stories in Basic Vocabulary;*** illustrated by Billy M. Jackson; Garrard; 1957; Grades 3 - 6

Lodge stories are the tales told by the Indian tribes living in the southwestern United States. Included are stories from the Cherokee, Creek, Alabama, Yuchi, Choctaw and Seminole. The stories are legitimate but are written in the halting style of a basic vocabulary book.

Note: There are some people who will criticize the telling of stories using basic vocabulary. It's true that in most instances they lose the lyrical quality of the oral tradition, but for many students who have reading difficulties, the books can have a favorable component. The reluctant reader can be invited to begin the process of reviewing books and analyzing them. With that in mind, the older student will feel that reading books at a primary grade level has a purpose. Notebook in hand, students can begin a learning process that will help them greatly in increasing reading levels while becoming critical thinkers.

Reluctant readers could be encouraged to read the stories aloud to give rhythm and inflection in the oral tradition, giving life to the tales. They could also practice telling the stories by memory using the oral tradition.

→←

Dolch, Edward and Marguerite; ***Teepee Stories in Basic Vocabulary;*** illustrated by Robert S. Kerr; Garrard; 1956; Grades 3 - 6

Stories of the Plains Indians are adapted to a basic vocabulary reader. Included are tales of the Blackfeet, Pawnee, Cheyenne, Wichita, Kiowa, Crow, Sioux and Arikara.

The book seems to be well researched. It can be beneficial for the older child to aid in reading as well as expanding knowledge of various Indian tribes.

See note with ***Lodge Stories.***

Dolch, Edward and Marguerite; ***Wigwam Stories in Basic Vocabulary;*** illustrated by Robert S. Kerr; Garrard; 1956; Grades 3 - 6

The book contains a collection of woodland Indian tales. Included are stories from the Menominee, Ojibway, Iroquois, Mohawk, Seneca, Algonquin, and Chippewa.

This is a basic vocabulary book with enough interest to be useful for an older child. However, the style is somewhat stilted because of vocabulary limitations.

See note included with ***Lodge Stories.***

Dorian, Edith and Wilson, W.N.; ***Hokahey! American Indians Then and Now;*** McGraw-Hill; 1957; Grades 6 - Up

Contributions of the American Indian have been great to our society. The book discusses the contributions and history of many tribes. It is an historical account as well as a sensitive attempt to portray the American Indian factually. It successfully tells how the Native people adapted to and lived in various geographical areas. Cultural traits of each group are listed at the end of each chapter, but the "traits" are limited in scope. A concluding chapter focuses on Indians "today" - 1957.

An understanding and appreciation of Native culture and traditions are apparent in the style and content of this well written book.

Black and white illustrations add appeal to the text. The book also contains a useful bibliography, an index and maps.

※

Eastman, Charles; *Indian Boyhood;* illustrated by E. L. Blumenschein; Dover; 1971; Grades 6 - Up

Originally published in 1902, the book is a record of impressions and experiences of Charles Eastman up to the age of fifteen years. The author, known as Ohiyesa, was a member of the Wahpeton Sioux tribe and shares his observations of the Sioux culture, social customs and beliefs. The book reflects a happy childhood filled with meaningful experiences and relates the adventure and tradition of the tribe.

The book is unaltered from the original publication. It is a first person account of high literary quality and would be valuable as a supplement book in the classroom. Highly recommended.

Adults could learn a great deal about the lives of Native people by reading the Eastman books. His books include: ***The Soul of the Indian*** and ***From the Deep Woods to Civilization.*** Eastman graduated from Dartmouth and from Boston University with a degree in medicine. He worked as a physician on the Pine Ridge Indian Reservation and was the doctor assigned the task of searching for the dead and wounded at Wounded Knee after the massacre.

Eastman's life was extraordinary. The Minnesota Historical Society is publishing a book on Eastman entitled: ***From The***

Land of the Sky Blue Water: Charles A. Eastman, Minnesota and the World of the American Indian by David Martinez.

⸻

Ehrlich, Amy; ***Wounded Knee;*** Holt, Rinehart & Winston; 1974; Grades 6 - Up

The book is an adaptation for young readers of Dee Brown's ***Bury My Heart at Wounded Knee.*** Tracing the white man's conquest of the Indians of the American West; it emphasizes the causes, events and effects of the major confrontation at Wounded Knee. It includes a bibliography, notes and index.

The adaptation is well done. The book is sympathetic to the plight of Native people forced to deal with the invasion of their ancestral lands. Illustrated with historical photographs. An excellent resource book.

⸻

Ekoomiak, Normee; ***Arctic Memories;*** illustrated by the author; Henry Holt and Co.; 1988; Grades K - 6

The bilingual text is written in both Inuktitut and English. Normee Ekoomiak says about himself: "I am an Inuk. I was born in a place of magic: at Cape Jones...I know all of the spirits of the land animals and the birds and the fish and the sea animals. I know their names and I can understand them and I can speak to them...I can remember everything. I grew up at Fort George in my grandfather's tent...I live and work in the South now. I am an Inuk of the city."

Arctic Memories is an outgrowth of memories, experiences and spiritual awakenings. The author's evocative text and bold, colorful illustrations transfers his past into our present and future. It is a journey that teaches and enlightens as he shares with the reader the life of the Inuit.

Acrylic paintings along with felt applique and embroidery depict children playing blanket-toss, men hanging fish, ancestral hunters and even a couple of nativity scenes. The author explains who the Inuit are, their language and art and concludes with a page about himself. A map is included on the back to show the geographical relationship of the Inuit with both Canada and the United States.

The book is an excellent resource that is imbued with dignity and a sense of values. It will be as fascinating for first graders as it will be to the older child as they become a part of "arctic memories".

⇥⇤

Ellis, Mel; ***Sidewalk Indian;*** Holt, Rinehart and Winston; 1974; Grades 6 - Up

Charley Nightwind is a "sidewalk" Indian, one who knows the ways of the city. When he is falsely charged with murder during an Indian protest in Milwaukee, he flees the city and seeks refuge on an Indian reservation to the north. He is pursued by the police and is aided by the Indians on the reservation.

Charley must learn to survive in the woods and he becomes acquainted with the ways of his ancestors. With the help of local Indians be manages to elude his pursuers but complications occur as he becomes involved in a dangerous plan to dynamite the dam at Spirit Flowage. It is a suspenseful tale and relates the dilemma faced by Native people in Wisconsin.

Though the tribe and place are not defined, the story is loosely based on the dilemma the Wisconsin Chippewa confronted with the Power Co. at Chippewa Flowage near Hayward, Wisconsin. (In the book, the town is called Sayward.)

Anishinabe sixth graders who read the book thought the story was okay even though the plot was contrived to heighten reader interest.

→←

Elston, Georgia, editor; ***Giving: Ojibwa Stories and Legends from the Children of Curve Lake;*** Waapoone Publishing; 1985; All grades

"The stories and pictures in this book are a gift to you from the children of Curve Lake Reserve. Giving and sharing are meaningful traditions of Canada's Native people - the Anishinabe." Thus begins the introduction that continues by giving background information that is helpful to the reader.

Children ages seven through twelve have written the stories of the Native people in their own inimitable style. Most of the stories range in length from a half page to a full page and are easily readable by young children. Interspersed throughout the text are illustrations by the Curve Lake children.

Georgia Elston, the editor and compiler, states: "Go back to a time when the land was quiet and the voices of nature could be heard. Let the children of the children of the elders of long ago tell their stories. Hush! Listen!" Children will enjoy this book.

→←

Elting, Mary; *The Hopi Way;* illustrated by Louis Mofsie; M. Evans; 1969; Grades 3 - 6

Louis grew up in New York knowing nothing of the heritage he received from his parents. His mother was a Winnebago Indian from the forests near the Canadian border and his father was a Hopi Indian from the Arizona desert. One summer the family goes to a Hopi village in Arizona that had been the boyhood home of Louis' father. It is during this summer that Louis begins learning the customs of his people.

The book presents a genuine picture of Hopi life. Louis, the principal character, has illustrated the text.

→←

Erdoes, Richard, ed.; *The Sound of Flutes;* illustrated by Paul Goble; Pantheon; 1976; Grades 6 - Up

The book is a collection of stories gathered from the Plains Indians, mostly Sioux. The stories range from the mystical to the heroic and have been shared with the editor by numerous people. The tale is transcribed as it was originally related with credit given to the storyteller.

The brilliant, stylized illustrations overflow with details of nature and Native life. The mixture of ancient Indian motifs with modern art result in a unique, affecting perspective of unexpected design.

→←

Esbensen, Barbara Juster; ***The Great Buffalo Race;*** illustrated by Helen K. Davie; Little Brown and Company; 1994; Grades 4 - 6

A note to the reader explains how a buffalo legend became part of the Iroquois Nation, a tribal culture of the eastern woodlands. In the note, the author explains: "This old tale, like all Seneca legends, was told during the long winter nights by Seneca storytellers. It was taken down by Arthur C. Parker, whose Seneca name was Gawaso Wanneh, and it can be found in his collection ***Skunny Wundy,*** where it is entitled 'The Buffalo's Hump and the Brown Birds' (Doubleday, 1926)."

Old Buffalo warns against following the first scent of rain. In this retelling of the ancient story, the Tribe of Buffalo face the rivalry between their chief, Old Buffalo, and Young Buffalo, who challenges the wisdom of the old leader. The two rivals lead their followers on a frenzied race over the drought ridden country to determine who will be the chief. "Hundreds fell to the earth, too tired to run any farther." Eventually the race ends, but "everywhere they looked, the grass was dry and sparse. Not a blade of green as far as their hot, tired eyes could see."

A climactic element is reached when Haweniyo, the Great Spirit, punishes the rebels, transforming forever the look of the buffalo. Brown Buffalo, son of the Old One, is the hero of the story. He stayed behind and is now the chief. Brown Buffalo is son of the Old One.

In this retelling, the story becomes a bit awkward because it lacks the cadence of the oral storyteller. The author and illustrator have collaborated on two other books.

→←

Esbensen, Barbara Juster; **Ladder to the Sky;** illustrated by Helen K. Davie; Little, Brown and Co.; 1989; Grades 3 - 5

Subtitled "How the Gift of Healing Came to the Ojibway Nation" the tale is based on a story preserved by George Copway in his book on history, legends and customs of the Native people. Published in 1850, **The Traditional History and Characteristic Sketches of the Ojibway Nation** honors the traditions and beliefs of the people. Also known as Chippewa, the "Ojibway" call themselves Anishinabe - "original people". George Copway was an Ojibway chief named Kah-ge-ga-gah-bowh and it is to his spirit that the book is dedicated.

"Long ago, in the old, forgotten time, Gitchi Manitou, the Great Spirit, created only strong, healthy people...Nobody was ever sick in those days. Nobody died." This wondrous tale tells of the "shining spirit-messengers" who would carry the old ones up to the sky where they would live forever - until one day when things began to change and sickness and death were sent to the people. The dramatic story tells how the people learn to cope with this new life, finding direction and power through the Midiwiwin - the Grand Medicine People.

The paintings by Helen Davie add vitality and beauty to the spirit of the narrative. Incorporating traditional Ojibway patterns to the illustrations gives an added dimension and strength to the tale.

Ladder to the Sky could be an introductory book to use with non-Native children to introduce them to Anishinabe stories and the tradition of the Midiwiwin, though children need to understand the serious spiritual aspects of the Midiwiwin. It is a lovely book, produced with sensitivity and respect. Anishinabe children and adults who read the book gave it a favorable report.

→←

Esbensen, Barbara Juster; ***The Star Maiden;*** illustrated by Helen K. Davie; Little, Brown and Co.; 1988; Grades 3 - 5

Ojibway chief Kah-ge-ga-gah-bowh, also known as George Copway, wrote a book telling the history, legends and customs of the people. The Ojibway are also known as Chippewa, but they call themselves Anishinabe - "original people". The book was published in 1850 and included in the text was the tale of "The Star and the Lily". ***The Star Maiden*** is a retelling of that story.

In the retelling of this lovely tale, Star Maiden has grown weary of wandering the sky and wishes to live among the people on earth. In her journey, she first becomes a rose, then a prairie flower and finally, a beautiful water lily. "Water lilies! They are stars that fell from the deep sky one night long, long ago. If you see them, touch them gently. Their petals shine in the sun like the stars that lived and sparkled in the sky once upon a time."

Watercolors by Helen Davie are wonderfully rich and maintain visual interest. Incorporated in each picture are traditional Anishinabe patterns that frame the work giving an added dimension to the history and authenticity of the story.

Children of all ages will enjoy the fine artistry of this book and delight in a truly remarkable tale. It is a welcome addition to the limited number of appropriate books that deal with the stories of Native people. Anishinabe students who reviewed the book gave it a satisfactory report.

Estep, Irene; *Iroquois;* illustrated by Robert D. Smith; Melmont; 1961; Grades 3 - 6

The book tells about the customs, dwellings, clothing and work of the Iroquois in a historical setting. The illustrations add clarity to the text.

There is no in-depth look at the Iroquois people.

Farguhar, Margaret C.; *Indian Children of America;* illustrated by Brinton Turkle; Holt, Rinehart, Winston; 1964; Grades K - 3

A disturbing aspect of the book occurs on page one where it says: "Many of these American Indians were cruel warriors."

The "cruel warrior" concept sets the tone for the book that is organized into various geographical areas and discusses the life style of the people in that location.

Not only is the book stereotypical in design, it is also superficial and simplistic. Illustrations fit the text.

⇥⇤

Feague, Mildred; *The Little Indian and the Angel;* illustrated by Ted DeGrazia; Children's Press; 1970; Grades K - 3

The book is a story of a little "Indian" boy who has an angel as a friend and playmate. The illustrations are beautifully done in color and quite imaginative.

This book does not deal with the culture or values of Native people. Rather, it gives an ambivalent view of "Indians", reinforces stereotypes and even ends with a confused look at Christmas.

Attempts are made to be cute but the result is not acceptable. The text presents a distorted view of children, religion, Christmas and Native people. There are aspects in the book that can offend a number of different groups.

⇥⇤

Feague, Mildred; *Little Sky Eagle and the Pumpkin Drum;* illustrated by Ted DeGrazia; Children's Press; 1972; Grades K - 3

It appears to be an imaginative tale of Little Sky Eagle and the pumpkin he has grown in his garden. In reality, it is a blatant distortion of the spiritual life of Native people. The religious aspects are handled in a confused manner and one illustration shows a person with a snake in his mouth but no explanation. In all the drawings, the mother is presented as a faceless person without an explantion as to why she is faceless. There are no ideas of tribe, culture, values or family life of Native people.

Because of the negative, confused image presented, this book will have a dreadful effect on the child reader.

Friskey, Margaret; ***Indian Two Feet and the Grizzly Bear;*** illustrated by John Hawkinson; Children's Press; 1974; Grades K - 3

Indian Two Feet wants a warm, furry robe for his bed. He decides it would be better to get one large animal skin than several smaller ones, so he sets out to awaken a sleeping grizzly. After his attempts to capture a grizzly fail, he returns home. He finds his mother has made a big, thick, warm, wooly blanket for him.

The whole text is filled with quite a few major flaws. The book does not deal with a specific Nation, culture or anything else for that matter. The people are treated impersonally and Native life is shown in a distorted fashion. The illustrations merely reinforce the anonymity of the people. It is unacceptable.

Friskey, Margaret; ***Indian Two Feet and His Eagle Feather;*** illustrated by John and Lucy Hawkinson; Children's Press; 1967; Grades K - 3

Indian Two Feet wants an eagle feather but learns it must be earned. When he saves his village from disaster in a flood, he learns that being wise is the first part of being brave.

A number of flaws in this book cannot be overlooked. It does not deal with any specific Nation or culture. They are "Indians", with the clothing, family life, and people to be totally one-dimensional and generic. The name "Indian Two Feet" is not a realistic name. The book ridicules the Nations that use eagle feathers as a way of honoring people that have exhibited courage.

The book is disrespectful and reinforces unhealthy attitudes.

→←

Fritz, Jean; ***The Double Life of Pocahontas;*** illustrated by Ed Young; Putnam; 1983; Grades 4 - 6

When it comes to truth and real knowledge, there actually isn't much known about Pocahontas. Indeed, what most non-Native people know about her is the fictionalized accounts written for the popular book market. And what continues to sell is the myth of an "Indian princess" and the "hero", John Smith. Unfortunately, this book brings nothing new to the accounts of Pocahontas, her father and the English invaders.

The book contains many verbal stereotypes, depicting the Native people as naive, savage and deceitful. "John Smith was the one who seemed to know most about handling the Natives... he figured he understood 'savages' pretty well. Gentleness was not the way to deal with them..." And here's another quote: "Yet other Indians were not one bit friendly. Once they killed an English boy and shot an arrow right through President Wingfield's beard. Often they lay in the tall grass...waiting for someone to come through the gate...Not even a dog could run safely. Once one did and had forty arrows shot into his body." And here's another quote: "...naked savages, they would have said-they were like herds of deer. How could they legally own land?" "When Pocahontas spoke of Okee, Mr. Whitaker explained gently that Okee was not a god but a devil...her magic was worthless." When Pocahontas and her friends dance for John Smith, "...he had never imagined that thirty girls could make what he called 'such hellish shouts and cries'." Powhatan is intrigued by the "power of guns".

The book continues in this vein, mixing fact with fantasy. And once again for those who may not know - most historians agree that John Smith's accounts were fabricated. Nevertheless, this book produces the standard version of the life of Pocahontas. Myth. Fable. It is neither insightful nor sensitive.

"Powhatan" was really a man named Wahunsonacock.

※

Fritz, Jean; ***The Good Giants and the Bad Pukwudgies;*** illustrated by Tomie de Paola; G.P. Putnam's sons; 1982; Grades 1 - 3

Jean Fritz has "combined fragments of old legends collected by Elizabeth Reynard in a book called ***The Narrow Land***

A Second Look, Native Americans in Children's Books

to write of the formation of Cape Cod, Martha's Vineyard, and Nantucket." The tale is about the good giants who are in conflict with some strange, mischievous little creatures called pukwudgies. The giant's five sons are killed, buried at sea and become five islands.

Originally, the Wampanoag people told the stories of Maushop, Quant and their five sons. Fritz has "adapted and added dialogue and scenes" and given Maushop some "yankee speech". With all the additions, deletions and change in speech patterns, the stories changed. In fairness, it does not seem that the author meant to be insensitive to Native people, but the end result is an altered story.

→←

Gebhard, Wilfried; ***What Eddie Can Do;*** illustrated by the author; Kane/Miller Book Publishers, Germany; 2004; Grades K – 1

Eddie has numerous adventures. On his imaginative journeys, he dives to a sunken ship, "discovers the secrets of dark caves", "travels through outer space", and "explores the rain forest". One thing he cannot do is tie his shoes. On his fabricated trips, he also "rides the prairie with great warriors".

The cover of the book shows Eddie in his bed, in the dark, flashlight pointed toward the ceiling. A cat is next to him and Eddie has an "Indian" headband and a single feather. In the pages of the book, he rides with the great warriors, straddles the arm of a chair, tomahawk in hand, headband and feather adorning his head. The "warriors", on horseback, gallop across the scene.

Stereotypes are reinforced with the idea that all any child has to do is don a paper headband, stick in a feather, and he becomes an "Indian warrior." The book continues the tradition of many children's books that puts an "Indian" someplace in the book to appeal to parents and children.

The author/illustrator lives and works in Germany.

><

George, Jean Craighead; ***Arctic Son;*** illustrated by Wendel Minor; Hyperion books for Children; 1997; Grades 2 – 4

"On the day Luke was born in December the wind bugled like a lost caribou calf. The temperature dropped to thirty below zero. The sun did not come up." The village leader, Aalak, gives Luke an "Eskimo name" and says: "His name may be 'Kupaaq,' for my Papa."

Aalak shows Kupaaq the Arctic landscape and introduces him to Inupiat Eskimo customs. "Kinuyakki" says Aalak. "Some call this brightness the northern lights." He tells the young boy, "You and I live where the lights are born." Luke (Kupaaq) learns many things. Iqaluk is fish. Siqluaq is a "pit dug twenty feet down into frozen ground of permafrost…my Eskimo refrigerator."

Kupaaq goes to a "Nalukatoq, the celebration to honor the whale." He dances Eskimo dances and sings Inupiat songs. He takes part in the blanket toss.

George's text is rich and honoring of the life of the Inupiat Eskimo. Descriptions, long summer days, long winter nights, and the connections of people and animals are detailed, bringing Arctic life into the grasp of children. The book honors the Arctic and the people who live there.

Both author and illustrator have won numerous awards for their work.

⸻

George, Jean Craighead; *The First Thanksgiving;* illustrated by Thomas Locker; Philomel Books; 1993; Grades 3 – 4

"*In a time so long ago* that only the rocks remember, the last glacier began to melt. As it turned to water, mountains of gravel trapped in the ice were dumped on the coast of New England."

A span of history is covered in the brief chronology of the story. Opening with the beginning of time and the formation of Plymouth Rock, the book progresses through the capture of Squanto, the settlement of the new colony, and on through the return of Squanto and his influence on the Plymouth Colony.

The account is straightforward, acknowledging the difficulties faced by the new settlers and the help given to the colonists by the Native people.

The story acknowledges that "The Pilgrims called the celebration a Harvest Feast. The Indians thought of it as a Green Corn Dance." Children need to know that Native people had Thanksgiving celebrations long before the arrival of the first Europeans.

Matching the narrative of Ms. George, Thomas Locker captures the New England setting realistically; the paintings reflecting the wide scope of people and place.

※

George, Jean Craighead; *Julie of the Wolves;* illustrated by John Schoenherr; Harper & Row; 1972; Grades 6 - Up

Miyax, also known as Julie, is a thirteen-year-old Eskimo girl. Circumstances cause her to leave the village and live alone among an Arctic wolf pack. Her experiences deepen her feelings and love for the traditional Eskimo life. She is horrified when a plane sweeps down and gunfire kills one of her beloved wolves. It is only the strong bond of love that causes Julie to return to her father.

A well written adventure story that captures the dilemma of a young Eskimo girl searching for her place in the world. It is written with sensitivity and is enhanced by exquisite black and white drawings.

In some later books, Ms. George uses the word Inuit.

Julie of the Wolves became a Newberry award winner in 1973.

※

George, Jean Craighead; *Nutik, the Wolf Pup;* illustrated by Ted Rand; Julie Productions; 2001; Grades 2 – 4

A Second Look, Native Americans in Children's Books

"In an Eskimo village at the top of the world lived a lively little boy." It is said that he was not very old, "but he could run as fast as a bird's shadow." His father is Kapugen, a great hunter. His mother is Ellen. His sister is Julie – Julie of the Wolves.

Julie told the boy stories of her adventures with the wolf pack and how the wolf family shared food with her. "The wolf's name was Amaroq. The little boy's name was Amaroq."

One day Julie brought home two sick, hungry wolf pups. She gives one to Amaroq to care for and she tends the other pup. She tells her brother that the wolves will come for the pups when they are well. Julie warns Amaroq not to love the pup, because the pup must return to the pack.

When the pup is strong and healthy, Amaroq returns him to his wolf home. "I am very strong," Amaroq said to himself. "He got home before his tears froze." In the end, the boy and pup become family. "...the wolves sang back, 'That is good.'"

George tells the story simply, capturing the cadence of an oral storyteller. The illustrations add clarity to the Alaskan landscape.

This story was first told in ***Julie's Wolf Pack;*** the sequel to ***Julie of the Wolves***, which won the Newberry Medal in 1973.

→←

George, Jean Craighead; ***Snow Bear;*** illustrated by Wendell Minor; Hyperion Books for Children; 1999; Grades K – 2

Young Bessie Nivyek sees a "huge block of ice near the shore. It looks like a ship." Bessie decides she wants to climb the ship formed by the upthrust of ice and "pretend she is sailing to beautiful places." She meets Snow Bear, a polar bear cub, and they begin a playful interlude. They are watched over by Bessie's older brother, Vincent, and Nanuq, Snow Bear's mother. As Bessie and Snow Bear work their way around the ice, a large male polar bear appears that is a menace to all. Vincent, Bessie's brother, sees that a bear is following his sister. Mother Bear fears her cub is in danger. In a scene reminiscent of **Blueberries for Sal** by Robert McCloskey, Bessie and Snow Bear "run back the way they came."

Some of the phrasing may seem overly poetic, but this is a poetic rendering of an imaginary story. Children should understand that this is "make-believe" and not true. (They should figure out very quickly that a child and bear cub will not imitate each other's movements.)

Exquisite watercolors by Wendell Minor capture the essence of the story in splendid detail. The Inuit parkas are filled with brilliant color; the landscape is alive with a richness that captures the Arctic beauty, and the story is a delight.

Jean Craighead George has won many honors for her books, including the Newberry Medal for ***Julie of the Wolves***.

※

Glubok, Shirley; *The Art of the Eskimo;* designed by Oscar Krauss; Harper & Row; 1964; Grades 3 - 6

A Second Look, Native Americans in Children's Books

The objects selected for inclusion in the book span more than a thousand years. Eskimo art provides a fresh impression of the Eskimo culture. The book provides clear explanations of Eskimo masks, drawings and figures.

There is a fine coordination between text and illustrations. The author skillfully interprets Eskimo art tradition in a clear, concise presentation for young people. Appropriate for all ages.

The copyright is an indication of the word Eskimo instead of Inuit.

→←

Glubok, Shirley; ***The Art of the North American Indian;*** designed by Oscar Krauss; Harper & Row; 1964; Grades 3 - 6

Photographs of Indian pipes, dolls, totems, masks, birch bark baskets, and other objects of art are presented. Included are objects from the Plains Indians and the elaborate double masks of the Northwest Coast People. Accompanying the photographs are background information and descriptions on the purpose, symbolism and location of these art objects.

A skillfully written book in clear concise language. Appropriate for all ages.

→←

Goble, Paul; ***Adopted by Eagles;*** illlustrated by the author; Bradberry Press; 1994; Grades 3 - 6

Paul Goble's books soar with energy, enthusiasm, and great respect for the stories of Native people. ***Adopted by Eagles: a Plains Indian story of friendship and treachery*** is based on a "more complex story which is said to have been a favorite of Chief Red Cloud (1822 – 1909)."

White Hawk and Tall Bear are *kolas,* friends; the friendship is a sacred one. One friend is left on a narrow ledge, alone with the eagles, "…to starve, and to fall to an awful death on the rocks far below." Tall Bear cries out to the Great Spirit "Have pity on me! *Wani wachin!* I want to live!" The story is an intense tale of love, friendship and betrayal that ends in renewal.

An author's note says: "There are two main ideas inside this Lakota story which appear often in North American Indian literature: treachery between two warriors or hunters when they are far from home, and animals or birds who help people in need."

Paul Goble's pictures are dazzling, bold, and filled with remarkable detail. They embody the feeling conveyed in the author's notes regarding the stories of Edgar Red Cloud. "The myths were his scriptures."

※

Goble, Paul; ***All Our Relatives, Traditional Native American Thoughts about Nature;*** illustrated by the author; World Wisdom, Inc.; 2005; Grades 4 and up.

Foreward by Dr. Joe Medicine Crow, Absaroke. "Dr. Joe Medicine Crow is the Crow Tribal Historian and the oldest living man of the Crow tribe." He is also an author.

The author's note states: "The title, All Our Relatives, is an often-repeated refrain in Lakota ceremonies and prayers: mitakuye oyasin, meaning 'all my relatives' or 'we are all related'."

Paul Goble has successfully joined authentic design and color with the tradition of the old stories. Throughout the book, illustrations are matched with quotes from Native people. Stories reflect the beliefs of the people and the sacred traditons that were an integral part of every day life. It is an exceptional book for students and teachers and parents. Through the book, everyone can learn from the Nations and their relationship with the earth.

Paul Goble is a Caldecott Medal winner. He breathes life into his stories; his paintings are bold, brightly colored, and carefully detailed. His work is a treasure.

→←

Goble, Paul; ***Beyond the Ridge;*** illustrated by the author; Bradbury Press; 1969; Grades 1 and Up

An old woman lies dying in her tipi, surrounded by her family. A voice leads her away from her home to a faraway, beautiful land. Even as she travels on her spiritual odyssey, she turns and sees "herself lying under her blanket..." After her death, the family prepared her for the "...journey along the Pathway of the Souls."

The vibrant, exquisite paintings give a power and vision of life "beyond the ridge." Portrayed is a world much like Earth, but with more abundance and beauty. Even though she could still hear her grandchildren crying, the old woman went to the people on the other side of the highland. "She felt strong again. The way down from the top was so easy and beautiful. She even wanted to run. There was no other path to take."

Prayers of the Plains Indian are included as Paul Goble sensitively melds story and art. It is a powerful, transcendent book. "Death? There is no death; only a change of worlds."

Note: There has been some question as to why Mr. Goble chooses to leave his people faceless. He has an answer to this in a note from the author at the beginning of the book. "Faces are drawn without any expression or features. (This follows the convention of traditional Indian hide and ledger-book painting, and even children's dolls.) I once asked a Lakota lady, who makes dolls dressed in every minute detail, why she left the faces without features. Her reply was that children give the dolls their own personality, and do not have it dictated to them by the maker."

→✣←

Goble, Paul and Dorothy Goble; ***Brave Eagle's Account of the Fetterman Fight;*** illustrated by Paul Goble; Pantheon Books; 1972; Grades 5 - 6

Paul Goble's pictures are brilliant and vivid and give a stunning account of the war. It is a meticulous report of the battle and events leading up to the actual fighting.

An author's note at the beginning tells some background information: "What is known of the fight was told in later years by the Indians who had fought in it, and so it seems appropriate that it should be retold by them. This account attempts to capture the spirit of the published Indian accounts, but because Indians told only what they saw and did, it has also been necessary to draw on the material of white historians, in order to give the reader a better understanding of the fight and the events that preceded it. Many of the words spoken by Red Cloud in this account are edited extracts from his recorded speeches."

Doane Robinson says: "Red Cloud's War is the only instance in the history of the United States where the government has gone to war and afterwards negotiated a peace conceding everything demanded by the enemy and exacting nothing in return."

December 21, 1866 - "Three commissioned officers and seventy-six privates...under the command of Captain William J. Fetterman were killed by an overwhelming force of Sioux under the command of Red Cloud. There were no survivors."

The Gobles have given a straight forward, honest account of the battle.

→←

Goble, Paul; ***Buffalo Woman;*** illustrated by the author; Bradbury Press; 1984; Grades 3 - 6

The story of Buffalo Woman has a power that comes from the respect the author has for Native people. It is the telling of the kinship between the tribes of the Great Plains and the buffalo, but it is also the story of the transforming power of love.

The hero of this story is a young hunter. He marries a beautiful maiden who is a member of the Buffalo Nation. They have a supernatural son, Buffalo Calf, but her husband's relatives reject the young wife. Through a series of tests and with the help of his son, the hunter is allowed to join the Buffalo Nation.

The ending is a poem from the Osage tribe: Song of the Buffalo Bulls. Gobles's use of color and style mirror the story that unfolds. As usual, Paul Goble has given us a lovely book.

→⊁

Goble, Paul; ***Death of the Iron Horse;*** illustrated by the author; Bradbury; 1987; Grades 1 - 6

"On August 7, 1867, a Union Pacific freight train was derailed by Cheyennes…The derailment was only a minor incident, but one that the Cheyenne people have remembered with pride and amusement."

In this retelling of the event, Paul Goble details the events brilliantly and in vibrant color. Sweet Medicine has a vision of the coming of the white men and of the destruction that was to be a part of their appearance. Because the "iron horse" caused fear among the people, some of the young men went out to protect their people. The result was the derailment of the train and the death of the trainman.

A particularly poignant part of the book is the illustrations on the first and last pages. It is the same area of land: On the first page, the land is pure and free with the new iron horse shown upon it. The last page is littered with cans, bottles, power lines, some jet planes and an Amtrak train.

In the introduction, the author states: "Like everything to do with war, the derailment had sad and unpleasant aspects. But from this distance in time, we can see that the Cheyennes were simply fighting for their lives, liberty, and their own pursuit of happiness."

The story shows a great deal of sensitivity and respect for the people. In so doing, the author helps children to understand the history of the country and the tragic ways in which non-Native people settled it.

Illustrations are intense, brightly colored, and give a moving range of perspectives.

→←

Goble, Paul; ***Dream Wolf;*** illustrated by the author; Bradbury Press; 1990; Grades K - 3

Tiblo and Tanksi are two young children who decide to quit picking berries and climb the hills nearby. Because they are so engrossed in their climb, they are unaware of the approaching darkness. When they are cold, hungry and tired, a wolf appears to the children as if in a dream. The wolf helps them return to the safety of their home and the Wolf People are forever revered and honored.

Paul Goble has written a beautiful book. The illustrations are full of stunning color that sweeps across the page in exquisite detail. ***Dream Wolf*** is a revised edition of ***The Friendly Wolf*** by Paul and Dorothy Goble that was first published in 1974. For this new edition, Paul Goble has rewritten the text, reproduced the original illustrations and created new artwork for the jacket.

>←

Goble, Paul and Dorothy; ***The Friendly Wolf;*** illustrated by Paul Goble; Bradbury Press; 1975; Grades 3 - 6

When two children are picking berries, they stray into the hills and get lost. Seeking shelter, they discover the cave of a wolf and spend the night. The wolf that lives in the cave is a friendly wolf and escorts them home the following morning. As a result, the tribe honors the animal.

The simply told tale gains added strength from its lovely, stylish drawings. The artistry of Paul Goble is brilliant; an expression of respect and honor.

In 1990, Paul Goble revised the narrative to produce a new book entitled: ***Dream Wolf.***

Mr. Goble has received numerous awards in his distinguished career, including the Caldecott Medal in 1978, the Regina medal in 2006, and he received an Honorary Doctor of Humane Letters from South Dakota State University.

>←

Goble, Paul; ***The Gift of the Sacred Dog;*** illustrated by the author; Aladdin Paperbacks; 1987; Grades 1 – 5

It was a time of great hunger among the people. Even the buzzards and crows and wolves were hungry. The dogs would no longer carry their loads and the people were too tired and hungry to continue their journey. Dances were held to bring back the buffalo and young men went in all directions searching for the herds.

A boy in camp was sad to hear the hunger cries and told his parents, "I am going up into the hills to ask the Great Spirit to help us. Do not worry about me; I shall return in the morning."

As he stood on the hilltop, wind and hail and thunderbirds came with a great force. The boy was afraid. A rider appeared before the boy riding "on the back of a beautiful animal. There was thunder in its nostrils and lightning in its legs; its eyes shone like stars and hair on its neck and tail trailed like clouds."

The rider says to the boy that the animal is "called the Sacred Dog. He can do many things your dogs can do and also more. He will carry you far and will run faster than buffalo. He comes from the sky."

The clouds closed and "suddenly the sky was filled with Sacred Dogs of all colors and the boy could never count their number." So it is that the gift of the horse is bestowed upon the people. "Life was good after that." And the people lived "as the Great Spirit wished them to live."

Paul Goble's prose and paintings are exquisite and riveting. If you have only one book about the gift of the horse, let this be the one. Magnificent.

⇥⇤

Goble, Paul; *The Legend of the White Buffalo Woman;* illustrated by the author; National Geographic Society; 1998; Grades 2 – 5

In an author's note, Mr. Goble says: "In this most important of all Lakota sacred legends, the Great Spirit gave the Sacred Pipe so that people could pray and commune with him."

Based on oral tradition, the retelling of the White Buffalo Woman is done with reverence and respect. In exquisite detail, the text relays the significance of the pipe to Lakota people. Goble states that he has "not illustrated the Sacred Calf Pipe, of which no likeness should be made." The text transports the reader through the end of the Old World through the age when the nation was reborn and into a time of war and suffering. It is then that the White Buffalo Woman appears. "She was a stranger, beautiful and, also mysterious." Throughout the story, the gift of the pipe is shown to be one of hope, regeneration, and a new way to pray to the Great Spirit. The woman says that the Great Spirit has given the gift of the pipe. She says: "Pray with it, and you will see your prayers rise up to him with the smoke, and you will know he hears you."

Some meanings of the pipe are shared at the end of the story with text and illustrations that add a deeper dimension to the pipe ceremony. Pipestone National Monument was a "place of pilgrimage" in the old days. This book shares a part of the important spiritual and cultural life of the Lakota people.

Paul Goble shares another story of the White Buffalo Woman in the book *The Return of the Buffaloes* also published by the National Geographic Society.

Paul Goble has received many honors for his books including the Caldecott Medal for *The Girl Who Loved Wild Horses.* Throughout his career, he has consistently shown respect and accuracy in depicting the clothing, customs, and spirituality of Native Americans. His illustrations are extraordinary, soaring with color and life.

→←

Goble, Paul; *The Girl Who Loved Wild Horses;* illustrated by the author; Bradbury; 1978; Grades 3 - 6

The young girl had a special relationship with a herd of wild horses. She spent her days among the horses as they grazed contentedly among flowers near her village. One day a thunderstorm drove the girl and the horses far from home. The girl lived with the wild horses, but eventually returned home. In a climactic ending, we witness her metamorphosis into a beautiful horse.

The brilliant, colorful paintings sweep and stampede across the pages and are matched with a well written text. Paul Goble does a splendid job of writing and illustrating. Understandably, it earned the 1979 Caldecott Medal.

Goble, Paul; ***I Sing for the Animals;*** illustrated by the author; 1991; Macmillan Publishing Co.; All ages

>Thoughts of our kinship with nature, living in peace and harmony, and respecting the environment shine through the pages of this book. It is not a "Native American" book, though the author says he is "undoubtedly influenced by the lifelong association."
>
>At the beginning of the book, the author says: "This book is for children and grown-ups who love wildflowers and grasses more than mowed lawns; who cry for the birds and animals killed for 'sport' or 'necessity' and imprisoned in zoos and cages. It is for all who guard, and champion, Father Sky and Mother Earth."
>
>Paul Goble's illustrations show astonishing talent, careful research, and keen observation. The pictures beautifully communicate the feelings of the text.

Goble, Paul; ***Iktomi and the Berries;*** illustrated by the author; Orchard Books; 1989; All grades.

>In reading the Iktomi stories, it is necessary that the introduction "About Iktomi" be read first along with "A Note for the Reader". Iktomi, the trickster, is both humble and conceited; foolish and clever; a loser and a cunning winner.

Iktomi is over his head in this retelling of some bright red berries he believes are growing in the river and his misadventures in trying to secure them. This book is Paul Goble's second Iktomi tale.

Goble's artistic style adds an energetic feel to the Iktomi story as they reflect the playfulness of the tale and the trickster aspect of Iktomi. The illustrations dance across the pages only to be interrupted by Iktomi and his opinions of himself.

→←

Goble, Paul; *Iktomi and the Boulder;* illustrated by the author; Orchard Books; 1988; All grades

Iktomi, the trickster of Plains Indian folklore, is cleverly introduced in this tale about a bouncing boulder, a blanket and a flurry of furry bats.

Because "Iktomi has no respect for the precise use of words", the stories are told in informal language. Storytellers wove variations around known themes, but they all started out the same way: "Iktomi was walking along…"

An introduction "About Iktomi" at the beginning of the book provides an added dimension for the modern-day storyteller. Iktomi skips delightfully across the pages with Goble's rich, stylized pictures setting the pace. Once again, Paul Goble has demonstrated his unique gifts. Have fun with the Iktomi stories.

Goble, Paul; ***Iktomi and the Buffalo Skull;*** illustrated by the author; Orchard Books; 1991; All grades

"Iktomi was walking along...wearing his best clothes...going to get his horse", because he was going to the next village to impress his girlfriends. He felt so proud, but he is married, you know. He returns home by way of the river, gets his head stuck fast in a buffalo skull and must ask his wife to get him out of trouble.

As the book jacket proclaims: "In this fourth funny story about the Plains Indian trickster, Paul Goble again reveals a painter's mastery of the great and the small in nature, from horse to mouse - with man in the middle making a fool of himself."

The illustrations are amazing - full of life, energy and stunning color.

Goble, Paul; ***Iktomi and the Buzzard;*** illustrated by the author; Orchard Books; 1994; All grades

"Iktomi was walking along…*Every story about Iktomi starts the same way.*"

Iktomi, the trickster, is once again having trouble with his behavior. In this story, he is all dressed up and going to a powwow. He is bragging and quite full of himself. When he comes to a river, he is not sure how to cross. Then "Iktomi spied

Buzzard circling in the sky" and the trickster began plotting. Buzzard agreed to fly Iktomi to the dance, but Iktomi cannot contain himself – he has to make rude signs and insulting gestures toward Buzzard. Unknown to Iktomi, Buzzard can see the impertinence by watching the shadows on the land below him. Buzzard tricks the trickster and Iktomi becomes victim to Buzzard's cleverness. Iktomi, as always, plans what to do next.

Paul Goble's engaging paintings and superb text capture the Iktomi stories masterfully.

※

Goble, Paul; *Iktomi and the Ducks;* illustrated by the author; Orchard Books; 1990; All grades

Caldecott Medallist Paul Goble tells another amusing tale of Iktomi, the trickster of Plains Indian folklore. Iktomi plans on having a meal of roast duck and so he lures some innocent ducks off the pond with his tricks. But he does not take the wind, a couple of trees and a cunning coyote into account.

Paul Goble gives us an entertaining tale that will be enjoyed by all ages. Iktomi speaks to the ambitions, vulgarities and insincerities present in everyone's lives, but he is a humorous, entertaining character. Multifaceted, colorful pictures amplify and extend the humor and are animated with the spirit of Iktomi.

Goble is flawless in his presentation of the Iktomi stories.

Goble, Paul and Dorothy Goble; ***Red Hawk's Account of Custer's Last Battle;*** illustrated by Paul Goble; Pantheon Books; 1969; Grades 4 - 6

> June 25, 1876 - The Battle of the Little Bighorn. Probably the best-known battle, this account is told through the eyes of a fifteen-year-old Oglala boy. Though the boy is fictional, the material is historically and meticulously accurate.
>
> An author's note gives some additional information: The account "is based on the published accounts of both Sioux and Cheyenne participants in the Battle of the Little Bighorn. These accounts do not give a complete picture of the battle because an Indian only tells of what he has seen or done. To give the reader a general view it has been necessary to include the explanatory passages printed in Italics…"
>
> Red Hawk's rendition of the conflict is both poetic and unemotional; it is an analysis of the fighting from a soldier's point of view. The pictures by Paul Goble add a vibrancy and realism to the story of the battle.
>
> Writing about war, especially for children, is always difficult. The Gobles have done so with honesty and sensitivity; in so doing, they have honored the memory of the people who fought at the Little Big Horn.

Goble, Paul; ***The Return of the Buffaloes, a Plains Indian story about famine and renewal of the Earth;*** illustrated by the author; National Geographic Society; 1996; Grades 3 – 6

> Buffaloes provided almost everything the people needed, but a time came upon the land when the buffaloes could not be found. "Everyone was hungry and the children were too weak to go out and play any longer." Day after day the hunters returned empty handed. "The leaders of the village chose two young men" to look for the buffalo. On their journey, they met a woman who promised to once again send the Buffalo Nation. The arrival of the thundering herd is full of energy and movement and "noises of snorting and bellowing and thundering hooves."
>
> Paul Goble tells the story with mastery, recognizing the spirituality of the Native people. The illustrations are bold, colorful, and capture the essence of the drama of the text. A glossary and author's note adds valuable information to the story.
>
> Goble concludes in the way of traditional storytellers: "That is the story the old people used to tell about those long-ago days. *Keyapi*, that is what they said."

→←

Goble, Paul; ***Star Boy;*** illustrated by the author; Bradbury Press; 1983; Grades K - Up

> ***Star Boy*** is the ancient story of how the Blackfeet were given the sacred knowledge of the Sun Dance. The hero of the story actually had two names: Star Boy and Scarface. As a baby, he lived with his mother in the Sky World and everyone knew that

his father was the Morning Star and his grandparents were the Sun and Moon.

Star Boy and his mother are banished from the Sky World and sent to Earth. The mysterious scar on his face causes people to be frightened, but eventually he falls in love with the chief's daughter and she helps him to return to the Sky World and seek forgiveness from the Sun.

Paul Goble has produced a rare book that is both visually and verbally gratifying. He closes with a poem - "Song of the Rising Sun" by Black Elk.

→⊁

Grossman, Virginia and Sylvia Long; *Ten Little Rabbits;* Chronicle Books; 1991; Grades K – 1

Counting books are one of the basics of early childhood education. Rhyming texts are elemental in beginning stories for young children. *Ten Little Rabbits* is counting and rhyme attached to rain dances, storytelling, tricksters, and smoke signals. A very brief glossary at the end of the book gives information about ten tribes.

Rabbits are dressed in a garment (a blanket) that is supposed to represent the Native clothing of the Sioux, Tewa, Ute, Menominee, Blackfoot, Hopi, Arapaho, Nez Perce, Kwakiutl, and Navajo. Each page is devoted to one number and one tribe. No clue is given as to the tribe represented by the blanket. "One lonely traveler riding on the plain." "Two graceful dancers asking for some rain." "Seven merry mischief-makers playing hide-and-seek." The mischief-makers are the Arapaho. It isn't until the brief glossary at the end of the book that a name is given to any of the tribes.

The result of this book is a superficial, insulting, dehumanizing, and demeaning image of Native people. It is a mixed bag of harmful images. (All in seventy-one words.)

The continued juxtaposition of Native people and animals in literature is unacceptable. Don't fall for the "cuteness" angle or any other excuse offered for such images.

Teachers, librarians, and parents will make the difference when they take a leadership role in understanding the damage done by stereotypes and hurtful images. Knowing why a book is toxic is an crucial first step. Refusing to buy a toxic book is wisdom.

Hader, Berta and Elmer; ***Reindeer Trail;*** Macmillan; 1959; Grades 3 - 6

The book is based on an historical event in Alaska during the 1890's. The Eskimo people of northwest Alaska were in danger of starvation. Young Ahlook is an Eskimo boy who lives the traditional Eskimo life with his family. Because the fishing and hunting grounds had been depleted, a plan was devised to bring reindeer from Lapland to Alaska. Leif and Ingri are young Lapp children who accompany their family to Alaska with a reindeer herd. When they arrive in Alaska, they meet Ahlook and the rest of the villagers who await their new friends.

Reindeer Trail is based on Sheldon Jackson's report of his trip to Lapland to bring the Lapp herders, their families and herds of reindeer to Alaska. The book presents a picture of Eskimo life. The actual route of the Lapp herders may be confusing to younger children but a presentation with a globe would effectively demonstrate the route.

Illustrations in black and white as well as full color pictures add completeness to the text.

In 1959, it was the norm to refer to Sami people as Lapp, and the Inuit as Eskimo.

⤞⤝

Harris, Christie; ***Forbidden Frontier;*** illustrated by E. Carey Kenney; Atheneum; 1968; Grades 6 & Up

Allison Stewart had been raised in the wilderness of British Columbia. Her father was the Chief Trader of the fort for the Hudson's Bay Company and of Scottish ancestry. Her mother was a high-ranking Haida. The first part of the book is devoted to Allison's story. In part two of the book we learn the story of Megan Scully, daughter of Irish immigrants. We watch as the two girls grow and eventually meet in the wilderness country of British Columbia in 1862.

The atmosphere of the story is rich with the exciting days of fur brigades and gold rushes in the Pacific Northwest. The book deals sympathetically with the Native people and their treatment in the days of frontier society.

Christie Harris has received the Book-of-the-Year Medal from the Canadian Association of Children's Librarians for two of her books.

❖

Harris, Christie; ***Once More Upon a Totem;*** illustrated by Douglas Tait; Atheneum; 1973; Grades 3 - 6

During the sumptuous feasting at the potlatches, many stories were told. Three of those stories are included in this collection. Also included are short chapters that set the mood for the feast and tell something about the life lived by the Native people of the North Pacific Coast.

The book is an outstanding collection of tales told with warmth and dignity that captures the beauty and imaginative spirit of the Native people who first lived on the area. Black and white illustrations heighten the effect of the narrative.

Christie Harris learned the stories while visiting the villages and the people of the Northwest Coast. She has written extensively for the Canadian Broadcasting Company.

❖

Harris, Christie; ***Once Upon a Totem;*** illustrated by John Frazier Mills; Atheneum; 1969; Grades 3 - 6

The Native people of the North Pacific Coast told stories that highlight their culture, the lavish potlatches, and their adaptabililty with the natural world. They lived in grand cedar lodges and carved totem poles with symbols of their traditions and historic distinction.

Five stories are included in the text: "The One-Horned Mountain Goat", "The Boy and the Sea Monsters", "The Wild Woman of the Woods", "The Giant Ogre, Kloo-Teekl," and "Fly again, My Proud Eagle".

Regarding North Pacific Coast people, the preface explains, "Isolated by mountains and fed by the bounty of sea and river, the unchallenged lords of the coast had ample leisure to develop rich artistic talents. Potlatch display provided a strong incentive. Greatest in the arts were the bold northern nations. Haida, Tsimshian, Tlingit, and Kwakiutl especially enriched their lives with painting and sculpture, song and dance, story and ceremonial."

The 1969 book is the Fifth Printing. First Printing was 1963.

Christie Harris learned the stories while visiting the people and their villages.

The black and white woodcuts that illustrate the text are representative of the art of the coastal people.

→✧←

Harris, Christie; **Raven's Cry;** illustrated by Bill Reid; Atheneum; 1966; Grades 6 & Up

The book is an historical novel whose setting is the Queen Charlotte Islands and British Columbia. It is a sensitive account of the Haida, a proud and cultured people. It begins in the year 1775 when the Haida encountered their first ship of white men. The book focuses on a family as they live the traditional Haida life, a life that is beautiful, producing one of the most art-centered cultures that ever existed. The death of the lovely young Maada at the hands of ruthless Captain Dixon is chronicled. The meeting of the Haida and the white men was bewildering to both sides, but the white men brought strong ships, firearms, devastating diseases, and a new religion. In less than two centuries, the Haida people were reduced drastically in numbers. The great chiefs of the Haida left a heritage of beauty that radiates vitality and strength.

The black and white illustrations reflect the art of the Haida. Bill Reid, a descendent of the last great Haida chief, turned to art he said, "because his spirit demanded it." Highly recommended.

Raven's Cry received the Book-of-the-Year Medal in 1967. The Medal is awarded by the Canadian Association of Children's Librarians for the best children's book by a Canadian author. Mrs. Harris also received the Medal in 1977 for ***Mouse Woman and the Vanished Princess.***

Haseley, Dennis; ***The Scared One;*** illustrated by Deborah Howland; Warne; 1983; Grades 1 - 3

Scared One is given his name by the other boys in the village because he is afraid of dogs and of the night. Most of all, because he is afraid of being alone, he allows the children to taunt him. It is when he finds an injured bird that his life becomes changed. His mother sends him to Old Wolf, an elder of the village to seek help, but Scared One finds it a negative experience. A little later, the boy is somehow transformed and cries, "I will never fear! I will never die!"

The author has chosen to give the reader a confused look at Native life. Old Wolf, the Elder, is not only ineffectual, but comes off looking like a malefactor. The Native people don't have a tribal identity, his mother is unable to help her son, and the transformation of Scared One is fraudulent. His whole visionary experience, if that in fact is what he had, is not dealt with successfully.

Deborah Howland has contributed some powerful drawings to the text, but her perception doesn't rescue the book.

⇥⇤

Hays, Wilma and R. Vernon Hays; ***Foods the Indians Gave Us;*** illustrated by Tom O'Sullivan; Ives Washburn; 1973; Grades 3 - 6

The Native people of the Western Hemisphere first used many of the delicious foods we enjoy today. These foods were then introduced to the people on the continents of Europe and Asia. The foods were accepted with little acknowledgement and, as a result, many people do not know the origins of the foods they partake of on a daily basis. The book is a fascinating story of these foods and a long overdue tribute to the people of North and South America. The book also includes a section of recipes that have been adapted from Indian cooking. According to the book, eighty percent of our present food plants originated in the Americas.

Black and white drawings illustrate the text.

※

Hays, Wilma Pitchford; ***Noko, Captive of Columbus;*** illustrated by Peter Burchard; Coward-McCann; 1967; Grades 3 - 6

Noko is a young Indian boy from Panama. He is the son of the chief and is the first to see the great ships of the white men. When the Spaniards found gold, they wanted to start a permanent settlement. Fighting breaks out and Noko and his family are taken hostage by the intruders. All but Noko manage to escape. It is an adventure story based in part on the diaries of Columbus' son.

In the context of history, the story, especially the ending, is not realistic.

※

Hays, Wilma Pitchford; ***Pilgrim Thanksgiving;*** illustrated by Leonard Weisgard; Coward-McCann, Inc; 1955; Grades 2 - 3

As the title indicates, the book tells the story of the Thanksgiving festival held by the pilgrims. Told by young Damaris Hopkins, it is a one-sided tale of celebration and encounters with "Indians". "This was the day the Indians would come. Governor Bradford had invited the Indians to come to a feast of thanksgiving...The Indians wore leggings and a kind of shirt made of deerskin... Their faces were painted in a wide stripe from the forehead down to the chin...A few of the older Indian braves sat at the table with Pilgrim men. Most of the Indians squatted on the ground."

Damaris did not want to be around the Indians, but young Giles made friends with a young "brave". When Giles gives the young man a knife, he appears naively amazed by the wondrousness of the gift.

As the celebration continues, the Indians begin to dance. "They made a circle. They hunched forward. They began to dance. High leaps. Strange yells. Raising their tomahawks high." The illustrations, in stereotypical fashion, match the text.

The author has based the book on writings of Governor Bradford and Master Winslow. Both men have written biased accounts that add to the Pilgrim - Indian myth. This book serves no purpose other than to perpetuate that myth and generate stereotypes.

❖

Hays, Wilma Pitchford; ***Pontiac, Lion in the Forest;*** illustrated by Lorence Bjorklund; Houghton, Mifflin; 1965; Grades 3 - 6

Pontiac was chief of the Ottawas. Growing hostility between the French and English made Pontiac realize he would have to choose sides if his people were to survive. He chose the French because he felt they had been more understanding of Indian values. Pontiac had great qualities of leadership and was a brilliant military strategist. The story line is predictable and includes some stereotypes.

Henry, Edna, Wechappituwen (Blue Star Woman); ***Native American Cookbook;*** Messner; 1983; Grades 5 - 6

> The book contains a tasty collection of recipes from a number of tribes. An introduction to each section includes historical and cultural information as well as personal anecdotes. For those unable to obtain the Native foods, the author gives readily available substitutes. For example, she suggests using brown rice for wild rice and spinach for lambs quarters. Though the fry bread calls for whole-wheat flour, a more traditional recipe would use white flour.
>
> Black and white drawings enhance the effectiveness of the book. Fry bread and Labrador tea were favorites among the children who tried these recipes, but everyone enjoyed cooking and sampling. Edna Henry is of Nipmuc and Cherokee ancestry.

Henry, Jeannette and Rupert Costo; ***A Thousand Years of American Indian Storytelling;*** Indian Historian Press; 1981; All Grades

> An informative introduction by the editors discusses the role of storytelling in the life and culture of Native people. "Among the American Indians, storytelling was an art, and those who were the best storytellers were respected and beloved." Included in the text are stories with humor, modern-day tales and some favorites of the storytellers.

More than forty stories are part of this collection that spans a broad range and covers a "thousand years". The illustrations vary in style depending on the story and fit the text well.

The editors also tell us "There's More to Come." "These stories should serve as an introduction to the huge body of literature existing as part of the heritage of the American Indian. There are thousands of them, historic and fictional, in the form of myths, fables and legends."

There is a wonderful wholeness to this book that will provide a very special experience for people of all ages.

※

Highwater, Jamake; ***Anpao, An American Indian Odyssey;*** illustrated by Fritz Scholder; Lippincott; 1977; Grades 6 & Up

The author has created an epic from the oral tales of diverse plains and Southwest tribes. The central character is Anpao whose love for the beautiful Ko-ko-mik-e-is is so powerful that he undertakes a long and dangerous quest in order to marry her. The reader meets Anpao's reverse twin Oapna, taken from the fascinating Plains' Indian conception of the Contrary. The story encompasses the Blackfeet story of Scarface. And, as the story explains, riding from village to village is the terrible stranger - Smallpox.

Jamake Highwater has woven together old and new in the classic tradition of the story. Old Wasicong is the storyteller.

Highwater, Jamake; *Many Smokes; Many Moons, A Chronology of American Indian History Through Indian Art;* Lippincott; 1978; Grades 6 & Up

Emphasis is on tribes in North America. It is the history of many different groups who developed distinct cultures before the invasion by the Europeans. Jamake Highwater uses the art and artifacts of various Native American cultures to illustrate historical events. The narrative is in chronological dated notes which accompany black and white photographs of ancient and modern Indian artifacts. The author stresses in the text that there is not one truth, but many, there is not one history, but different ways of looking at events. Most of what has been written about Indians has been from the viewpoint of the dominant culture. Mr. Highwater offers a significant insight at events from the perspective of those who were truly the first people on the North American continent. It is an accurate account of the unique realities that are part of art history of Native people.

Hill, Kay; *Badger, The Mischief Maker;* illustrated by John Hamberger; Dodd, Mead & Co.; 1965; Grades 3 - 6

The stories of Badger come from the Micmac Indians of the Algonquin nation. Badger lives by his wits playing tricks on Medoc the mountain lion and Mooin the bear. Glooscap, the wise and kindly god, must watch Badger closely, for sometimes he goes too far with his clever pranks. Eventually he is captured by those he has tricked and he comes to learn the meaning of kindness.

Kay Hill has skillfully adapted the stories to make them suitable for the young reader.

In 1969, Kay Hill received the Book-of-the-Year Medal from the Canadian Association of Children's Librarians for ***And Tomorrow, the Stars.***

Hill, Kay; ***Glooscap and his Magic;*** illustrated by Robert Frankenberg; Dodd, Mead & Co.; 1963; Grades 3 - 6

No one knows where or when Glooscap was born. Possessed of wondrous, magical powers, it was Glooscap who made the people and animals of the eastern woodlands. The Wabanaki tell many stories about Glooscap and his adventures with spirits and magical animals. Glooscap is a mythical hero whose stories all end happily while telling a worthwhile moral.

An enjoyable book imaginatively illustrated with black and white drawings.

Hill, Kay; ***More Glooscap Stories;*** illustrated by John Hamberger; Dodd, Mead & Co.; 1970; Grades 3 - 6

A collection of tales based on legends of the Wabanaki people of North America's eastern woodlands. Great Chief Glooscap, with his huge size and wondrous powers, does roaring battle with giants and wizards and instructs the people and animals how to live wisely and well.

It is a well-written retelling of Canadian Indian legends. Black and white drawings heighten the effect of the text.

Hirschfelder, Arlene; *Happily May I Walk, American Indian and Alaskan Natives Today;* Charles Scribner's Sons; 1986; Grades 5 - 6

The text contains such a wide range of material that it is more encyclopedic than narrative. Included are chapters on tribal governments, reservations, Alaska Natives, language, daily lives, religious ways, dance and music, sacred healers, elders, children and education, Native Americans in cities, reservation resources, economic life and so on through twenty-two chapters.

The very large scope of the contents make it necessary to leave out essential information in some areas. This in no way takes away from the book as a valuable resource. Instead, the book could be a springboard for a child to search out materials with greater depth. Black and white photographs from various sources illustrate the text.

Hirschfelder, Arlene and Beverly R. Singer; *Rising Voices, Writings of Young Native Americans;* Ivy Books; 1992; All ages

Essays and poetry by young Native Americans shine through the pages of this book. The words are heartfelt and memorable, rooted in community and tribes. Each piece in this anthology speaks to the writer's joys and sorrows, hopes and visions, giving us a heart-song of their lives.

Carla Willeto, Navajo, writes: "The Voice – our Voice - is getting stronger/ Rising to the turquoise sky - /Listen! You will hear it soon…/very soon."

Janadele Baker, a member of the Crow Tribe in Montana, relates this feeling: "As I look at my people, it's as if I can feel their love and caring desires for one another. My people……..are one."

Arlene Hirschfelder is a teacher and writer. Beverly Singer, a Santa Clara Pueblo, is a teacher, artist, and independent film producer.

―――

Hodgers, Margaret; *The Fire Bringer: A Paiute Indian Legend*; illustrated by Peter Parnall; Little, Brown & Co.; 1972; Grades 3 - 6

The Paiutes long ago told stories that explained the origins and wonders of the world. They told of Coyote, the Friend and Counselor of men. Fire was one of the first gifts Coyote gave to the people. The story, a retelling of the ancient tale, tells how Coyote and a young Indian boy led the Paiutes on a mission to take fire from the Fire Spirits of Burning Mountain. Their journey makes an exciting adventure.

The tale is simply written and is faithful to the spirit of the original story. Illustrations enrich the text. Mr. Parnall is the recipient of numerous awards for his work.

※

Hofsinde, Robert; ***Indians at Home;*** illustrated by the author; Morrow; 1964; Grades 3 - 6

The book deals with various types of dwellings used by the Indians. The text includes descriptions of the different styles of homes, the life and customs of each home and the transition to modern times.

Black and white illustrations add clarity to the text and show how to experiment in building some of the dwellings. The book will be helpful for research and as a supplementary classroom text. However, there is no in-depth look at the tribes or cultures discussed.

The book uses the expression "Indian" throughout the text. This is a reflection of the 1964 copyright. The book can be useful for children as an investigative tool, but certainly should not be the only text used.

※

Hofsinde, Robert; ***Indian Fishing and Camping;*** illustrated by Robert Hofsinde; Morrow; 1963; Grades 3 - 6

A serviceable book for research although it may have a limited audience. The author relates the skills used by the "Indians" in fishing, camping and making gear. A description of spearfishing by Woodland Indians is included along with text devoted to how the Pacific Coast Indians made their fish traps from natural fiber. Ice fishing by the Eskimos is related to the reader along with information on preparing fish and cooking it outdoors. A chapter devoted to trail safety concludes the book.

The book is well researched and will appeal to those interested in this specific subject. The contents are well organized making it practical as a social studies supplement. However, it must be noted that this is a cursory look and by no means complete.

Black and white drawings accompany the text.

Hofsinde, Robert; ***Indian Hunting;*** illustrated by the author; Morrow; 1962; Grades 3 - 6

A straightforward introduction to hunting skills of the American Indian. Hunting, as practiced traditionally by the Native people, is discussed in simple language. The hunting customs were influenced by the needs the animals fulfilled. Wild animals supplied the people with food, clothing, shelter and fuel. Mr. Hofsinde describes the weapons, hunting methods and ceremonies connected with the hunt.

The black and white drawings add clarity to the descriptions and explanations in the text. It is important that the child reader as well as adults realize that this book is a beginning text and does not cover the subject in the depth needed for research.

This book, along with the other books by the author, should be just one part of inquiry.

※

Hofsinde, Robert; *Indians on the Move;* illustrated by the author; Morrow; 1970; Grades 3 - 6

The book is a survey of the methods of travel employed by American Indians throughout history. Included are types of travel by foot, horses, and water. The author also discusses travel in winter and concludes with a chapter on travel used in the modern age. The book is limited in its detail, but will appeal to those who are interested in the subject.

The illustrations aid the reader in a general understanding of the basic information. Illustrations are in black and white.

The book contains an index which is helpful. Anyone reading the book must be aware that there is no in-depth look at the culture or life of Native people. This text should simply be one part of inquiry; not used as the only source of research.

※

Hofsinde, Robert; *Indian Warriors and their Weapons;* illustrated by the author; Morrow; 1965; Grades 3 - 6

The author has chosen seven tribes to discuss in relationship to methods used in battle. The seven tribes are: Apache, Crow, Blackfoot, Iroquois, Sioux, Navajo and Ojibwa. Descriptions of clothing, weapons, charms and life of the representative tribes are discussed.

The narrative gives a limited account of this specific area of "Indian" life. Black and white drawings illustrate the text. Utilized for its information content, the subject matter may appeal to a limited readership.

Children must clearly understand that the book in no way can cover the depth needed in researching the tribes mentioned.

Holberg, Ruth Langland; ***Luke and the Indians;*** illustrated by Joshua Tolford; Hastings; 1969; Grades 3 - 6

Luke Clark, a ten year old Puritan boy, longed to be free of the endless labor, harsh discipline and stern schooling of life in Gloucester. He disobeys his father, runs away and joins a band of Wampanoag Indians. He strikes up a friendship with Teona, an Indian boy his age. Luke makes the transition from one culture to another.

The author has created a story of extremes. Luke "loves" his Indian family and "understands" their culture. At the end of the book, Luke happily returns to his Puritan family. The Indians eat his beloved white dog and Luke is shocked and repulsed by it. Luke thinks of them as heathens and returns to a "better" life in Gloucester.

The book lacks sensitivity and insight.

Holling, Holling C.; ***The Book of Indians;*** illustrated by Holling C. and Lucille Holling; Platt; 1962; Grades 3 - 6

> North American Indian groups are divided into four broad categories: people of the plains, people of the deserts and mesas, people of the forest and lakes, and people of the rivers and sea. The reader becomes acquainted with each group by accompanying a child in the daily life of the people. The history, culture, customs and life style of each group represented is explained.
>
> Brown and white drawings on each page add to the mood of the book. Full color illustrations are also displayed throughout the pages.
>
> Because of the broad nature of the text, the narrative lacks depth and definition. Even so, a child involved in investigative methods of research could use the book.

Hood, Flora; ***The Turquoise Horse; Prose and Poetry of the American Indian;*** illustrated by Marylou Reifsnyder; G.P. Putman's Sons; 1972; Grades K - 3

> The text is a collection of songs and poems of the North American Indian. The origin of each poem appears in an index at the end of the book rather than on the page with the poem. Children could find this confusing and may not even look at the

index. The tribal origin should have appeared with the poem. No cultural information is presented.

Illustrations are cartoon-like and do not represent the culture included. Stereotypes are reinforced through the drawings. When this book is weighed in the balance, it is definitely found wanting.

Houston, James; ***Akavak, An Eskimo Journey;*** illustrated by the author; Harcourt, Brace & World; 1968; Grades 3 - 6

Akavak and his grandfather faced a hazardous journey as they set forth to reach the distant land of Kakjuak. Grandfather had promised to see his brother once more before he died. They face incredible hardships as they make the terrifying trip over the frozen mountains. The wisdom of old age and the strength of youth are united in a story of Eskimo skill and courage.

Mr. Houston has written a powerful story with sensitivity and poetic feeling. Beautiful charcoal drawings enhance the text. It is worthwhile for older students as well.

The author has said that it is very difficult for a non-Inuit writer to capture Inuit stories. Therefore, some of the legends he recounts may have changed in translation.

Mr. Houston has received many awards and honors. Among those honors are the American Indian and Eskimo Cultural Foundation Award, the Queen Elizabeth Silver Anniversary Medal, and many, many awards for his books. Over half of his books have won international awards. The number of awards he has received is significant.

Houston, James; ***Eagle Mask: A West Coast Indian Tale;*** illustrated by the author; Harcourt, Brace & World; 1966; Grades 3 - 6

Skemshan, a young prince of the Eagle clan, is to face the trials of endurance, the rituals and celebrations that signal his coming of age. Skemshan, and his friend Kaibu, must make a trip without food, shelter or fire as a test of their courage and skill. The story climaxes with the potlatch and Skemshan understands the responsibilities of manhood.

Mr. Houston's powerful prose makes this a worthwhile book. An authentic description of the culture and life of the West Coast Indian is provided in word and picture. The black and white illustrations add vitality and vigor to the narrative.

Native people in Canada, who responded to students' letters of inquiry, stated they found it an authentic and worthwhile story.

Houston, James; ***Frozen Fire;*** illustrated by the author; Atheneum; 1977; Grades 6 - Up

Matthew Morgan's father was a prospecting geologist. When Matt's mother died, Matt accompanied his father to Frobisher

Bay in the Canadian Arctic. Mr. Morgan and his helicopter pilot set out prospecting and fail to return after a massive Arctic storm hits the area. Determined to find his father, Matt and his Eskimo friend, Kayak, search for them by snowmobile. The two boys struggle against storms, starvation and wild beasts as they battle for their own lives.

A vivid sense of the traditional Eskimo way of life is dramatized in the story. It is a well-written tale filled with realistic detail of Eskimo culture and environment.

Mr. Houston has received three Book-of-the-Year Medals from the Canadian Association of Children's Librarians. The award was given in 1966 for *Tikta' Liktak,* in 1968 for *The White Archer;* and in 1980 for *River Runners.*

>✤<

Houston, James; ***Ghost Paddle: A Northwest Coast Indian Tale;*** illustrated by the author; Harcourt, Brace & Jovanovich; 1972; Grades 3 - 6

Hooits is a young man of the Raven clan. He has lived fifteen winters, but he has never known a time of peace. A constant state of warfare exists between his tribe and the people of the Inland River. His father, Sea Wolf, decides to seek peace. Inspired by a dream, Sea Wolf skillfully carves a paddle for his son and begins the dangerous trek into enemy territory. In a dramatic climax, Hooits is forced to use his ghost paddle in an unequal battle.

The book is a well-written adventure story. The beauty and dignity of the people is displayed in the sensitive charcoal drawings.

For his work as an artist, writer, and administrator, Mr. Houston was made an Officer of the Order of Canada. Mr. Houston was also a master designer for Steuben Glass.

※

Houston, James; *Ojibwa Summer;* Photographs by B. A. King; Longman Canada Ltd.; 1972; Grades 3 - 6

One hundred photographs are combined with a noteworthy text to record the journey of the Ojibwa from an ancient heritage to their emergence into a new world. The book covers one summer among the Ojibwa in central Ontario. The narrative tells of the long history of the "people of three fires" and of the Ojibwa way of life. The photographs brilliantly and sensitively portray the pride, vitality and metamorphosis of the Ojibwa.

As it states on the book jacket, "***Ojibwa Summer*** preserves and predicts." Appropriate for all ages.

※

Houston, James; *Songs of the Dream People: Chants and Images from the Indians and Eskimos of North America;* illustrated by the author; Atheneum; 1972; Grades 3 and Up

The book is a collection of songs and chants that have a remarkable vitality and passion dancing through the text. It is a richly varied selection of song-poems, reminiscent of the stroke of a paddle, the flutter of wings or the thump of the corn-grinding stone. The reader feels the rhythm of life of the Indian and Eskimo. The beautiful song-poems are grouped regionally and each is identified by tribal origin. A map of tribal locations is included.

The illustrations are in an exquisite fluid style making the book a visual delight. Drawings of artifacts, art objects and weapons offer moving reflections of America's past. Recommended for social studies and literature classes at the secondary level as well as elementary grades.

The awards and honors received by Mr. Houston are significant.

※

Houston, James; *Tikta' Liktak: An Eskimo Legend;* illustrated by the author; Harcourt, Brace & World; 1965; Grades 3 - 6

A beautiful legend about a young boy set adrift on an ice floe is retold by James Houston. Tikta' Liktak, a young Eskimo hunter, resigned himself to die. In a dream, the sea spirit comes to his aid. In a constant battle with the elements, wild animals and utter despair, he survives to return to his home on the mainland.

The story is retold with simplicity and poetic feeling. Striking illustrations add to the appeal of the book.

In 1966, *Tikta' Liktak* was awarded the Book-of-the-Year Medal from the Canadian Association of Children's Librarians. The

Medal is presented for the best children's book by a Canadian author.

><

Houston, James; *The White Archer: an Eskimo Legend;* illustrated by the author; Harcourt, Brace & World; 1967; Grades 3 - 6

Raiding "Indians" captured his sister and killed his parents. Kungo, a young Eskimo, was filled with a fierce desire for revenge. Kungo heard of Ittok, a strange old man, who had great skill as an archer and wisdom with men and animals. He would share his knowledge with Kungo. With a restless hatred, he attempts to rescue his sister and avenge the death of his parents. When Kungo has a chance to kill, he achieves a far greater triumph than revenge.

The shapes and scenes of James Houston's exquisite illustrations fold earth and people and animals together into the oneness of which he writes so eloquently.

><

Houston, James; *Wolf Run: A Caribou Eskimo Tale;* illustrated by the author; Harcourt, Brace & Jovanovich, Inc.; 1971; Grades 3 - 6

Punik's father had drowned the previous summer. Now his people faced famine because the caribou herds failed to return in the spring. Punik sets out alone to find food for his starving family and almost dies of starvation himself. Wolves, the spirits of his grandparents, aid him in securing caribou meat for his family.

It is a well written book which realistically portrays the Eskimo culture and environment. It is a dramatic story, strikingly illustrated by the author.

⇥⇤

Hoyt-Goldsmith, Diane; ***Buffalo Days;*** photographs by Lawrence Migdale; Holiday House; 1997; Grades 3 – 6

A lovely kaleidoscope of visual impressions and engaging text, ***Buffalo Days*** follows ten-year-old Clarence Three Irons, Jr. and his family as they remember the days when great herds of buffalo roamed their lands.

Clarence's father is a manager of the Crow Nation's buffalo herd, part of an effort to bring the buffalo back to Crow lands. The Crow have a perfect place for a buffalo pasture, a wilderness of thirty thousand acres. "The pasture is twelve miles wide, and it is surrounded on three sides by deep canyons. Along the fourth side, the tribe has built a giant, ten-foot-high fence."

Appealing, full-color photographs include pictures of the buffalo, the land, and the people who care for them. Celebrating Buffalo Days is something that everyone looks forward to all year long. The people put up tipis, hold a powwow, and have "dance contests, drumming, and giveaways." Rodeo competitions and horse races are part of the celebration as well as a colorful parade.

The pictures are marvelous and capture the spirit of the Crow Nation as they are engaged in everyday life and the spirit of celebration as they recall the glories of the days when the buffalo roamed the land.

A glossary at the end of the book provides meaning for words and their pronunciations. Boarding school, brucellosis, and buffalo jump are some of the words in the glossary along with Iilappaach Ahoo amd Apsaalooke. Kids have fun learning the new words.

Joe Medicine Crow says: "The buffalo means everything to the Crow." He tells of the importance of the return of the buffalo: "It just makes us feel Indian again. We lost a part of our way of life, our culture. Now it makes even little kids happy to know we have buffalo running up there."

→←

Hoyt-Goldsmith, Diane; *Pueblo Storyteller;* photographs by Lawrence Migdale; Holiday House; 1991; Grades 3 - 6

At the end of the book, ten-year-old April says: "I am a pueblo child and I love to listen to my grandparents tell stories. From their example, I learn to take what I need from the earth to live, but also how to leave something behind for future generations. Every day I am learning to live in harmony with the world. And every day, I am collecting memories of my life to share one day with my own children and grandchildren."

April follows in the tradition of storyteller as she tells of her life in the Cochiti Pueblo near Santa Fe, New Mexico. Her grandparents teach her to play golf and sculpt the clay Storyteller figure. It is from her grandmother that she learns the skill of making round loaves known in the Keres language as ba'a. Her uncle is a drum maker who shows April how the drum is constructed and tells her that each one "has its own special sound, its own voice".

Included in the text is a legend: "When I was very young, my grandparents told me a legend about how our ancestors found the place where we are living today, our pueblo along the Rio Grand River. They call it 'How the People Came to Earth', and it is still one of my favorite tales."

Full color photographs add immeasureably to this multifaceted, outstanding documentation of the Cochiti Pueblo. It is a tribute to the people who live there; to the extended family and to the strong sense of a shared community. As April says about her people: "I am thankful that they have given me this rich history." Everyone who reads this book will share in her thankfulness.

⤻⤺

Hoyt-Goldsmith, Diane; ***Totem Pole;*** photographs by Lawrence Migdale; Holiday House; 1990; All ages

David, a young member of the Tsimshian tribe, tells the story of his father who is a carver of masks, fish hooks, animal figures and totem poles. The book focuses mostly on the carving and raising of a totem pole through a first person narrative by David. He says of the event: "I am proud to have a father who can transform a straight cedar log into a magnificent totem pole.

In the forest, it was a beautiful tree. Then my father saw in it the shapes of Thunderbird, the Klallam, Raven, Whale, Bear, and the Chief. He brought them all to life with his skill. I am proud of my people. I am proud to be the son of a Tsimshian carver."

Vibrant colored photographs with informative captions give a clear idea of the step-by-step procedures of the carving and ceremonies that are taking place. Included in the text is the "Legend of the Eagle and the Young Chief - A Tsimshian Tale" with an accompanying illustration that enriches the story.

The carver, David Boxley, speaks of his art: "Our art from 1886 to 1950s was outlawed, along with our potlatches, blankets, and totems. It is important to me for our people to understand that this is our art and that we should be proud of it."

Sensitively produced, this book can teach and enlighten.

→←

Hudson, Jan; *Sweetgrass;* Scholastic Books; 1984; Grades 5 - 6

At fifteen, Sweetgrass is still unmarried, but desperately wanting a husband. She is the spoiled and pampered daughter of Shabby Bull, a warrior of the Blackfoot Nation. The book is basically two parts - the first part dealing with the overwhelming desire of Sweetgrass to get married and the second half tells of a smallpox epidemic that strikes her people.

The author seems unfamiliar with tribal life and has chosen some deplorable statements to include in the text. The whole obsessiveness with men and marriage seems like a teenage Made-for-TV Movie and the smallpox scene is unrealistic. The family would not be off alone in the winter; that is simply author orchestration to put action in the story line.

The story is told in the first person with Sweetgrass saying: "Aside from my obnoxious almost-brother Otter...there have only been babies in our tipi. And when they die young, they are not counted." And - "My aunt waddled toward us, panting from the heat. Her buckskin underclothes must have been sticking together." (Buckskin underclothes? Oh. My. Goodness.)

There are many demeaning statements referring to women throughout the narrative. "Bent-Over-Woman always walked like she was tired...with graying hair sticking out from her braids like dirty feathers, she looked just like a crow." One girl is given to be a "slave wife" and the women must be married young "to tan the buffalo robes for trading".

In reference to a family in the text tipi: "The first loud sound of the day snarled from the tipi nearest us...His fat wife was snoring!...A snore like a buffalo snort..."

At one point, Sweetgrass is called a "...bad puppy."

When the people are sick, there's lots of stench, gagging, pus and bad smells. This is Sweetgrass growing into a mature woman - "All I wanted to do was leave all these sick people, go out on the clean snow and puke them all away." "I pulled her body to me so that her head rested on my left shoulder and my mouth was full of her rotten smell of pus." "A stench rode on the wind twisting through the poplars. I had to spit a lot because it made me gag."

The people deal with the epidemic in this manner - "Others died because no one had nursed them." "...you remember, the fat one with the scar on her neck - she was luckier and only lost her children."

Yes, a smallpox epidemic is horrible, but Native people dealt with each other compassionately. The heavy hand of plot manipulation is evident and Native people take the brunt of negative stereotypes.

Incredibly, ***Sweetgrass*** received the Canada Council Children's Literature Prize and received the Book-of-the-Year Medal from the Canadian Association of Children's Librarians. The book is inaccurate, demeaning and totally lacks insight.

→←

Hunt, W. Ben and Burshears, J.F.; ***American Indian Beadwork;*** Collier; 1973; Grades 6 - Up

The book is an excellent handicraft guide and study of design and methods. Introductory pages give a short history of beadwork, discuss the use of bead designs and explain how to do loom beading and sewed beadwork. Many original examples of beadwork are shown through the use of black and white photographs. The latter part of the book focuses on actual beadwork designs. The designs are shown in full color with a brief explanation of the tribe who used them. Examples of Apache belts are shown as well as Sioux, Cheyenne, Ute, Ojibwe and others.

The book is well organized and easy to read. It would be an excellent classroom resource book; useful in art classes and social studies research. The Anishinabe adults who read this book found it helpful in explaining beadwork to school children. Students, under the guidance of Anishinabe adults, used the book to create belts, armbands, bracelets, and necklaces.

→←

Hunt, W. Ben; *The Complete Book of Indian Crafts and Lore;* Golden Press; 1972; Grades 3 - 6

An excellent book that clearly describes articles that children can make, the introductory chapters present background information about Indian tribes and lore. Also included is a list of Indian names and pronunciations. Some of the crafts in the book are instructions for making moccasins, sunburst bustles, dance hoops, drums, capes, vests, and peace pipes. A representative sampling of dance costumes and dance steps is also discussed. Beadwork designs and symbols and directions for making a teepee are also outlined.

All illustrations are in full color with detailed instructions. It is authentic and well researched, but certainly not "complete." Anishinabe elders who read the book thought it was a good introductory book for children. The designs and directions were used to make sunburst bustles, capes, and vests for the dance group at Grand Portage Elementary School.

→←

Hunt, W. Ben; *The Complete How-to Book of Indian Craft;* Collier; 1973; Grades 6 - Up

>   The book is compiled from several of Mr. Hunt's books that were published in the late 1930's and early 1940's. The book is very well researched and methods for making things are correct. Included in the book are chapters on Indian Clothing, Indian Music, Basic Tools and Materials, Indian Ceremonies, Headdresses and Necklaces, Around the Campfire and more.
>
>   The book is readable with easy to follow directions. It is a remarkable source of information about the artistry, design, crafts, beliefs and traditions of the American Indian. All illustrations are hand-drawn diagrams in black and white.
>
>   The book also contains an index, bibliography and glossary of Sioux names with pronunciations. Children should be made aware that the word Sioux is not appropriate for the people.
>
>   It should be explained to children that this is not "complete" as the title suggests. Anishinabe adults found it helpful in classroom presentations. The Anishinabe elders clarified the need for using appropriate tribal names and explained how the term Sioux came to be used in our language.

→←

Hunt, W. Ben; *The Golden Book of Crafts and Hobbies;* Golden Press; 1969; Grades 3 - 6

>   The book contains a number of projects suitable for children to do themselves or with adult supervision. Most of the articles can be made with a few simple tools and materials that are

easily obtained. The chapters contain basic information on nature study, boats, camping equipment and craft projects. Two chapters deal with projects specifically relating to Indians. The chapter on Indian ornaments discusses moccasins, capes, dolls, fans and other crafts. Under the heading of sleds, the author demonstrates how to build an Eskimo sled and a Cree trail toboggan.

All of the drawings are clear and complete. Full color illustrations appear on every page and give detailed visual instructions for the accompanying text.

Hurley, William; ***Dan Frontier with the Indians;*** illustrated by Jack Boyd; Benefic; 1971; Grades K - 3

The book is a controlled vocabulary reader. It relates the story of Dan Frontier and his encounters with the "Indians" led by Chief Black Fish. The Indians speak in a halting stilted style. The book does not speak of Indian values or culture.

The narrative and illustrations are stereotypes. The book is still available through garage sales, used book stores, and on the Internet.

Israel, Marion; ***Apaches;*** Melmont; 1959; Grades K - 3

This book could serve as an introduction to the Apaches and their history. It tells about the people, their food, land, clothing and dress. It is written in simple language and could appeal to younger children also.

>—<

Israel, Marion; ***Cherokees;*** illustrated by Henry Timmins; Melmont; 1961; Grades K - 3

Every day life of the Cherokees is described before the coming of the Europeans. The book tells the events of one year from one fall to the next. It conveys the importance of ritual and respect for other beings. Written in simple and direct language, the book provides a general introduction to the Cherokee. The illustrations give clarity and add to its appeal.

>—<

Israel, Marion; ***Dakotas;*** illustrated by Paul Sousa; Melmont; 1959; Grades K - 3

The Dakotas are described in their everyday life. It tells where they lived, describes the hunt, daily tasks of women, their food and their dwellings. The book is an introduction to the young reader to the way of life of the Dakotas.

>—<

Israel, Marion; ***Ojibway;*** illustrated by Harry Timmins; Melmont; 1962; Grades K - 3

A well-researched, yet simple book on the history of the Ojibway. Every day life of the Ojibway is described as the book follows the activities of the seasons. Included in the book are the events at a sugar camp, the details of homes and tools.

The book provides a basic introduction to the Ojibway in easy to read language. It could be useful with younger children as well. The illustrations add understanding to the text.

⇥⇤

Jackson, Garnet; *The First Thanksgiving;* illustrated by Carolyn Croll; Scholastic, Inc.; 2000, Grades K – 3

The book is a **Hello Reader!** text directed toward helping students increase skill, fluency, and independence in their reading. At the beginning of the book, there is a message for parents to help children before, during, and after the story.

Because the story is simply told and the vocabulary controlled, children will find the book easy to read. It begins: "On September 6, 1620, a small, wooden ship, called the *Mayflower* sailed on its way to America. It had left England with 102 people. These people came to be known as Pilgrims." Another bit of information is shared: "The Pilgrims docked the ship and came ashore. They were on the land of the Wampanoag Nation. This was the village of Patuxet." The text identifies Samoset as Abenaki and acknowledges that Squanto "had been kidnapped and brought to England in 1614. Five years later, he made it back home."

These sentences can be momentous teaching moments to share with children the realities of what was happening to

Native people as Europeans began to settle in the Western Hemisphere.

Pictures in full color accompany the text.

><

James, Harry C.; *A Day in Oraibi: A Hopi Indian Village;* illustrated by Don Perceval; Melmont; 1959; Grades K-3

Honau and his sister Poli are Hopi children from Oraibi in northern California. A young white boy, Jon Carter, visits the village to learn more about the Hopi. Honau and Poli give Jon a tour of their village and Jon learns about their gardening, livestock, weaving, pottery and jewelry making. Jon also meets the chief and learns about the Kiva.

The text reflects the 1959 copyright.

><

Jeffers, Susan; *Brother Eagle, Sister Sky; A Message from Chief Seattle;* illustrated by Susan Jeffers; Dial Books; 1991; Grades K-3

Eloquent words begin the book: "How can you buy the sky? Chief Seattle began. How can you own the rain and the wind?" The moving, poetic words continue through the book with a dynamic message for the young people who are the intended readers - take care of the environment, preserve it and cherish it. The book's jacket gives some sketchy information about Chief

Seattle and end papers briefly describe the events leading up to the speech itself.

Susan Jeffers, the creator and illustrator of the book, has written a note of explanation at the end of the text to explain a little about the "origins" of the speech. She says: "The origins of Chief Seattle's words are partly obscured by the mists of time". She also writes that "What matters is that Chief Seattle's words inspired - and continue to inspire - a most compelling truth: In our zeal to build and possess, we may lose all that we have."

Though the words and illustrations strongly link the philosophy of Native people to the present-day ecological movement, there is one overwhelming problem: Most scholars challenge the authenticity of the speech. A number of historians claim that Chief Seattle neither said nor wrote the words ascribed to him. According to a German scholar, Dr. Rudolf Kaiser, the speech attributed to Chief Seattle may really have been written by a screenwriter in Texas by the name of Ted Perry - in 1971. Dr. Kaiser claims the original speech remained unaltered until the new speech by Perry appeared in a film on ecology. Later, the Perry speech began showing up in magazines and books as part of a strong environmental message aimed primarily at children. Many notable scholars concur with that assessment.

Historians do agree that Chief Seattle was a skilled diplomat and great orator. Born in 1786, See-ahth, his name in the Lushootseed language, was Suquamish, one of the Coastal Salish tribes of the area near the Puget Sound. He made a dramatic speech in 1854, citing the differences between the way of life of the Native people and that of the European settlers. More than a thousand of his people heard the presentation that was delivered in the Salish dialect. The only known translation of that speech was by Dr. Henry Smith who published it in 1887. The National Archives contain only two short documents attributed to Seattle.

Brother Eagle, Sister Sky is a perpetuation of a manufactured myth. Yes, we need to be responsible stewards of the planet and Native people exemplify the spirit of responsible living in harmony with the land. What is deplorable is that people feel it's all right to put words into Seattle's mouth if it's for a good cause. Native people have been used by business for years to sell products from automobiles to margarine. Now environmental groups feel justified in using a great chief like Seattle to sell their ideas.

The unfortunate part of the whole affair is that writers did not feel that Chief Seattle's speech was marketable. His words were adapted, rewritten and reinterpreted until it was a saleable item, fit for the business of selling ecology, but it was no longer his voice.

The illustrations match the text - romanticized visions of "Indians" teaching the ecology lesson. It's too bad the creator of the book didn't tell what happened to the people. Why didn't the author mention that Chief Seattle died in 1866 at the age of 80...one year after the city named for him made it illegal for "Indians" to live in Seattle?

Translator Smith attributes Seattle, a baptized Roman Catholic, as saying: "And when the last red man shall have perished from the earth and his memory among the white men shall have become a myth, these shores will swarm with the invisible dead of my tribe. The white man will never be alone. Let him be just and deal kindly with my people for the dead are not powerless."

※

Johnston, Basil; ***How the Birds Got Their Colours;*** illustrated by Del Ashkewe; Kids Can Press; 1978; Grades 3 - 6

The text of this book is bilingual: Anishinabe and English. This story revolves around Papeekawiss, the great dancer, and the birds of the world which were all one color: white. Papeekawiss invites all the animals to his feast of Thanksgiving. The birds, being very plain, were envious of the splendid finery of all the animals. They ask Papeekawiss to make them "handsome like the animals." He agrees and instructs them to come to his house the next morning. When they all line up the next morning, crow behaves foolishly much to the chagrin of all the others.

The story is delightful and funny. Del Ashkewe's vibrant pictures widen the appeal of this exceptional book.

※

Johnston, Johanna; ***The Indians and the Strangers;*** illustrated by Rocco Negri; Dodd, Mead & Co.; 1972; Grades 3 - 6

The book deals superficially with several well-known "Indians". Included are glimpses of Squanto, Powhatan, Pontiac, Sacajawea, Tecumseh and others.

Though the book is written simply and is accompanied by woodcut illustrations, it does not deal in depth with each individual represented.

The stereotyped storyline nullifies the effectiveness of the book.

→←

Johnston, Patronella; ***Tales of Nokomis;*** illustrated by Francis Kagige; Charles J. Musson Ltd.; 1970; Grades 3 - 6

Patronella Johnston is an Ojibway from the Cape Croker Reserve on Manitoulin Island. It was her desire to preserve the Native culture and to teach the young generation the stories of her people. The seventeen tales that she has chosen to share are well written and imaginative. They are important for their entertainment value as well as for the moral truths they teach.

The delightful paintings, all in full color, capture the mood of the tale. The illustrator is an Ojibway from the Wikwemikong Reserve on Manitoulin Island.

→←

Jones, Hettie; ***Coyote Tales;*** illustrated by Louis Mofsie; Holt, Rinehart & Winston; 1974; Grades 4 - 6

Four tales adapted by the author concern the many facets of Coyote, the trickster. The first tale, "Coyote Steals the Summer" tells how Coyote received his powers from the Sky Spirit. In "Coyote Loses His Dinner", Coyote learns that matching his wits with Fox means to go hungry. Coyote gets into serious trouble in the third tale when he tricks a young girl and in the final story Coyote saves an entire village.

The stories are adaptations of legends from the Assiniboine, Dakota and Skidi Pawnee people. In the introduction, the author states: "No matter what he is doing, though, Coyote is there to be laughed at...At the end of each story he disappears, which is also part of his charm...Like the old men who used to go from village to village to tell his stories, he merely turns up, and gives everyone a good laugh before he leaves".

Louis Mofsie is of Hopi and Winnebago ancestry. The illustrations reflect the character and spirit of the Coyote stories.

→✂←

Jones, Hettie, ed.; *The Trees Stand Shining: Poetry of the North American Indian;* illustrated by Robert Andrew Parker; Dial; 1971; Grades K - 3

The song-poems collected in the book are authentic and reflect the Indians reverance of nature. The poems selected are short which make them effective for introducing Native American song-poems to young children. The translations are clear, concise and evocative of the Indian worldview. Some of the tribes included are the Chippewa, Pima, Iroquois, Teton Sioux, Kwakiutl, and the Papago. (Today, the Papago are known as Tohono O'Odham.) The tribal source of each poem is identified at the conclusion of the poem.

A Second Look, Native Americans in Children's Books

Full color paintings lend an imaginative vitality to the moods and images of the poems. The illustrations reflect the life style of Native people in a historical setting.

※

Jones, Weyman; ***Edge of Two Worlds;*** illustrated by J. C. Kocsis; The Dial Press; 1968; Grades 6 & Up

Calvin Harper was on his way East to law school when his party was attacked and he remained the lone survivor. After two days, he meets an old Indian man named Sequoyah. Sequoyah is sick and needs Calvin's help. Together, they make the long, perilous journey and in the end Calvin must make a difficult decision.

Throughout the book, Sequoyah is referred to as "the Indian". Whenever Sequoyah talks, it is "the Indian". Calvin wonders what the gold case is that the Indian carries around his neck. "A locket, maybe, from some white woman, perhaps with the miniature pictures of her children inside. Calvin wondered where this Indian carried his scalps."

One of the men in the story says: "…we read your bootheels stomped in the mud to say there was a lone white man afoot in this Injun country." Later the two hunters wonder why Calvin wants to go back to find Sequoyah. One man says: "I saw a little girl once who had been captured. When we got her back from the Apache all she did was sit and look straight in front of her all day. Didn't cry or smile or say nothing. Brain scalded, like a rabbit watching a weasel, too scared to move."

In the end, Calvin looks around at all the grass and boulders and "smiled downwardly, in the Indian way, feeling as if he owned it all."

The book is based in part on Sequoyah's walk halfway across Texas. A concluding chapter discusses the invention of the Cherokee alphabet. Nothing new is added to the Sequoyah story. Children need to know that the book is a fictionalized account of a great leader.

→←

Jones, Weyman; *The Talking Leaf;* illustrated by E. Harper Johnson; Dial Press; 1965; Grades 3 - 6

Atsee is a young Cherokee who wishes to follow in his father's footsteps and become a great scout. As he grows up, Atsee sees the times changing as more white settlers invade the land. He eventually decides to put aside his "bow and arrow" and learn more about the ways of the white man. The book is based on the life of a real person who became a teacher and the earliest translator of English into Cherokee.

In the story, Atsee decides to set aside some of the traditional values of the Cherokee. Indeed, there was cultural conflict with the invasion by Europeans, but the story line makes it appear that the people chose a "better" life. The child reader must be made aware that the changes were a matter of survival in the midst of tremendous struggles.

Black and white illustrations add meaning to the text.

>✦<

Katz, Jane B.; ***This Song Remembers: Self-Portraits of Native Americans in the Arts;*** Houghton; 1980; Grades 6 - Up

Tape-recorded interviews by the author capture the voice and vision of twenty-one gifted Native American artists. The art forms are diverse - from theater to graphic arts. The book, divided into three parts, includes Visual Arts, Performing Arts and Literature. ***This Song Remembers*** truly lets the artists speak for themselves as the editor simply provides background information and an introduction. Photographs of the artists and their creations are an integral part of the book.

The quality of the art is outstanding and the artists voices speak of art as a "fundamental activity in tribal cultures, an integral part of the daily life of ordinary people...an expression of the basic need of people in all times..."

A brief summary cannot do justice to this book. It is a valuable resource and can be used as an antidote for much of the negative books that have been written about Native people.

>✦<

Katz, Ruth J.; ***Pumpkin Personalities;*** illustrated by Sharon Tondreau; Walker & Company; 1979; Grades 4 – 6

The focus of the book is to create unique jack-o-lanterns by using an assortment of commonly used household items. There are step-by-step directions for making "fruit and vegetable beasties", "a furry owl", "cookie and candy creatures", a couple of presidents and "an Indian brave" along with an "Indian maiden".

The directions are fairly simple. You need some jute, feathers, a chandelier light bulb, five beads, a shoelace and some buttons. You also need "glittery sugar sprinkles" - for war paint. After you've gathered your materials, you glue the jute on for hair, tie the beads onto the shoelace for a headband, attach the feathers to the back of the head, use the light bulb for the nose and finally, "Mark war paint designs on cheeks. Cover lines with glue and coat with colored sprinkles." Those directions are for the "brave", but the "maiden" is similar except you make braids out of the jute and place the feathers behind one braid.

There are no redeeming qualities at all in a book like this. The author should have stuck to the "space monsters" concept and left Native people alone. It is crass, embarrassing and ridiculous. Referring to people in this way is dehumanizing and leaves children with the impression that it's all right to mock a certain segment of society. This is not art, it's arrogance.

→←

Keats, Ezra Jack, editor; **God is in the Mountain;** illustrated by the author; Holt, Rinehart & Winston; 1966; Grades K - 3

Mr. Keats has selected a group of eloquent phrases from diverse religions of the world. They are poetically expressed insights into spiritual experiences of different cultures. Two pages are devoted to the renderings from American Indian people. One passage reflects the deep reverence for Mother Earth by Native people.

This is a significant contribution to literature for a young reader. It will help children conceive the beauty in differences. Illustrations are on every page. The depth of thought and insights of the phrases make the book appropriate for all ages.

Keats has been the recipient of many awards including the Caldecott Award in 1963 for ***The Snowy Day.***

Kimball, Yeffe and Anderson, Jean; ***The Art of American Indian Cooking;*** Doubleday; 1965; Grades 6 - Up

A superb collection of American Indian recipes including delectable seafood entrees of the Northwest Coast, turkey and corn dishes of the Southeast, and vegetable recipes from the Southwest. The foods are indigenous to the North American continent and familiar as basic foods. The recipes have been carefully researched and expertly presented.

Yeffe Kimball is an "Oklahoma Osage", an artist and a consultant to magazines. Jean Anderson, a journalist, was with the food department of the Ladies Home Journal for seven years.

Kjelgaard, Jim; ***Buckskin Brigade;*** The Junior Literary Guild and Holiday House; 1947; Grades 6 - Up

Buckskin Brigade tells the story of the frontiersmen who "blazed the trails" across the North American Continent and opened the land for settlement. "As the westward march of civilization made its slow way over and through successive barriers of forest and prairie and mountain until it had spanned three thousand miles from ocean to ocean, it followed the moccasined paths of nameless men in buckskin". (They're not talking about Native people here.)

The beginning is 1506 with a chapter entitled "The Tree" and continues with "Croatan" in 1588, "The Medicine Bag" in 1615, "Savage Trek" in 1661, and so on through successive years until 1844 - "End of the Trail". Based on the lives of real people, the book is arranged chronologically to give an historical perspective.

In the chapter "Croatan", the character known as Tom feels he must have been "born to a life like this. Maybe he was half savage". Assurances are given that the "savages" got along all right. "The savages had the right idea. They worked when they felt like it, and loafed when they didn't. And nobody was more stealthy in a forest or more quiet in a thicket…But certainly no savage would work in a London cobbler's shop…"

"The Medicine Bag" chronicles the story of Father LeCaron, who "saved his first soul from pagan savagery and committed it to God's mercy…one simple savage had listened to and believed the Truth." In dealing with a wounded man, "…he knew that none had wanted to bother with the wounded man…The savages had been much more interested in the two Iroquois scalps which the war party had also brought. In a most heathenish and unseemly manner they had exulted over their grisly trophies. …The savages' was an un-Christian faith, so far removed from the True Belief…"

In the same chapter, there is reference to "an old squaw" and the amazing "instinct woodsman and savages had for water and wilderness ways". There is an Indian village composed of bark-thatched huts: "Slender poles were erected before all of them, and a varying number of scalps fluttered from the poles...The butchered carcass of a dog hung before one of the huts..." The women are "heathen devils" and "Their stringy black hair was plastered to their heads with the grease of some forest beast... The venom that had taken possession of their souls showed in their snapping black eyes".

Even the staunchest Jim Kjelgaard fan must realize that the references to Native people throughout the book are insulting and unfair. Like Laura Ingalls Wilder, Mr. Kjelgaard has favored author status which makes it difficult for people to comprehend the damaging effect of this book. Anyone reading the narrative must understand that the prevailing attitude toward Native people is reflected in the text of this book - the feeling that the continent was inhabited by savages prior to the settlement by Europeans and free for the taking. Children need to know this is wrong.

It's still available via Internet sites, used book sales, and through regular ordering channels. And, in June of 2007, it was still available on shelves in public and school libraries.

The books children read, and have read to them, do affect their perceptions of people and history as well as their place in the overall scene. This book continues to hurt.

→✦←

Kjelgaard, Jim; ***Kalak of the Ice;*** Holiday; 1949; Grades 6 - Up

> Elements of Eskimo culture and religion are woven into the story of Kalak and Agtuk. Kalak is a polar bear known for her cunning and great strength. Agtuk is the Eskimo Chief who wants to catch her.
>
> It is an interesting story as Kalak tries to raise her young while eluding capture. The struggle of man and beast in a hostile northern environment is realistically portrayed.
>
> Anishinabe sixth graders who read the book thought it was great. One Anishinabe adult responded to the text by saying: "This Kjelgaard book seems all right."

Kjelgaard, Jim; ***Wolf Brother;*** Holiday; 1957; Grades 6 - Up

> A young Apache, 16 year old Jonathan Wolf, returns to his home reservation after five years of school. It is the 1880's and his people are destitute. Circumstances cause him to flee the reservation and he joins the renegades who have rejected reservation life. He is eventually captured, makes a successful escape and returns to his people determined to help them.
>
> The book is written with the usual Kjelgaard flair for storytelling. The Anishinabe children who read it thoroughly enjoyed it, but wondered if they'd have the same feelings about it if they were Apache.

The readers didn't seem to notice the passage that described Manuelito as being "fat and flabby". "He wore cast-off clothing which must have come from some white man's trash pile..."

>—<

Kleitsch, Christel and Paul Stephens; ***Dancing Feathers;*** Annick Press, Ltd.; 1985; Grades 4 - 6

Tafia Shebagabow, who lives on an Ojibway reserve in northern Canada, tells her story - "...sometimes some pretty exciting things happen to me. Like one time last summer - I sure got myself in a lot of trouble..." Thus begins the story of a pow-wow, a jingle dress, a stolen painting, and a couple of kids lost in a big city. Black and white photographs add understanding to the text.

There are a couple of places that may bring up some questions, such as the dancing being a "hop, hop, hop," and a white friend saying (as a compliment?), "You know, Frank I never think of you as being Indian". However, the characterizations are real, with meaningful lives and a sense of community. Sensitively written, it provides an honest insight into the lives of Native people living in Canada.

"It's an old dance that I do..." Tafia is talking. "The dance of my people. I feel brave and strong and I'm flying...Flying like dancing feathers in the wind." This is a good book.

>—<

Kleitsch, Christel and Paul Stephens; ***A Time to be Brave;*** Annick Press Ltd.; 1985; Grades 4 - 6

> The setting of the story is the Shebagabow family's trapping cabin deep in the bush. Tafia Shebagabow is an eleven-year-old Ojibway girl who must overcome her fear and go for help when her father is injured at their winter camp.
>
> Tafia comments: "You've got to keep your wits about you all the time when you're in the bush. Lots of unexpected things can happen and you have to think fast and make the right decisions. Sometimes a wrong decision could cost you your life, or that of the person who's with you."
>
> The relationships depicted are warmhearted and responsible. Elders are valued. Black and white photographs contribute a positive dimension.

→←

Kohn, Bernice; ***Talking Leaves: The Story of Sequoyah;*** illustrated by Valli; Hawthorn; 1969; Grades 3 - 6

> As a boy, Sequoyah was small and walked with a limp. The book tells of Sequoyah's long years of work to develop a syllabary for the Cherokee. With the aid of his ten-year-old daughter, Ahyoka, he dramatically presented his discovery to the Cherokee Tribal Council.
>
> It is a well researched biography. The boldly colored illustrations add vibrance and vitality to the text. Additional drawings in delicate black and white are sensitive and beautiful.

Kostich, Dragos; *George Morrison, The Story of an American Indian;* Dillon Press; 1976; Grades 3 - 6

George Morrison was born in a small Chippewa community in northern Minnesota. He soon demonstrated his ability as an artist and studied in Minneapolis, New York and Paris. An internationally known artist, George was filled with exceptional energy and dedication to his art. He was a member of the Grand Portage Band of Chippewas.

The book is simply written and illustrated with black and white photographs. Because of the biographical nature of the book, it would be appropriate for all ages.

Krasilovsky, Phyllis; *Benny's Flag;* illustrated by W.T. Mars.; World; 1960; Grades K - 3

In 1926, the Alaska Flag Contest was launched to choose an official flag for Alaska. Young Benny Benson, an "Indian" boy, was a student in the Territorial school at Seward. The book is based on the true account of how Benny designed a flag of the country he loved. In May, 1927, Benny's flag was adopted as the official flag of Alaska.

The black and white drawings vividly illustrate the people and geography of Alaska.

Lacapa, Michael (retold); ***The Flute Player, An Apache Folktale;*** illustrated by Michael Lacapa; Northland Publishing, 1990; Grades 2 - 4

Michael Lacapa acknowledges: "…the White Mountain Apache storytellers I listened to and learned from as I was growing up." His "stories were learned from elders of the tribes, and he is dedicated to their preservation."

The Flute Player is the tale of a boy and girl who become "very, very interested in each other" during the hoop dance. As time goes by, he goes up the canyon and plays his flute and the girl places a leaf in the water. She tells him, "When you see the leaf float past you, you will know that I like your song." Time after time, music from the flute echoes from the canyon walls and each time the girl places the leaf in the water. The boy must leave for a while without being able to tell the girl, a misunderstanding arises and tragedy strikes. Today the Apache continue to tell the story of the two young people.

A centuries-old Apache folktale, Lacapa has captured the essense of the story with clear text and stylized, colorful illustrations.

Lacy, Dan; ***The Lost Colony;*** Franklin Watts; 1972; Grades 3 - 6

The book chronicles the events leading up to the mysterious disappearance of the settlers on Roanoke Island. The politics of England and Spain that encouraged colonization and exploration is discussed. John White was one of the originators of the colony and grandfather to Virginia Dare, the first English child born in the "New World." John White kept a fascinating journal of "Indian" life and also was an excellent artist who sketched the Native people, their villages, and cultural life. He was not among the colonists when they disappeared.

The book is illustrated with black and white photographs and reproductions of rare engravings. A valuable asset of the book are the references to Thomas Hariot's thorough accounts and writings. Included also are reproductions of John White's paintings.

Parts of the book contain the usual renderings of screaming Indians: "One of their leaders, George Howe, went off to hunt crabs a mile or two from the others. He stripped off his outer garments and went wading in the shallow waters on the sound side...As he went near a thicket...an arrow whistled from the reeds and struck him. Before he could run, another dozen had pierced him. As he fell, Indians ran from their hiding place screaming war cries. They beat him to death with their clubs, and then ran to their canoes and paddled swiftly to the mainland before the colonists could reach them." The "Indians" are "bitterly hostile", "timid, but friendly", and "dressed in strange costumes".

Adults could use this book for historical reference, but be aware of the impact of negative adjectives and one-sided reporting. This book perpetuates many stereotypes. Keep it out of the hands of children.

>←<

LaFarge, Oliver; *Cochise of Arizona;* illustrated by L.F. Bjorklund; E.P. Dulton; 1953; Grades 6 - Up

The book is a fictionalized account of one of the greatest of all American Indian chiefs, Cochise of the Chiricahua Apaches. Cochise sought peace but was forced into war by the white men. Once they were at war, Cochise and his small band of warriors held the United States Army at bay for more than ten years. Cochise was a brilliant and courageous leader, a man of extraordinary military consciousness, and warm human relationships. The story also relates how Major General Howard and Cochise secured peace between their people.

Oliver LaFarge writes with power and sensitivity about a truly great American. He was involved in designing an alphabet for writing Navaho and served as President of the Association on American Indian Affairs twice. He is best known for his novel *Laughing Boy*, which won the Pulitzer Prize for Novel in 1930. LaFarge is of French and Narragansett ancestry. Narragansett is more accurately the Nahahiganseck Sovereign Nation.

>←<

LaFarge, Oliver; *A Pictorial History of the American Indian;* Crown Publishers, Inc.; 1956; Grades 6 and up

"The New World was settled slowly, by driblets of people crossing from Siberia to Alaska from time to time over a period of fifteen thousand years and more." In the next column it says: "If a discovery was made in the central part of the Old World, in China, India, Asia Minor, or around the Mediterranean, the news spread all through in a thousand years or less. So the knowledge spread at how to plant grain, how to make bread and beer, and how to work metal."

La Farge goes on to explain how things were different in the "New World" because of natural barriers. He writes: "The immigrants were not all alike. Some were tall, some short;...some are darker than others." He also explains that the fact that "in the course of fifteen thousand years many different peoples came into the New World is shown also by the Indian languages." "People often ask white men who live among Indians, 'Do you speak Indian?' It is a foolish question, like asking, 'Do you speak European?'"

Children are fascinated with the descriptions of the "old ways". In a world of technology, children marvel at the inventiveness of old cultures. The book is alive with pictures, allowing children to visualize the message of the text.

LaFarge explains the confusion on names: A "famous example is Young Man Afraid of His Horses, whose name really said that he had stampeded the enemy's horses." He writes that "...names that were short in the native language became long in translation so the white men shortened them."

On the negative side however, La Farge writes extensively about the warring of some of the tribes and spends considerable space describing various methods of extreme torture. One chapter is called, "Mothers and Torture". The book could have been wonderful for children if the grim, vicious accounts of war and torture had not been included. One might ask: What purpose does that serve? How much was motivated by the publisher wanting to sell books?

At first glance, many teachers and parents may think it's appropriate for a child. After all, it's a "pictorial history". The brutalities in the text are not suitable for young students. Leave this book in the hands of historians to study and weigh in the balance. There is an abundance of material for someone wanting to do research if they will do so in an honest manner.

Oliver LaFarge received the Pulitzer Prize for Novel in 1930 for **Laughing Boy.** He is of French and Narragansett ancestry. Narragansett is the Nahahiganseck Sovereign Nation.

⟶⟵

Lampman, Evelyn Sibley; *Half-Breed* ; illustrated by Ann Grifalconi; Doubleday; 1967; Grades 5 - 6

Pale-eyes, angry that his mother is remarrying, sets off to find his father. The son of a Crow Indian mother and a white father, Pale-eyes decides he will live with the father who left the Crow long before. He becomes Hardy Hollingshead, the name bestowed on him by his father. After an arduous journey he finds the white settlement where his father lives. Hardy is confronted with many difficult situations and must make a place for himself in the frontier society. In the end, he decided to stay with his white family.

The book is filled with stereotypes and distortions. Hardy must learn to eat like a white man, not with his fingers…and his hair must be cut. In reference to the "medicine bag" the reader is told that "Of course, he doesn't believe in it any more. He knows better now."

In speaking of the "Indians" - "They poor tribe...weak." "They're beggars, and they steal anything they can get their hands on to trade for liquor." " 'They stink,' agreed Courtney, wrinkling his straight nose."

This book is an example of how children learn prejudices while adults look on and wonder how it happened.

>*<

Lampman, Evelyn Sibley; ***Navaho Sister;*** illustrated by Paul Lantz; Doubleday; 1956; Grades 5 - 6

Sad Girl is a young Navaho who is sent to a government boarding school for Indians. She bravely confronts the challenges, sorrows and heartbreaking sacrifices at the school. Because she had been the only child in her grandmother's home, she worries about her grandmother living alone. The book ends on a bright note with Sad Girl and Grandmother being reunited with family with whom they had lost contact.

As with the other Lampman stories, this one is filled with stereotypes. There is an uncomfortable feeling to this book with distortions and manipulation of the material.

>*<

Lampman, Evelyn Sibley; ***Squaw Man's Son;*** Atheneum; 1978; Grades 5 - 6

Thirteen year old Billy Morrison's father sent his mother back to live with her own Modoc tribe. Later, his father married a white woman who detested Indians and Billy leaves his home in Oregon to join the Modocs. Captain Jack, an outstanding leader and tribal chief, realizes the futility of war with the U.S. Army. Nevertheless, the peace is broken and the Modocs seek refuge in the natural fortress of lava rock. Billy's story is one of a boy caught between two worlds in a tragic struggle.

Stereotypes abound - "As sure footed as wild goats, the Modocs descended the ledge..." "The medicine man, his painted face distorted with suspicion...his narrowed eyes were watching Billy..." When his father takes Billy to the barber to have his hair cut - "You cut Billy one more time...me take scissors. Use them to scalp you with." A visit to the store is no better. "Course we want underwear...What you figure my son to be? Some kind of heathen that runs around without underbritches?" In the end, Billy goes to California. Who can blame him?

><

Lavine, Sigmund; ***The Games the Indians Played;*** Dodd, Mead & Co.; 1974

American Indian games generally fell into two classifications. One category consisted in games of chance, the other in games of dexterity. These two classifications could be further divided into types of games. The book is well organized with the chapters describing the types of games, the tribes involved, and includes some interesting history about the background of the games. The book is illustrated with photographs and old prints.

A well-written book covering a subject that is rarely written about for the general publishing market. The subject area makes it suitable for all ages.

LeGarde, Amelia; *Aseban;* illustrated by Julie Borgen; Anishinabe Reading-Duluth: 1978; Grades K - 2

Aseban is the Ojibwe word for raccoon. The tale revolves around two blind men, Nanaboujou, Nokomis and raccoon. In this beautifully told tale we learn why raccoon has rings around his tail and a dark mask around his eyes. The setting is a "time remembered by grandparents." It is a fine example of a pourquoi story.

Full color illustrations are on each page. This is a delightful tale that has been set down in the fashion of true storytelling. Text in English accompanies the illustrations and Anishinabe (Ojibwe/Chippewa) text is written on concluding pages. Amelia LeGarde is Anishinabe.

Lenski, Lois; *Indian Captive: The Story of Mary Jemison;* illustrated by the author; Lippincott; 1941; Grades 6 - Up

Mary Jemison, a young colonial girl from Pennsylvania, was captured by Seneca Indians in 1758. Mary attempted many escapes, but she never succeeded. She learned to love her Indian family and later could have returned to the settlements of the white people. Mary chose to remain with the Indians she loved dearly.

Writing in 1941, Lois Lenski wrote what many felt was an honest, sensitive portrayal of Native life. The nature and content of the book gives an insight into the expectations of children's literature in 1941. The Native people are depicted as cruel and naive. The women do all the work. The book abounds with all the stereotypes that have been standard fare for too long. "...the greedy looks on the faces of the Indian women...Log-in-the-Water, the laziest Indian in the village...Gray Wolf, sullen and leering, demanded fire-water."

This book will be frightening for children and could be especially harmful for children who are adopted from other countries.

Lois Lenski was a noted, popular author of her time. She wrote over sixteen regional books including **Strawberry Girl** which won the Newberry Medal in 1946.

→✣←

Lenski, Lois; **Little Sioux Girl;** illustrated by the author; Lippincott; 1958; Grades 3 - 6

Eva White Bird lived with her family on an Indian reservation in the Dakotas. In the winter they live in Black Horse and in the summer they move to the river bottom. The family struggles with blizzards, hunger, floods and poverty. When Eva loses her Sioux doll, Prairie Rose, she walks alone to the reservation to find it. The doll was a gift from Grandmother.

It is not until the following winter during the Christmas party that the mystery of the lost doll is solved.

Miss Lenski has attempted to write a sympathetic book about the "Sioux". Unfortunately, there is a feeling of white superiority throughout the book and a number of stereotypes appear.

⸻

Leonard, Jonathan Norton; *The First Farmers;* Time-Life; 1973; Grades 6 - Up

The discovery of planting appears to be relatively simple, yet the cultivating of food led to more complex societies and higher civilizations. The rise of agriculture fostered larger populations and permitted these groups to settle permanently in one place. The book discusses types of seeds developed and containers for cooking and storing. The reader observes the development of farming in Mexico and Peru and the changes in the civilizations of the people involved. Some of the religious ceremonies observed are chronicled along with colorful illustrations of the ceremonies and planting techniques. The text also answers some questions about the origin of corn that scientists have researched for a number of years.

The book is well organized and illustrated with colorful photographs, drawings and charts.

Children involved in research will find this book helpful.

Lerner, Marguerite Rush; ***Red Man, White Man, African Chief: The Story of Skin Color;*** illustrated by George Overlie; Medical Books for Children; 1960; Grades K - 3

In very simple language, the book explains the reason for varying degrees of skin color among the people of the earth. It also presents the scientific names for a few words such as carotene, chlorophyll and melanin. The pronunciation of the words is given along with an easily understandable definition.

Colored illustrations on every page add interest and clarity to the text. The simple phrasing, though scientifically correct doesn't help alleviate racist attitudes. It does, however, explain skin color. The title is unfortunate.

→><←

LeSueur, Meridel; ***Sparrow Hawk;*** illustrated by Robert DesJarlait; Holy Cow! Press; 1987; (original copyright 1950); Grades 5 - 6

The "Black Hawk War" is the background for this story that is seen through the eyes of Sparrow Hawk. The year is 1832. Sparrow Hawk and his white friend, Huck, experience many changes in their frontier lives as the Sauk people try to retain their homeland. By the end of the book, Sparrow Hawk is seriously wounded and many of the people are dead, including Sparrow Hawk's mother. Their land has been treacherously taken from them, but Sparrow Hawk and Huck continue "putting the white man's knowledge and the red man's knowledge together."

Vine Deloria, Jr., discusses some of the "discordant notes" that some "cultural purist may find...unsettling." He states that "LeSueur provides a serious look at some old and familiar questions in a manner that should...provide...food for thought about the nature of the life journey they are undertaking." The stylized drawings by Robert DesJarlait add strength and validity to the novel.

Meridel LeSueur was a social activist and writer all her life. She was blacklisted during the McCarthy era "as a radical from a family of radicals." She deserves and needs to be read.

Lewis, Richard; ***All of You Was Singing;*** illustrated by Ed Young; Atheneum; 1991; All grades

All of You Was Singing is a retelling of the Aztec myth of how music came to Earth. It is a lyrical translation of how the sky sends the wind to steal music away from the sun, "And the wind, hearing my plea, gathered into itself all of your earth's silence and, in a great rush of air, swept past the roof of my sky, where it found the sun and the melodies of its music, playing in a nest of light."

The story is animated with love and respect through the vibrant, prismatic images of Ed Young as well as the poetic text by the author. Richard Lewis shares the spirit of the book when he says: "My own sense of this myth is the profound importance of music to the well-being of life. To sing is an affirmation of the melody and rhythm of life. And such singing continues... even after us".

There is a power and wondrousness to this tale that is immeasureable; the dedications are lovely.

⁂

Lewis, Richard, ed.; *I Breathe a New Song: Poems of the Eskimo;* illustrated by Oonark; Grades 3 - 6

A collection of Eskimo verse and song presented in modern English poetic forms. The scope of material ranges from magical songs and lullabies to songs for taunting enemies. An introduction by Edmund Carpenter, an anthropologist, describes the people, their beliefs and their ways of forming poetry. The origin of each poem is identified.

The book is illustrated with bold graphic drawings by Jessie Oonark, mother of eight children who lives in the Northwest Territories. It is a noteworthy selection of verse. Appropriate for all ages.

⁂

Lewis, Richard, ed.; *Out of the Earth I Sing: Poetry and Songs of Primitive Peoples of the World;* illustrated with photographs; Grosset & Dunlop; 1968; Grades 3 - 6

Original people have a universal language in their poetry. In this varied collection of song-poems we see people whose imaginations give rich meanings to the universe and who respond to their instincts through songs of celebration and prayer. The poems come from throughout the world and include selections from American Indians and Eskimos.

Illustrations are photographs of reproductions of primitive paintings, carving and weaving.

The song-poems give an excellent feeling for the rhythm of life as it is felt by Native people of the world. Recommended for all ages.

→←

Longfellow, Henry Wadsworth; ***Hiawatha and Megissogwon;*** illustrated by Jeffrey Thompson; National Geographic Society; illustrations copyright 2001; Afterword by Joseph Bruchac; Grades 4 – 6

Longfellow's poem is based on stories from the Anishinabe Nation. The episode with Megissogwon, the mightiest of magicians, is filled with fiery serpents, ghosts, and black-pitch water. It is Megissogwon who sends pestilence, disease, and death to the people. Hiawatha is the hero, following the wise words of his grandmother into a barren land to challenge the evil magician.

The works of George Copway, a Chippewa writer, and Henry Rowe Schoolcraft, a man who had collected many of the stories of the Anishinabe, influenced Longfellow. Jeffrey Thompson captures the spirit of the Anishinabe stories in his realistic illustrations. The designs are well researched giving freshness and renewed meaning to an old story. At the end of the book, Thompson explains the patterns he used.

In the afterword, Joseph Bruchac addresses the question: "Is Hiawatha an authentic Native American Story?" Bruchac examines the influence of Copway and Schoolcraft on Longfellow's work, and states: "*Hiawatha* can be seen as the start, a century and a half ago, of literary respect for the oral traditions of Native Americans." Mr. Bruchac further explains the flaws in the story. "And Longfellow made a big mistake. **The Song of Hiawatha** isn't about Hiawatha at all." He states, however, that the epic poem is "important even if it isn't authentic." The story "…brought our consciousness one small step towards the appreciation and acceptance of Native American cultures and Native American literature."

⸺※⸺

Luenn, Nancy; **Nessa's Fish;** illustrated by Neil Waldman; Atheneum; 1990; Grades K - 2

"At autumn camp, Nessa and her grandmother walked inland half a day to fish in the stony lake. They jigged for fish all afternoon and evening." Because they catch more fish than they can carry home, they "piled stones over them to keep away the foxes. Then, tired out, they fell asleep".

Grandmother becomes sick during the night and it is up to Nessa to help her grandmother while guarding the fish from a fox, wolves, and even a bear. When Nessa's parents and grandfather find them, "everyone hugged her" and "grandmother woke up and smiled".

The illustrations are in soft-tone watercolors that reflect the spirit of the narrative.

Children who read the book, and those who had the book read to them, felt it was a satisfying story. The author and illustrator have shown the special relationship that exists between a child and her grandmother. Though the story line is contrived, there is nothing in the book that will damage a child's self-image or contribute to negative feelings about Native people.

※

Lyons, Grant; ***Pacific Coast Indians of North America;*** Messner; 1983; Grades 3 - 6

Though the title indicates Pacific Coast Indians, in reality the book mainly discusses the Northwest Coast People. One of the most complex societies to be found on the North American continent is dealt with in a superficial manner and lacks sensitivity to the history, culture and economy of the Northwest Coast people.

There is an overall desolate feeling to the book that neither enlightens nor enriches. The black and white photographs that accompany the text are authentic, but they do not make up for the overall negative impact of the book.

※

Lyons, Oren; ***Dog Story;*** illustrated by the author; Holiday House; 1973

The boy first saw the dog tied up behind a friend's house. She was being teased and stood at the end of the chain snarling and barking. He writes, "I didn't know what kind of dog she was, but I know she was not like the dogs I was used to. Most of our Indian dogs are sort of mixed up, mongrels I guess." His friend gave him the dog. It took a great deal of patience but the dog was finally gentled and trained. A warm friendship developed and when the dog is shot beyond saving the boy feels the loss deeply.

Black and white drawings by the author, sensitively evoke the mood of the story.

Mr. Lyons, a traditional Faithkeeper, is a chief of the Turtle Clan of the Onondaga Nation. He is a member of the Onondaga Nation Council of Chiefs and has received the Elder and Wiser Award of the Rosa Parks Institute for Human Rights. Other honors include the Ellis Island Congressional Medal of Honor and the First Annual Earth Day International Award of the United Nations.

Maestro, Betsy; The ***Discovery of the Americas;*** illustrated by Giulio Maestro; Lothrop, Lee & Shepard Books; 1991; Grades 2 - 4

At first glance, the book appears to have been written as a curative for all the Columbus hoopla. The book jacket and the first few pages indicate that the reader will learn about all the people who discovered and "rediscovered" the Americas.

There are thirty-five pages of total text, all of which contain a half page or less of narrative. Eight of these pages are devoted to the journeys of Columbus, five to Magellan, two to Balboa. Other European "discoverers" given space are Saint Brendan,

Leif Ericsson, Bjarni Herjolfsson, and Prince Madoc of Wales. There are pages of general interest that discuss the migration or "wandering people, or nomads" across "...a natural bridged formed between the land mass we call Asia and what is now North America."

Native people are given four short pages and on one of these we are told: "...most Native American cultures were more short-lived." The illustration showing the arrival of Columbus has the obligatory naked Natives behind bushes looking at the newcomers.

There are some fascinating comparisons between the "Old World" and the "New World" on one page that shows similarities between various objects. A pottery house from Indochina has much in common with a pottery house from South America. An elephant on wheels from India is shown by a dog on wheels from Central America. There are pottery pieces from Japan and South America that show striking similarities, as do the string crosses from India and South America.

Concluding text includes a "Table of Dates" that has some valuable information, a short discussion of some of the people of the ancient and early Americas as well as a page devoted to "The Age of Discovery".

Giulio Maestro's panoramic illustrations sweep across the page in lovely detail.

In the end, there is a feeling for wanting more – wanting a book that is a celebration of people before and beyond Columbus.

Maher, Ramona; *Alice Yazzie's Year;* illustrated by Stephen Gammell; Grades K - 3

> In a seamless record of Alice Yazzie's year, the superb book enables the reader to enter the Navajo world. Alice and her grandfather live in a hogan where they can see Black Mountain, a Navajo holy place. Alice finds a lamb to shelter from the cold in January and in July walks six miles for cupcakes and strawberry pop. Each month is recorded through poetic images of Navajo life. Alice and her grandfather's richness of spirit, their love and their joy are recorded throughout the text. Their sorrow and their regret for a past that is gone is also shared.
>
> This is a quiet story told with simplicity and beauty. The illustrations catch the warmth and charm of the Southwest and the quality of life among the Navajo. Every part of this novel is wonderful.
>
> Carl Gorman writes an afterward, "Notes About the Navajo Country and Ways of Life." It makes a lovely closure to this beautiful and sensitively produced book.

Marriott, Alice Lee and Rachlin, Carol K.; *American Indian Mythology;* Crowell; 1968; Grades 6 - Up

> Presented is a compilation of thirty-six stories from various tribal groups. Brief descriptions of the cultures appear at the beginning of each selection with mention of tribal names,

geographical location, language group and cultural traits. The four sections of the book presents representative tales from tribes across the North American continent.

The book includes a bibliography and an excellent introduction. Black and white photographs are found throughout the text. The reading level is high. For younger children, the stories could be read aloud.

→←

Marriott, Alice; ***Sequoyah, Leader of the Cherokees;*** illustrated by Bob Riger; Random House; 1956; Grades 3 - 6

The book chronicles the life of Sequoyah (Sik-wa-yi) from birth to his death. Included also is a chapter on the history of the Cherokee. Sequoyah, "the lame one", had a dream to devise a form of written communication for the Cherokee. The reader is involved in the fulfillment of that dream against the backdrop of Cherokee history and culture.

In 1824, Sequoyah was presented a silver medal by the Cherokee legislature in honor of his achievement.

Historical note: "The Five Civilized Tribes", the Cherokees, Choctaws, Chickasaws, Creeks, and Seminoles, invited missionaries to open schools for them with the hopes of proving they were peaceful, progressive, and hard-working. It was the missionaries who felt that Indian languages could never be written.

The book is written with accuracy and fidelity to the Cherokee people. Text and illustrations convey the quality of life among the Cherokee and give insights into the personality of Sequoyah.

※

Marriott, Alice; *Winter Telling Stories;* illustrated by Richard Cuffari; Crowell; 1947; Grades 3 - 6

The book is a collection of some of the wise and humorous Saynday stories of the Kiowa Indians. Saynday was the one who made the world the way it is. He put the sun in the sky and brought the buffalo to the Indians. It was Saynday who tried to marry a whirlwind and sometimes he suffered the most from his own magic.

The black and white illustrations flow with the spirit of the text.

※

Martin, Bill, Jr. and John Archambault; *Knots on a Counting Rope;* illustrated by Ted Rand; Henry Holt and Co.; Text copyright 1966 and 1987; illustrations copyright 1987; Grades 1 - 3

The counting rope is a metaphor for the passage of time. A boy sits with his Grandfather by a campfire one evening and says - "Tell me the story again, Grandfather. Tell me who I am." Each time Grandfather recounts the night of the boy's birth, the fierce storm, and how the child was very weak and almost died, another knot is added to the counting rope. As the story emerges, the reader learns of the boy's greatest challenge, his blindness.

Knots on a Counting Rope is a poignant, eloquent story. Because of this, it has some disturbing aspects that may be overlooked by a first reading. One distressing point is the boy's constant interruption of an Elder. The question also must be asked - how did such a young boy obtain the right to wear an eagle feather? The dialogue spoken is overly poetic. Furthermore, there is no mention of the Nation of people that the story is about and the spiritual aspect of the "Blue Horses" is inappropriately dealt with.

The original copyright date of 1966 gives a clue as to the nature of the book. The mid-Sixties was a time when it was "in" to romanticize and write about Native people.

>⊰

Martin, Patricia Miles; ***Indians, The First Americans;*** illustrated by Robert Frankenberg; Parents Magazine Press; 1970; Grades 3 - 6

A general introduction to American Indians is given, as well as discussing traditional values, reservations and contemporary city life. The book is organized into geographical areas. A concluding chapter discusses some of the contributions the "Indian" has made to modern society.

The illustrations throughout the book add clarity to the text. There is no in-depth study of tribal groups. Children should be encouraged to look at books that deal with Native people in a much more enlightened way.

⇥⇤

Martinson, David; editor; ***A Long Time Ago is Just Like Today;*** illustrated by John Peyton; Photographs by J.P. Savage; Duluth Indian Education; 1976; Grades 6 - Up

> The subject matter is as varied as the experiences of those who share them. The book is the written culmination of interviews with a number of Chippewa people, both young and old. The voices of the Chippewa speak to us on the pages as they share their culture, traditions and reverance for all life forms.
>
> The vibrant illustrations add warmth and imagination to the narratives. The photographs share the life of the people.
>
> This is a deeply satisfying book and recommended reading.

⇥⇤

Martinson, David; ***Cheer Up Old Man;*** illustrated by Vince Cody; State of Minnesota; 1975; Grades K - 3

> A simply told tale of a Chippewa grandfather; the story reflects his dreams of yesterday and the joys of his old age.
>
> It is primarily a picture book with bold color illustrations on each page. The illustrations vividly portray Chippewa culture, costumes, designs and dwellings in a historical setting.

⇥⇤

Martinson, David; ***Manabozho and the Bullrushes;*** illustrated by John Peyton; State of Minnesota; 1975; Grade K - 3

The story is about Manabozho, the hero and trickster of the Chippewa. (Ojibwe/Anishinabe.) The simply told tale revolves around Manabozho and a night of dancing. With the approach of dawn, Manabozho saw with whom he was dancing. The trick was on him!

An enchanting, enjoyable tale simply written. Black and white illustrations on each page add to the fun and beauty of the narrative.

In the bilingual book **Be-Inabin,** the storytellers, Billy Blackwell, Liza Thibault, and Ogimabinaysik, have made this request: "These are traditional Ojibwe stories collected from the 'Anishinabeg.' We ask that in keeping with our Ojibwe customs they are not read in the summer or late spring or early fall. Nanabozho stories can only be told when snow is on the ground, and the thunders have gone to the south. The other stories, other than Nanabozho stories, can be told anytime."

Manabozho is spelled many ways, including Nanabozho.

※

Martinson, David; ***Real Wild Rice;*** illustrated by Vince Cody; State of Minnesota; 1975; Grades K - 1

The book is written in rhymed verse in the style of a beginning reading book. It is a short story about wild rice gathering. Black and white illustrations add much understanding to the text. Chippewa floral designs outline the pages.

It is a fun book for children - especially the young reader.

>‹

Martinson, David; ***Shemay, The Bird in the Sugarbush;*** illustrated by Carl Gawboy; State of Minnesota; 1975; Grades K - 3

Based on a true account of Liza Thibault as a young Chippewa girl living at Grand Portage in the early 1900's, the setting is a maple sugar bush camp of the Chippewa. Maple sugar making is woven into the story of Liza and her grandmother.

The simply told narrative is enhanced by the vivid color paintings of Mr. Gawboy. The illustrations are effective in their design, their reflection of Chippewa culture and their vitality. Carl Gawboy, a Chippewa, has shown his artistic skill and sensitivity in the pages of Shemay.

>‹

Marvin, Isabel Ridout; ***Josefina and the Hanging Tree;*** Texas Christian University Press; 1992; Grades 4 - 6

Fourteen-year-old Josefina and her best friend Maxi become involved in the conflict of the Cart War in Goliad, Texas. The year is 1857 and Mexican freighters are being captured, tried on phony charges and then hanged on the "hanging tree" in front of the Goliad courthouse. The freighters, who haul goods from the Gulf Coast to San Antonio, include Maxi's father who is ambushed and killed by outlaws. When Josefina's father is captured and taken to the hanging tree, Josefina and Maxi stall the hanging while waiting for the Texas Rangers to come to the rescue.

Based on actual occurrences in Goliad, Texas, the author has included suggested readings for those interested in learning more about the Cart War. A plaque, placed by the Texas State Historical Survey Committee, stands underneath the Hanging Tree. Also included is a "Glossary of Spanish Terms" that will aid the reader in understanding parts of the text. An Afterward gives additional information on the Cart War and the repercussions it had on the Mexican people.

This book can teach and enlighten about a part of Texas history that impacted the Native people that lived through the Cart War. Here is an example of good intentions resulting in a book with plenty of interest to hold the attention of a young reader. It is a worthwhile book that children will enjoy.

The author lived in Goliad, Texas, during her high school years and later became a teacher of English, Spanish and journalism. She now lives in Minnesota but spends her winters in Texas.

→←

Mathers, Sharon, Linda Skinner and Terry Tafoya; ***The Mamook Book: Activities for Learning About the Northwest Coast Indians;*** illustrated by Roger Fernandes; Daybreak Star Press; 1979; Grades 4 - 6

The Mamook Book is a concise, attractive book that presents a number of activities for children. It does not deal with one Tribe, but instead deals with several Native groups. There are directions, diagrams and patterns for a longhouse, a mobile, transformation masks and a salmon game. Vocabulary is carefully explained so the meaning to Native people remains uncorrupted yet is easily within the understanding of the child audience. Historical and contemporary scenes are both included which helps the reader keep things in perspective.

Mamook means "to do" in the trading language used by Northwest Coast people and this is a genuine "to do" book.

The book is an excellent resource. It is available through various Internet sites.

Max, Jill; ***Spider Spins a Story: Fourteen Legends from Native America;*** illustrated by Robert Annesley, Benjamin Harjo, Michael Lacapa, S. D. Nelson, Redwing T. Nez, Baje Whitethorne; Rising Moon; 1997; All ages

"You hold this volume in your hands because American Indian culture has a rich history of storytellers and stories." Authors Kelly Bennet and Ronnie Davison, writing under the pseudonym of Jill Max, have given us a collection of stories that is a true gift to the reader. There is *"The Great Flood: A Kiowa Legend." "Rainbow Makers: An Achomawi Legend." "Wichio Meets One of the Little People: A Cheyenne Legend." "How the Spider Got It's Web: A Wiyat Legend."* Traditions of the Tewa, Zuni, Osage, Muskogee, Navajo, Cherokee, Hopi, Kiowa, Lakota, and Muskogee Nations are included in the book.

The illustrators: Robert Annesley is Cherokee. Benjamin Harjo is Seminole and Cherokee. Michael Lacapa is Apache, Hopi, and Tewa. S. D. Nelson is Standing Rock Sioux. Redwing T. Nez is Navajo. Baje Whitethorne is Navajo.

The stories are respectful and impeccably researched. The pictures are genuine, wonderfully detailed, and alive with color.

>·<

Mayne, William; ***Drift;*** Delacorte; 1985; Grades 5 - Up

Tawena, the Indian girl, and Rafe Considine, who wants to go with her to see a hibernating bear, are introduced in the first two paragraphs of the book. "Tawena was throwing down little balls of suet from a lump of fat she had in her hand. Now and then she ate some herself. She had a fatty face...and brown eyes deep in the fat. He was sure she had stolen the suet."

And here is how Tawena carries on a conversation: "Indian womans come...They kill Indian girl right off...Tawena go away, you ever see Tawena again, ever see Tawena, ever. This white boy fire. Tawena ever at village." And so on.

The story line deals with Tawena's "instincts"; her sniffing and smelling, rather than crediting her intelligence. Throughout the book the people are not given a tribal identity.

The book is well written, richly visual and has some scenes of great humor which will appeal to children. This is unfortunate since it will leave the reader with bizarre impressions and reinforce negative stereotypes. People who write children's books have an obligation to write honestly and not succumb to stereotypes. This book is neither sensitive nor honest.

>✦<

McDermott, Beverly Brodsky; **Sedna: An Eskimo Myth;** illustrated by the author; Viking Press; 1975; Grades K - 3

Sedna, the mother of all sea animals, did not send food to the Inuit. They had neglected the custom of honoring her and so they were hungry. Angakok, the man of magic, was called upon to ask Sedna for mercy. It was then than Sedna rose from the depths of the sea, "…ignoring the pleas of the Angakok…she told a story to the man of magic."

Deceived by a bird, her father abandoned her and she lived alone in a cave at the bottom of the sea. "The Angakok was moved by Sedna's sad story." In helping the lonely Sedna, he finds a way for the people to be fed.

In bold illustrations of violet and indigo, the Inuit story is retold with a sense of drama.

>✦<

McDermott, Gerald; **Arrow to the Sun;** illustrated by the author; Viking Press; 1974; Grades K - 3

Arrow to the Sun is a re-creation of a profound and touching tale from the Pueblo Indians. In ancient times, the Lord of the Sun sent the spark of life to earth, where it entered the dwelling of a young maiden. In this way, the Boy came into the world of men. When others mock him because he has no father, the Boy sets out on the Trail of Life to search for him.

The bold, colorful illustrations capture the qualities of Pueblo art. A vibrant and unique rendering of an ancient tale, the book is superb for its power and abstract beauty. Mr. McDermott received the Caldecott Award in 1975 for the book.

McDermott, Gerald; ***Coyote, A Trickster Tale from the American Southwest;*** illustrated by the author; Harcourt Brace and Company; 1994; Grades K – 3

Stories of Coyote's misbehaving have been used for centuries to counsel and teach about the dangers of egotism, gluttony, and thievery. Coyote is a trickster, causing trouble, intruding on others lives, and generally being an example of human narcissism.

In this story, Coyote was "going along, following his nose. He had a nose for trouble." He found trouble with a Badger, a Woodpecker, and a Snake. When he heard a flock of crows chanting and laughing and then taking off in flight, Coyote decides he must learn to fly. The Crows share their feathers with Coyote and teach him to fly, but as usual, Coyote became impudent and boastful. The Crows had enough, took back their feathers, and left Coyote on his own. Because of this adventure, Coyote today is the color of dust and his tail has a black tip.

McDermott's colorful, dramatic art is bold and vivid, showing great respect for the original Coyote tales. The prose is rhythmic and direct, splendidly conveying the nature of Coyote. It is a wonderful pourquoi story.

Winner of the Caldecott Award for ***Arrow to the Sun,*** McDermott has received many honors for his storytelling and illustrations.

→✕←

McDermott, Gerald; ***Musicians of the Sun;*** illustrated by the author; Simon and Schuster Books for Young Readers; 1997; Grades K – 3

The Lord of the Night came out of the starry night, "…invisible, untouchable." The Lord of the Night was "King of the Gods. Soul of the World." A magic mirror, his third eye, let him see the entire world. He said: "The world is gray and joyless." He saw that the people were without laughter and dancing and singing. Lord of the Night decided to change that. He instructed the Wind to "fly to the house of the Sun and free four musicians…. Red, Yellow, Blue, and Green." The journey is made to capture light and music and dancing and joy, but Wind faces many obstacles before the world was "filled with color". In the end, "All give thanks to the Lord of the Night."

A note from the author says: "Musicians of the Sun is a lost fragment of the mythological tradition of the Aztecs…"

The bold, wondrous illustrations are in "…acryllic fabric paint, opaque inks, and oil pastel on paper handmade in Mexico."

McDermott, Gerald; ***Raven, A Trickster Tale from the Pacific Northwest;*** illustrated by the author; Harcourt Brace & Company; 1993; Grades K – 3

> Raven is the main character in Native American myths and stories of the Pacific Northwest. In this retelling, Raven flies through darkness, because the people lived in a world without light and warmth. Searching for light, Raven sees light coming from the house of the Sky Chief. The Chief's daughter is beautiful; Raven changes into a pine needle and falls into the water that the woman is drinking. Later, the woman gives birth to a baby who is the transformed Raven. As the grandson of the Sky Chief, Raven finds the source of light, steals it, and throws it into the sky. "This is how Raven stole the sun and gave it to all the people."
>
> McDermott's careful examination of Native American cultures and beliefs is evident in his storytelling. Bold, colorful, stylized illustrations complement the text. As with many other trickster tales, this one ends with light and joy and thankfulness.

McGaw, Jessie; ***Little Elk Hunts Buffalo: As Little Elk Tells it in Picture Writing;*** Nelson; 1961; Grades K - 3

> The hungry Cheyennes had found no buffalo and it was already the tenth day of the hunter's moon. Little Elk left camp alone to look for buffalo. Finding a large herd, he rode back with the news. He was jubilant when he thought his arrow had brought

down the first buffalo. But was it his arrow? He learns the truth at the feast of celebration.

Written in pictographs, the English translation appears below each picture.

The story is grossly oversimplified and the people are generic. ***Tales of the Iroquois*** by Tehanetorens is by far a superior book on Indian pictographs.

→←

McGaw, Jessie Brewer; ***Painted Pony Runs Away: As Little Elk Tells it in Picture Writing;*** Thomas Nelson & Sons; 1958; Grades K - 3

Little Elk, a young Cheyenne boy, searches for his pony that has run away. He is captured by a group of Sioux, but escapes. He rescues a Sioux boy who has had a serious accident and the Sioux and Cheyenne make peace.

The book is written in pictographs on tan paper with each picture translated into English. A section at the end of the book discusses facts about picture writing.

This is an oversimplified story with a contrived plot. An excellent book on Indian pictographs is ***Tales of the Iroquois*** by Tehanetorens.

→←

McGovern, Ann; *If You Lived With the Sioux Indians;* illustrated by Bob Levering; Four Winds Press; 1972; Grades 1 - 4

Ann McGovern attempts to write about the Sioux in a sensitive manner. She describes daily life, the clothing, food, games, customs, religion, travel and on through a list of thirty-nine questions. The format of the book has a question at the top of the page and then it is answered as simply as possible in a page or two.

Some of the disturbing aspects of the book are the types of questions that are asked: "Did the Sioux Indians scalp their enemies?" The answer includes references to the Sioux feeling there was "…special meaning in an enemy's scalp. It was round like the sun, so for the Sioux it had power, like the sun…A Sioux kept a scalp all his life, the way a soldier of today might keep his medals." The child reader does not have sufficient maturity to handle the issues discussed here. Instead it will further alienate children from the truth. "Did the Sioux like war?" "What would you eat?" It is here that she writes: "Buffalo, buffalo and more buffalo…and sometimes raw buffalo. You would even drink the blood of buffalo." You know what kids will do with that one. The questions on religion will be confusing for children and do not correctly portray the ceremonies and beliefs of the people.

The author has tried to give insights and understanding to the Lakota peoples, but these insights are negated by the stereotypes included.

McGovern, Ann; ***Little Wolf;*** illustrated by Nola Langner; Abelard-Schuman; 1965; Grades K - 3

Little Wolf is taught the skills of hunting by his father, but he refuses to hunt. His father becomes angry with Little Wolf but Grandfather says to let him be. There are other ways. Father insists he hunt. Little Wolf knows the ways of the woods, the animals and the plants. He knows the plants that make people sick and the plants that heal. Little Wolf will not hunt. In the dark night, Little Wolf finds the Chief's only son dying in the woods. Since Little Wolf knows the secrets of the forest, he finds the plants that make the boy well again. In this way, Little Wolf wins the respect of the tribe.

Brown and white drawings add warmth and charm to this quiet tale. Though no specific tribal group is named, the story contributes a positive look at Indian life. It also presents the statement, through story form, that we may not all be the same, but we all have valuable contributions we can make to our group.

The lack of tribal identification is a negative factor in the book, but the Anishinabe children who read it thought the story was satisfying.

⸻ ❖ ⸻

McGraw, Eloise Jarvis; ***Moccasin Trail;*** Puffin Books; 1986; (Originally published by Coward-McCann, 1952); Grades 6 - Up

Jim Keath had run away from his family eight years earlier to spend time in the wilderness of the Oregon territory. After a near-fatal battle with a grizzly, he had spent six years living with the Crow Indians who rescued him. Jim receives a message of desperation from his two brothers and a sister telling him they are moving west and need his help. The story tells how Jim makes the hard journey back to reconcile with his family.

The book is dedicated to "Peter and Laurie - My Own Little Wild Indians".

As the story opens, we meet Jim Keath: "His eyes were not black, but so light brown they looked almost golden against his bronzed skin; yet they had the Indian's wild, unsettled, wary look in them." In describing his joy in killing the bear: "That joy was his first step toward savagery."

"Something happened inside the boy as he watched one of the warriors...waving his coupstick from which a blond scalp dangled...His own mother's hair had been that color..." The warrior had "flaunted the blond scalp".

When Jim leaves, he meets some other Indians. "The older Indian, hearing his name, bobbed his head and grinned. Jim felt disgust as he pushed out of his thicket and joined the group. Diggers were poor excuses for Indians. Look at them. Bandy legged, grinning like skinned coyotes, stinking of the fish they lived on."

Jim has trouble in adjusting to his new found family as his sister shouts at him: "...he don't deck himself out like a savage to prove it!...You ain't in Absaroka now, you're in a civilized valley with civilized folks, livin' in a house again the way you was meant to. You ain't a Injun, you're a Keath...Why won't you cut off them braids and quit lookin' like a heathen?"

There is talk of an Indian uprising. "No, not these sleepy Chinooks or Multomahs, but real wild Injuns. No telling what kind, they'd only got a glimpse of one of them and that was enough - riding naked, he was, on a horse swifter than an antelope, and yelling bloody murder and shooting in all directions and scaring the wits out of the stock."

Jim happens upon a lot of "Indians" throughout the book. "But this time his hands were like ice and his mouth dry with fear, one terrible picture before his eyes - a line of sullen Indians with flat, blank eyes...The Umpquas - who kept slaves."

It is interesting to note that The New York Times and the Library Journal have written glowing reviews of this book. It is also a Newbery Honor book which is awarded annually for "the most distinguished contribution to American literature for children."

Jim's journey carries enormous momentum and implications that convey strong feelings of superiority on the part of the settlers and relegates the Native people to the role of burdensome, troublesome "heathens".

The book is demeaning and inaccurate, but with the new edition, will find a new generation to contaminate.

>✛<

McNeer, May; ***War Chief of the Seminoles;*** illustrated by Lynd Ward; Grades 3 - 6

Osceola was an intelligent and courageous chief of the Seminole Indians. During the Seminole War, Osceola was fighting

A Second Look, Native Americans in Children's Books

to win justice for his people. Because of Osceola's brilliant leadership, the U.S. Army faced the most difficult campaign ever undertaken against the "Indians." The book describes the events leading up to the war and the eventual capture and death of Osceola.

The book appears to be well researched, but it places emphasis on the "warring" aspects of tribal life. Unfortunately, children were immediately drawn to the "war chief" theme.

→←

Meadowcroft, Enid LaMonte; *Crazy Horse, Sioux Warrior;* illustrated by Cary; Garrard; 1965; Grades 3 - 6

Crazy Horse was a bold and brilliant leader. His story is one of courage and the proud freedom of the plains. He was a "war chief" of the Oglala Sioux and fought to defend the lands that were rightfully theirs.

The entire book emphasizes the warrior life of Crazy Horse. Children sensed a glorification of war and that all of this was unavoidable. In discussion, they concluded it was indeed avoidable because the Europeans did not have to settle on tribal land. That concept isn't handled in the text.

→←

Meadowcroft, Enid LaMonte; *The First Year;* illustrated by Grace Paull; Crowell; 1946; Grades 3 - 6

It was a difficult first year for the pilgrims. The voyage on the Mayflower was hazardous and exhausting for the passengers and crew. When they reached land, they were faced with loneliness, hunger and a strange new land. Many of them died that first year. It was only through the kindnesses of the "Indians" that the Plymouth Colony survived the harshness of their new home.

Regrettably, the book is replete with negative images and ethnocentric biases. History becomes manipulated, the Native people are treated in a condescending manner and only when the "Indians" help the settlers are they presented as having any value. The word "savage" appears throughout the text.

Some quotes from the narrative:

"Me Samoset. Me chief of Indians..."

In speaking of the "Indians": "They don't look very clean. I am afraid my pillows will be ruined."

"We have paid them for the corn we took...and they have returned the tools they stole."

In speaking of Massasoit eating some turkey: "...and gnawed it as if he were a dog with a bone."

The illustrations of Native people are cartoon-like and insensitive. The effect of the drawings as well as the narrative is to portray the people as unintelligent, inarticulate, and naive.

This book presents nothing new to the story of the Plymouth Colony, but instead is an offensive retelling that reflects the ambiguity with which the European invaders dealt with the

Native people. The author has not created a legitimate exchange between two diverse groups of people, but has, like too many authors, evaded the real issues.

→←

Meigs, Cornelia; *The Willow Whistle;* illustrated by E., Boyd Smith; Macmillan; 1931; Grades 3 - 6

The story centers on two children, Mary Anne Seabold and Eric Thorveg along with their "Indian" friend, Gray Eagle. It is a tale of the "opening of the West" and the continuing adventures the children have on the American Frontier. Mary Anne is taken by "the Indian", Gray Eagle, to visit his tribe. There is a search for Mary Anne because no one knows what became of her or to Gray Eagle's tribe since they "have disappeared". There is also a race between Eric and an "Indian boy" and a "grand buffalo hunt". A new schoolhouse is built, but the "Indians" mistake it for a Medicine Lodge.

In reaction to the "Indians", Mary Anne "…was not in the least afraid of them. At first all the dark faces looked to her just the same, but soon she learned to know this one or that…But Mary Anne's mother could not learn so quickly to put aside her dread of these wild creatures belonging to a new country."

"The red-skinned newcomer seated himself upon a boulder beside the stream and remained there…" Further descriptions of "Indians" contain this sentiment by the author: "Indians have strange ways, such strange ways that white men come to understand them very slowly. In some respects the red men are more like children than grown people…"

References are made throughout the book about what "Indians" do: "It is not the fashion of Indians ever to say thank you, nor did these still sullenly hostile Arickarees seem to care for making friends with the white men..." Also, "With Indian quickness... he swung himself up on the pony's back." And - "But like all Indians she was most unwilling to show that she knew anything of the strangers' speech..." In describing the skill of the "Indians" on horseback: "He stooped from the horse's back as he flashed past, swung low as only an Indian can, and thrust the point of his lance through a small crumpled object that lay upon the ground. It was the Blue-Backed Speller."

The "Dance of the Omahas" begins: "Every squaw came out of her lodge wearing all her beads, her chains of elks' teeth and of bears' claws...The skin drums thumped...the tall warriors went round and round them in a great circle, dancing their strange slow, stamping shuffle and calling the long Ah-ha-ha, Ah-ha-ha, of their solemn chant."

The text is written strictly from the European settler's point of view and the people are "Indians", "squaws", "braves" and "papooses". Native people are described as childlike and naive, who will never be able to understand school and books and civilization. The illustrations match the stereotypical text. This book is still on the shelves and considered a literary treasure for children. Don't believe it. It is a source of negative, harmful images. It is understandable that it was published in 1931, but it is chilling that it remains on library shelves today.

Miles, Miska; ***Annie and the Old One;*** illustrated by Peter Parnall; Little, Brown; 1971; Grades K - 3

The cactus does not bloom forever. The sun rises from the edge of the earth to shine over the Navajo world. Then it sets. There is a time for all things to return to the earth. The Old One understands these things, but Annie cannot. The Old One shares time with Annie. Times of tending sheep, playing and laughing together and the special times of story telling. Time for Annie and the Old One will end. When the new rug on the loom is finished, Grandmother will go to Mother Earth. The rug on the loom becomes Annie's enemy and she plots to stop her grandmother's weaving.

A simple yet wise and poignant tale set in the contemporary world of the Navajo. Beautifully sensitive drawings emphasize the strength of this heartfelt story.

There are some flaws, however, in the book. For instance, it was noted that Grandmother was called "the Old One" which in reality would not be how an Elder is addressed. In the illustrations, when walking to the mesa, there is no blanket - at the mesa, a blanket appears for Grandmother. Also, Annie wears "traditional" clothes to school which is not how Native children usually dress when attending class.

None of these flaws negates the feeling that generates from this book. Noting the flaws is informational, not necessarily critical.

Mr. Parnall has received numerous awards for his work, including three Caldecott Honor Books. The books honored are: **The Desert is Theirs,** 1976; **Hawk I'm Your Brother,**

1977; ***The Way to Start a Day,*** 1979. He has written and/or illustrated over eighty books.

→←

Miller, Luree, and Scott Miller; ***Alaska; Pioneer Stories of a Twentieth-Century Frontier;*** Cobblehill Books; Dutton; 1991; Grades 6 - Up

Dramatic stories of pioneering men and women of Alaska come to life in the pages of this book. The reader is given an intimate sense of the Alaskan experience as the Miller's describe the challenges of every-day life and the exhilaration of living in the largest and northern-most state.

One of the chapters, entitled "Willie Hensley: Bridging Alaska's Two Worlds", deals with the success story of the leader of the Northwest Alaska Native Association, a multi-million dollar organization. Willie Hensley was born in an Inupiat village north of the Arctic Circle. Because his father died when he was young, he was adopted into the large family of his uncle. Later, his uncle died and he lived with his aunt, Naungagaq, also known as Priscilla.

His "adopted mother" taught him about "the Ilitqusiat - the Inupiat Spirit...It is a value system, a way of behaving that includes cooperation, sharing, humility, collective living, and respect for our elders."

Willie left home when he was fourteen years old and went away to school in Tennessee. "But I didn't have any problems...I knew who I was." He credits his mother, Priscilla, "...for his Inupiat spirit that sustained him in this strange white world."

"Our heritage is rich," says Willie, "and we must not lose it...We have our families, our traditions, our language, and our land, which are so much a part of our lives. At the same time, we have access to education and the Western political and economic world to do the other things we need to do. So we can have the best of both worlds."

The book is illustrated with photographs and a map. The people are real and the story of Willie Hensley is optimistic. This is an outstanding book, and if only one chapter is read, let it be the one on Mr. Hensley. The chapter closes with: "If our people are to survive, they must keep and foster the Inupiat Spirit. If we protect our spirit and protect our land, we will endure."

The book can be adapted for younger children by reading portions of the book aloud and discussing the elements of the story.

※

Mitchell, Barbara; ***Tomahawks and Trombones;*** illustrated by George Overlie; Carolrhoda Books; 1982; Grades K - 3

Around the year 1755, a group of Moravians living in Bethlehem, Pennsylvania were living peacefully with the Delaware Indians. When tension builds between the two groups of people and escalates toward war, the Moravians defeat the Indians by playing their trombones from the roof of one of the houses.

The Indians become so frightened by this "heavenly music" that they run away and hide in the woods.

"A note from the author" states that "Some of this story comes from a 225-year-old diary kept by the Moravian sisters. Some... from a peace talk given by Bishop Spangenberg...Some of it is legend. And some of it is imaginined. It may not have happened exactly as it has been told..."

So...which part is imagined? Which part is legend? The part that says: "They began to burn barns and houses all around Bethlehem." Or the section that shows the men on the top of the roof blowing the trombones and the frightened "Indians" gaping in fear - "The Indians had never heard anything like it. The Indians were frightened. 'Music up in the sky!' they said. 'It must be the voice of the Moravians' God!' "

In the "Afterword" it states: "Did the trombones make the Indians go away on the Christmas day? No one really knows. But according to legend, a Delaware later told a sister it was the strange music in the sky that made them lower their tomahawks."

Once again, there is a story conjured up from "legend" and "imagination" at the expense of Native people. Young children will not be influenced by the explanations at the beginning and end of the text, if anyone even reads it; they will take the book literally. Children will see "Indians" as a source of ridicule and condemnation, while affirming the value of the Moravian settlers.

Unless there is adult intervention, children make negative presumptions about the "Indians" in the tale. Don't let that happen. Intervene.

→←

Momaday, Natachee Scott; *Owl in the Cedar Tree;* illustrated by Don Perceval; University of Nebraska Press; 1992, Reprint of 1965 edition published by Ginn; Grades 3 - 6

Haske is a young Navajo boy who has a deep reverance for nature and an intense desire to draw the things he sees. Haske attends school and learns the language of the white men. Old Grandfather tells him he must choose between the new ways and the old ways, that choosing the ways of the white men offends the Navajo gods. Haske is confused and hurt. Riding Woman, his mother, explains that he must keep the best of the old ways and learn the best of the new.

The warmth of Navajo family life and dignity of the culture are presented in this well written story. The book deals with the cultural conflicts faced by many Native children. The book is enhanced by the brown and black drawings that illustrate the text.

Natachee Scott Momaday, Kiowa/Cherokee, received the Western Heritage Award in 1976 for *Owl in the Cedar Tree.* The award was presented by the National Cowboy and Western Heritage Museum in Oklahoma City. She is the mother of writer N. Scott Momaday. Mr. Momaday won the Pulitzer Prize for fiction in 1969 for his book *House Made of Dawn.*

Montgomery, Elizabeth Rider; ***Chief Seattle, Great Statesman;*** illustrated by Russ Hoover; Garrard; 1966; Grades 3 - 6

Seattle was a Puget Sound Indian of the Suquamish tribe. As a boy, Seattle learned to fish, hunt, swim and to be a distinguished speaker. When the Muckleshoots attacked, Seattle displayed brilliant leadership and became a great war chief. When settlers arrived, Seattle helped them in every way possible.

It is a simply written biography that will appeal to students.

It's too bad the author didn't tell that Chief Seattle died in 1866 at the age of 80 - one year after the city named for him made it illegal for "Indians" to live in Seattle. For more information, read the review on ***Brother Eagle, Sister Sky*** by Susan Jeffers.

Moon, Grace; ***Chi-Wee;*** illustrated by Carl Moon; Doubleday; 1925; Grades 6 - Up

Little Chi-Wee lives with her mother in one of the great stone pueblos that was home to many Indian families high on a mesa overlooking the desert. A number of exciting things happen to her: a kidnapping in which a goat takes part, an accidental excursion into the holy place called a Kiva, and a trip to an ancient ruined pueblo where she and her playmate capture a bear. It is a book of sunshiny days, blue sky and the space of the desert.

The book is arranged in episodes, which makes it quite adaptable for reading aloud. The black and white drawings by Carl Moon add to mood of the text.

※

Moon, Grace and Carl; ***One Little Indian;*** Whitman; 1967; Grades K - 3

Ah-di is a young Indian boy who lives with his family in the desert country. One morning he awakened to a feeling that the day was going to be special. It was the day of Ah-di's fifth birthday and Ah-di must search for the surprise which awaits discovery. While searching, Ah-di has a marvelous time and finds two surprises instead of one.

The story is well written and will delight the young reader. It is a lovely story, suitable for reading aloud and sharing. Beautifully stylized drawings heighten the effect of the narrative.

It's unfortunate the ***One Little Indian*** title was chosen.

※

Morrow, Suzanne Stark; ***Inatuk's Friend;*** illustrated by Ellen Raskin; Little, Brown & Co.; 1968; Grades 3 - 6

When the seals did not come to the hunting grounds, Inatuk's father told the family they must move to town. Inatuk did not want to leave his friend Soloquay and he did not want to live in Point Barrow. Soloquay gave Inatuk a piece of soapstone and a small carving, telling him that with those things he would find a friend.

The delightful illustrations give depth and grace to this realistic story about a modern Eskimo boy and his family. It is a well-written yet simple tale.

If the book were written today, perhaps the author would have called the people Inuit instead of Eskimo.

>＜

Munsch, Robert and Michael Kusugak; ***A Promise is a Promise;*** illustrated by Vladyana Krykorka; Annick Press, Ltd.; 1988; Grades 1 - 3

Since the Inuit spend a lot of time on the ice at sea, they have devised an imaginary creature called a Qualluppilluit to keep small children from the dangerous crevices formed in the ice. The Quallupilluq wears a woman's parka made of loon feathers, and, according to the stories, grabs children when they venture too close to the cracks in the ice.

Allashua tells her mother she is "going fishing in the cracks in the ice". When she is warned of the dangers of the Qualluppilluit she promises "to go fishing in the lake and not in the ocean and a promise is a promise".

Well, it doesn't turn out that way and Allashua finds herself in trouble. Mother, however, is able to make promises work for them and in the end everything turns out fine.

The book is a pure delight, blending a warm, loving family into an adventurous story that will enchant children. Even the scary parts are handled with the competency of Mother outwitting the Quallupilluit with intelligence and good humor. Their home is an ordinary house and Allashua's family is typical and up-to-date. The illustrations are lovely and filled with color. It is an absolutely wonderful book.

Annick Press was a believer in Robert Munsch and his stories. Mr. Munsch became Canada's number one author. Mr. Kusugak is Canadian Inuit (Eskimo) who builds stories on the oral traditions of the Inuit people.

→←

Murphy, Claire Rudolf; *A Child's Alaska;* photographs by Charles Mason; Alaska Northwest Books; 1994; Grades 3 – 6

In a delightful combination of narrative and photographs that mingle on every page, the child reader is introduced to images of the spectacular landforms, animals, and people of Alaska. Cultures and everyday lives of Alaskan people are the focus of this multi-faceted book.

Opening the book is a map of Alaska with graphics of animals of the state. On the first pages there are two pictures on two pages; an eagle on one page and on the other page is a lake with the Alaska Range in the background. The captions are grouped together with triangles pointing to the picture being described. Most children found no trouble figuring out the format.

In simple phrasing, the book examines the everyday life of Alaska's children. "Whether they live in the city or in the bush, young Alaskans might do ordinary things like belong to Scouts, ride bikes, or watch television. But since this is Alaska, children might also stand in their yards and watch green and pink northern lights dance across the evening sky or look out their bedroom windows to see a thousand-pound moose chomp its way through the family garden."

Glaciers, tundra, magnificent mountains, and Alaska's amazing animals breathe with life in the pages of the text. Human lives are also examined respectfully with appreciation for the contributions of various cultures. A glossary at the end of the book is very helpful and gives pronunciations for many words. A coffee-table style book, it would be great for a child's room.

Claire Rudolf Murphy lives in Alaska and is the author of many books and articles. She lives in Fairbanks with her family. Charles Mason is an award winning photojournalist who also lives in Fairbanks.

→←

Nabokov, Peter, ed.; ***Native American Testimony, An Anthology of Indian and White Relations: First Encounter to Dispossession;*** Crowell; 1978; Grades 6 - Up

Peter Nabokov has selected material from a variety of sources and presents a series of powerful and illuminating documents. It is a history of relations between Native people and Europeans as observed by the Indians who lived the experience. The documents come from government records, letters, speeches and autobiographies. The voices of Indian America are assembled in a remarkably vivid collection.

An old man recalls his first glimpse of a creature who "looked like a man...but had wool all over its face." A Chickasaw Elder remembers his boyhood experiences on the tragic Trail of Tears. A Micmac Indian relates the story of how one Indian turned the tables on his aristocratic audience. Native Americans share their responses to the stranger, the settlers, the government, and the invader.

The book is illustrated with photographs and maps which present a legitimate and moving record of American history. The reality and power are honest.

→><←

National Museum of the American Indian; ***When the Rain Sings, Poems by Young Native Americans;*** Smithsonian Institution in association with Simon & Schuster Books for Young Readers; 1999; All ages

An exceptional collection of thirty-seven poems by young Native Americans is included in this book. Students aged seven to seventeen participated in a writing program sponsored by the Wordcraft Circle of Native Writers and Storytellers. The poems are vibrant, honest, and profound. Photographs and artifacts from the Smithsonian's National Museum of the American Indian (NMAI) were inspirations for the poetry and serve as illustrations for the text.

Nations represented are Ojibwe, Lakota, Omaha, Navajo, Cochiti-Kiowa, Tohono O'odham, Hopi, and Ute. Much information is included in the Forward, "About Wordcraft Circle and This Book", Introduction, Acknowledgements, Indian Nations Represented, Object Information, and Photo Credits.

The poems and artifacts are incredible. "Empty Cradleboard" (Ojibwe) is a touching poem opposite a picture of a cradleboard from the Michilimackinac region. A beautiful Akimel O'odham basket is facing the poem "Beautiful Flower". A fourteen-year-old Cochiti-Kiowa student writes about "Bingo Bread…I watch their hands work unconsciously, pounding and kneading the dough, making immaculate round loaves."

In the introduction, Elizabeth Woody (Confederated Tribes of the Warm Springs Reservation of Oregon) has this to say about the project: "So full of self-knowledge, health, and expressive designs of their own making, these young people and their poems articulate the future of our communities."

This book is a treasure.

→✦←

Naylor, Phyllis Reynolds; *To Walk the Sky Path;* Follett; 1973; Grades 6 - Up

Billie is a ten year old Seminole boy caught in a world between the modern and traditional. Billie must resolve inner conflicts and decide what role he will take as a Native child living in a modern world. At school he learns the tools necessary for acceptance in the dominant society while at home he learns the legends and rituals important to the Seminole. Gently interwoven into the story is the role of Billie's beloved Grandfather and the influence he has on Billie's life. The death of the Grandfather and the impact on Billie is dealt with compassionately and with insight.

The book competently deals with the conflicts of cross-cultural living yet retains the entertainment effect to hold interest.

Anishinabe children reported satisfaction with the book.

Ms. Naylor has written one-hundred-twenty-five books and has established The Phyllis Naylor Working Writer Fellowship.

Norman, Howard; ***Who-Paddled-Backward-With-Trout;*** illustrated by Ed Young; Little, Brown & Co.; 1987; Grades K - 3

A young Cree boy, Trout-With-Flattened-Nose, is not happy with his name. He wants a name he "can be proud of." He thinks of several. Perhaps he will be "Who-Can-Sneak-Up-On-Owls", but that doesn't work out so he thinks of more. His final choice is "Who-Paddles-a-Canoe-Better-Than-Anyone" and he sets out to earn his new name.

The humor in this story is engaging and right. It will have strong appeal to children's sense of fun-loving adventure. Ed Young's black and white illustrations are strong and add to the over-all pleasure of this book.

An introduction by Howard Norman tells us: "This story was told to me by George Wesukmin ("Sour Berry") when he was eighty-two years old. He lived in a Cree Indian village near Gods Lake in northern Manitoba, Canada. In his village, if you were not happy with the name your parents chose for you, you could try to earn a new name."

Mr. Young received a Caldecott Medal in 1990 and Caldecott Honors for two books.

→←

North American Indian Travelling College; *Legends of Our Nations;* North American Indian Travelling College; 1984; Grades 5 - 6

Twenty-six legends are included in the book. These legends present us with a lesson or tell us why or how things in the world came to be. On first reading, the stories may appear to lack fluidity, but that is because these stories are oral traditions, not just prose. Read these and imagine the storyteller's pauses and nuances and it all makes sense.

"Become immersed in the stories of how the corn was originated, how the robin received his song or how the world was created. Let the stories or legends carry you away into another world and enjoy the fantasy, the unknown and in some cases the truth. Let these stories and legends open a new horizon…" The storytellers hope this book will "become your favorite book and the stories and legends will be passed on…" Let's hope so.

The black and white line drawings are marvelous.

O'Dell, Scott; ***Black Star, Bright Dawn;*** Houghton Mifflin; 1988; Grades 5 - 6

Bright Dawn lives in Womengo, Alaska, with her mother, Mary K. and her father, Bartok. Black Star is the white dog, part husky but mostly wolf, who Bright Dawn chooses to lead her father's dog sled team. "He was the purest white, with a black star on his forehead and black slashes under big eyes. But of everything, it was his eyes themselves that captured me...They were ice blue..."

It isn't until Bartok is trapped on an ice floe and loses some fingers as well as his courage that Bright Dawn's life changes dramatically. The family moves to Ikuma and some of the men of the town ask Bartok to represent them in the Iditarod, the 1,000 mile Anchorage to Nome dogsled race. Unfortunately, Bartok breaks his shoulder and Bright Dawn takes his place in the grueling race.

Children will probably like this story even though there are some truly improbable events in the plot. First of all, it would be highly unlikely that such a novice would be in a race such as the Iditarod. Bright Dawn is attacked by moose, loses half her team, becomes stranded on an ice floe and wins the $2500.00 Sportsmanship Award.

Bartok's character is one-dimensional; not the kind of man who would be called "chief man of our village...the one that everyone listens to." And as far as being the best hunter in the village, when Black Star wouldn't move, Bartok "took the whip to him... Then my father walked on the frozen creek and fell through the ice up to his neck." Overall, the manipulative hand of the author is evident.

⸻

Ortiz, Simon J.; ***The People Shall Continue;*** illustrated by Sharol Graves; Children's Book Press; 1977; Grades 1 - 6

Harriet Rohmer, the series editor, sums up the book well: "This is an epic story of Native American people. It extends in time from the creation to the present day; it touches all aspects of life; it speaks in the rhythms of traditional oral narrative. Essentially, this is a teaching story…It's purpose is to instill a sense of responsibility for life…the words of the story transmit the spirit of the people."

Simply and honestly, Ortiz presents a narrative of creation, survival and hope. It is a story he "realized they must share" with all people. Sharol Graves, who is Ojibway, has illustrated every page in bold, wondrous color. Ortiz is Acoma. This is a book that should be read by children everywhere. Available via Internet sites, this book would be a wonderful gift to a family.

⸻

Osofsky, Audrey; ***Dreamcatcher;*** illustrated by Ed Young; Orchard Books; 1992; Grades K - 2

Woven around the Ojibway dreamcatcher is a story of a baby in the cradleboard dreaming good dreams. "In the moon of the raspberries in a time long ago a baby sleeps, dreaming. Dreaming on a cradleboard wrapped in doeskin soft and snug…"

The Ojibway (Anishinabe), wove nets called dreamcatchers to protect their babies from bad dreams. The nets let only the good dreams through.

The book jacket says that Audrey Osofsky became "fascinated with an old dreamcatcher in the Hinckley Fire Museum" that led to "extensive research about the Ojibway culture."

Ed Young's stunning, colorful pastels powerfully reflect the life of the Anishinabe. Mr. Young received the Caldecott Medal in 1990 and Caldecott Honors for two books.

>*<

Paige, Harry W.; *Johnny Stands;* Warne; 1982; Grades 5 - 6

Johnny Stands, a fourteen year old "Sioux Indian" lives with his elderly Grandfather in a "tar-paper shack" on a reservation. A strong bond grows between them that is rooted in the traditions of his grandfather. A social worker arrives to inform Johnny that he must live with an aunt in the city because his grandfather is too old to care for him. It is then that Johnny and his grandfather decide to "run away". Thus begins a series of adventures.

The book is cause for concern in a number of areas. For instance: "A chorus of hau's...answered his questions." "A scattering of hau's ran through the crowd." "And now the Indian people... break into our place...and call us prisoners and talk of shooting." The medicine man "would give money...to tell them things that were not as true as his grandfather's words." In reference to ceremonies - "The younger children screamed, frightened by the darkness and the wild cries of the singers." "…among them a few Indians, in their ragged jeans and denim jackets...There were men in neat suits.." The men in neat suits is in reference to the white men.

And in the end Johnny "would learn what was right and good, and he would come back and tell his people." These are not occasional stereotypical phrases - the book is filled with them.

>‹

Parish, Peggy; **Good Hunting, Little Indian;** illustrated by Leonard Weisgard; Addison-Wesley; 1962; Grades K - 3

The book is intended as a lighthearted picture book for young readers. Little Indian ventures forth with his bow and arrow to hunt. When he is not successful, he turns to go home only to be chased by a wild boar, which he ends up riding. His father kills the boar and everyone has a feast.

Native people are depicted as comic, one-dimensional characters. Customs and values of Native people are distorted, inaccurate and pejorative. The book suffers from a defect of focus. Say "no" to this one.

>‹

Parish, Peggy; **Granny and the Indians;** illustrated by Brinton Turkle; Macmillian; 1969; Grades K - 3

Granny is one of those indomitable people who can handle all situations. When the "Indians" give Granny trouble, she takes on the whole tribe all by herself. Of course, Granny wins.

Insulting overtones permeate the book. Native people are characterized as silly, childish and ridiculous. Young readers thoroughly enjoy this book which makes it even worse. The illustrations are a source of ridicule and mockery which heightens the negative effect. The book is totally void of sensitivity.

Peggy Parish is author of the popular Amelia Bedelia books. Her nephew continues writing the Amelia Bedelia books.

→←

Parish, Peggy; ***Let's Be Indians;*** illustrated by Arnold Lobel; Harper and Row; 1962; Grades 3 - 6

Craft projects centered on "Indians" is the basis of the book. The reader can make and wear a complete "Indian" costume and then learn the rules for "Indian" games. There are directions for making ceremonial masks, musical instruments and a cooking rack.

This book is definitely off the track. The title suggests that all it takes to be an "Indian" is a construction paper headband and some wallpaper beads. The crafts do not use materials that real people would have used, but instead focuses on things around the home. There is not a look at the tribes or culture of Native people. It would seem from the book that all "Indians" are alike. The illustrations all focus on white children dressing up in their "Indian" costumes.

The corruption of the material is unacceptable. Negative stereotypes abound and are reinforced via the superficiality of the text. It is an offensive, demeaning, inaccurate book. Can you imagine a book - "Let's Be Italians" or "Let's Be Swedes"?

Arnold Lobel, favored artist, a master of the whimsical and imaginative, somehow got mixed up with this one.

Parish, Peggy; ***Little Indian;*** illustrated by John E. Johnson; Simon and Schuster; 1968; Grades K - 3

"Little Indian" goes into the forest to find a name for himself, but finds it isn't easy. He has some encounters with animals that are not successful. When his father discovers a turtle clinging to his pants, he gives him the name Little Turtle.

The book is a distortion of the name-giving customs of some tribes and a mockery of the beliefs of Native people. An image of "Indians" being laughable characters with little human value will be reinforced.

Parker, Arthur C.; ***Skunny Wundy, Seneca Indian Tales;*** illustrated by George Armstrong; Whitman; 1970; Grades 3 - 6

Presented in the book is a series of Seneca Indian tales. The stories reflect the importance of the forest animals in Indian culture. Different creatures took on special traits as shown in the retelling of these tales.

Arthur Parker writes with authority. He was a well-known anthropologist and museum director whose father's family belonged to the Seneca tribe. There is a moral to each tale. It is an excellent book to share orally or to use for storytelling.

Exquisite black and white drawings heighten the effect of the narrative.

⸻

Parnall, Peter; *The Great Fish;* illustrated by the author; Doubleday and Co.; 1973; Grades K -3

"Charlie sat at his grandfather's feet, enjoying the warmth of the old cabin. Outside a cold wind blew. It was the time of year when yellow leaves dipped and bucked through the air. It was the time of year when dry corn stalks chattered, and the air was heavy with the smell of fermenting apples."

Charlie's grandfather, William Three Feathers, tells many stories to Charlie, "Tales of the Great Elk of the West Mountain," "The Tale of the Winter when the Wolves Lost their Fear of Man" and "The Tale of the Night Demon Owl". In this story, Grandfather tells of the King of the Fish and how the Indians were saved from starvation.

The book jacket informs the reader that "Peter Parnall has created a fable that serves as a particularly poignant reminder of a heritage we have all but lost". It is obvious from reading the text that Mr. Parnall has an "intense interest in conservation". Clearly, this fable has been created to send a message to children about the need for responsibility in caring for the earth. To sell this idea, Mr. Parnall has selected Indians as the messengers.

The great fish "...loved the sun and the sparkling gravel, as does the Indian. He loved the freedom to hunt and move with the current, as does the Indian. He loved the clean sight and smell of the water, as does the Indian." The people are never referred to other than as Indians - no tribal identity is given.

As it stands, **The Great Fish** is written for the cause of ecology. There is no feeling of tribal life, and the boy and his grandfather appear to be historical Indians in a contemporary setting. In order to make a strong environmental message, the author has chosen to use Indians as manufactured prophets. While it's true that Native people lived the philosophy espoused in the story, the book is selling a cause.

Parnall has quite a background in illustrating books dealing with Native people. He is a sensitive and insightful writer and treats the Native people with respect and honesty.

Mr. Parnall is the recipient of a number of awards including three Caldecott Honor books written by Byrd Baylor and illustrated by Mr. Parnall. The books honored are: **The Desert is Theirs,** 1976*;* **Hawk, I'm Your Brother,** 1977*;* **The Way to Start a Day**, 1979. He has written and/or illustrated over eighty books.

→✦←

Penner, Lucille Recht; *The True Story of Pocahontas;* illustrated by Pamela Johnson; Random House; 1994; Grades 1 – 2

The book is an easy reader designed for young children to be successful and excited about reading. Introductory pictures show Pocahontas in a very skimpy dress and tells how her father has many wives and "more than a hundred children." In simple text, the Powhatans appear bewildered and watch as the Englishmen begin "chopping down trees. They build a fort, a church, and little houses." A gun is referred to as a "big stick" that goes "Boom! Boom! Smoke and fire shoot out. A bird falls down dead. Is this magic?"

The Powhatans trade corn for "pretty glass beads, belts, and little mirrors." Later when Captain John Smith is with Powhatan, he is pushed down and men "raise their heavy clubs." As the story continues, Pocahontas rushes forward, throws her arms over Smith's head, and the chief calls back his warriors. "Pocahontas has saved the life of Captain John Smith."

The book continues in this vein and then people wonder how children come by their stereotypical attitudes. In reality, Powhatan's name was Wahunsonacock; the name of the village was Powhatan. Historians deny the story of Pocahontas saving John Smith and believe that Smith made up the story. Of Smith, many historians report that he was "a liar."

When Pocahontas marries, she goes to England. According to the book, "Pocahontas stayed in England for the rest of her life. But the people of America will always remember her."

The text leaves out the part about Pocahontas dying at a very young age. Historians believe that it was smallpox that killed her.

The fact that the book is called "The True Story of..." is incredible. Children will have a head full of stereotypes and misinformation.

※

Perrine, Mary; ***Nannabah's Friend;*** illustrated by Leonard Weisgard; Houghton, Mifflin; 1970; Grades K - 3

Nannabah is a young Navajo girl who must face the task of taking the sheep to the canyon. It is the first time she must go alone. Grandfather said a Navajo prayer to help her, but she was still afraid. Nannabah creates a small hogan and two dolls from mud to keep her company, but she is still lonely. Eventually she meets another young girl who is also tending sheep with whom she can share companionship.

The author perceptively writes about a different step each child must go through in the growing process. The story is told in a sensitive yet simple manner while also dealing accurately with Navajo life.

The illustrations create an aura of color and convey the sense of the desert and the quality of life among the Navajo.

※

Perrine, Mary; ***Salt Boy;*** illustrated by Leonard Weisgard; Houghton, Mifflin; 1968; Grades K -3

Salt Boy is a young Navajo boy. He wanted something only his father could give but he was afraid his father would be against it. When he finally did ask, he was told the time had not yet come. Salt Boy must continue tending the sheep as he had always done. One day a big storm came and Salt Boy showed his courage by saving a small helpless lamb. Thus he gained his father's respect and earned his greatest wish.

This simply told tale draws added strength from dramatic illustrations in red, brown and black. The children who read the book found the name Salt Boy confusing and wondered about the origin of the name. No explanations were found.

⇥⇤

Phillips, W.S.; ***Indian Campfire Tales;*** Platt & Munk; 1963; Grades 3 - 6

The book comprises the retelling of several Indian stories about various animals. The book is vague on tribal origins of the tales and adds no depth to a child's knowledge of Native people. "Indian" drawings are used throughout the text. The drawings are numbered and are explained at the back of the book.

This collection of stories is an example of generic "Indian tales". The introduction states that "…the stories are histories of the tribes", which is extremely misleading for the child reader. There is nothing in this book that distinguishes it from the abundance of over-simplified books about Native people.

The introduction states "…the stories are histories of the tribes." What tribes? Children will not understand that there are Nations of Anishinabe, Iroquois, Tohono O'Odham, and other strong tribal groups across the country.

Pine, Tillie S. and Levine, Joseph; ***The Eskimos Knew;*** illustrated by Ezra Jack Keats; McGraw-Hill; 1962; Grades K - 3

> The Eskimos had to cope with a harsh, severe environment. The geographic location of the Eskimos seems bleak and unrelenting. The Eskimos showed ingenuity and inventiveness in solving the problems related to the environment. The books shows how the Eskimos did things and how we use those same principles in our present times. Each basic principle is illustrated using a simple experiment.
>
> The book also includes some details of Eskimo life, the environment and shows the resourcefulness of the Eskimo.
>
> The pictures are stereotypical and the information is sparse.

Pine, Tillie S. and Levine, Joseph; ***The Incas Knew;*** illustrated by Ann Grifalconi; McGraw-Hill; 1968; Grades K - 3

> The Incas of Peru had a phenomenal culture. The book tells some of the amazing things the Incas knew and did centuries ago. They knew how to construct suspension bridges, they dug underground irrigation systems for their crops and they devised a calendar. The book tells of many more impressive inventions of the Inca Indians. It also shows how we apply those same ideas to our present day living. A few simple experiments demonstrate the techniques employed by the Incas.

The Anishinabe, Asian and white children who reviewed the book didn't think it was bad. They thought the author and illustrator had attempted to deal honestly with a book for primary age children.

⇥⇤

Pine, Tillie S.; ***The Indians Knew;*** illustrated by Ezra Jack Keats; McGraw Hill; 1957; Grades K - 3

The Indians knew how to do many things and this book shows how they did some of them. There are examples of how they could build canoes, preserve food, use the moon as a calendar, start a fire without matches, make paints and dyes, fertilize plants and make an arrow fly straight.

It would appear that the author has attempted to deal sensitively with the material presented, but it is too simplified. All the Native people are categorized as "Indians" without any tribal affiliation.

The format of the text is threefold. First the "Indians" are shown in the past doing an activity, then the reader is shown how things are done today followed by some simple science experiments "you can do". By using "Indians" in the past tense, "you" becomes the unstated non-Native child and the "Indians" are relegated to history.

The science experiments are typical primary grade lessons. In spite of the shortcomings, the Anishinabe children who reviewed the book enjoyed it. They took "you" as referring to themselves in the present day and they became vigorously involved with the activities.

※

Pistorious, Anna; ***What Indian is It?*** Follett; 1956; Grades 3 - 6

Each page of the book poses a question that is of interest to the young reader. There are questions such as, "Who invented the only Indian alphabet?" or "What Indian invention was used by the Navy?" Many questions are asked and the answers are given on each page. Full color illustrations accompany the questions. The book would be a way to stimulate class discussion on the contributions Native people have made to society.

The book is simplistic in approach and children need to realize there is no depth to the material. It's like the Sunday comics page with a learning section that includes a question and short answer. It picques the interest, but that's all.

※

Poatgieter, Hermina; ***Indian Legacy: Native American Influences on World Life and Cultures;*** Julian Messner; 1981; Grades 5 - 6

The scope of information included in the book is so large that the text is more a listing than a narrative. There are sixteen chapters that include a standard formula - articles on government, conservation, helping the first Europeans in the Americas, cotton and other fibers, Indian inventions and the arts. Corn and potatoes each have their own chapters while another chapter is devoted to other foods.

A wealth of valuable material is contained in the book that deals with the many contributions Native Americans made to the world. It is the type of book that children seek out when doing "research" on "Indians". Children need to be encouraged to seek out an array of materials when doing research projects and this book may be one of those selections. Since the book is historical in nature, children should be made aware of the fact that issues dealing with contemporary Native people are absent. When using this book, the child reader needs to realize the limitations.

→←

Rachlis, Eugene, (narrative by); *Indians of the Plains;* American Heritage Publishing Co., Inc.; 1960; Grades 5 - 6

Part of the American Heritage Junior Library, the book is filled with historic photographs, drawings, rare prints, reproductions of color paintings, maps and documents of the time period. The purpose of the book is "to help encourage a sense of history in young readers..."

What sense of history will young readers have when they read the following passages? - "War was the Indian's career and his hobby, his work and his play. With the possible exception of the buffalo hunt, no activity of the Plains Indians was more important than the business of warfare." And "Tribe ruthlessly massacred neighboring tribe. Enemies were often scalped, tortured, and killed in pure revenge." And "Indians were generally poor fighters. They tended to scatter and run." Or "...were planning a scalp dance to celebrate."

The matter of religion is handled unsatisfactorily: "Or that death in battle could be prevented, by rites performed over a bundle of sacred objects - even if those objects were only a pipe, tobacco, some grains of corn, and a feather? Or that the gods would respect a man who fasted and tortured himself? This trust in supernatural magic was given many names by the Indians." "Sun Dances of other tribes featured like tortures."

Throughout the text, when referring to religious practices, the author chooses words that are demeaning to Native beliefs. Objects "were supposed to protect the entire group." The pipe "was supposed to have been given". Spirituality involved a belief system not a supposition. There is a feel to the narrative that is insensitive to the religion of Native people.

Many of the historic photographs show warriors holding "enemy scalps", women doing all the work, the Sun Dance being a form of torture, and "Indians" murdering innocent families.

Overall, there are sweeping generalizations made that overlook the family, cultural and religious life of Native people.

→><←

Radford, Ruby L.; ***Sequoya;*** illustrated by Unada; G.P. Putnam's Sons; 1969; Grades K - 3

Sequoya was the Cherokee man who designed an alphabet for the Cherokee language. When he was young, his mother told him, "Wise Medicine Men say that lame people can sometimes work great magic." This biography tells about the astounding gift that Sequoya gave his people.

The book is easy to read and well illustrated, but it is slim in content.

⇥⇤

Raskin, Joseph and Edith; ***Indian Tales;*** illustrated by Helen Siegl; Random House; 1969; Grades 3 - 6

A number of stories dealing with the origins of the natural world are retold. Each tale is illustrated. The origins of the tales are not clearly defined nor are we told specifically the tribal group from which they came.

The flaws are probably unintentional, but nevertheless, they are apparent.

⇥⇤

Reid, Dorothy M.; ***Tales of Nanabozho;*** illustrated by Donald Grant; Henry Z. Walck, Inc.; 1963; Grades 4 - 6

Nanabozho is the creator-magician-trickster of the Anishinabe. (Chippewa/Ojibwe) In this book from Canada, the people are Ojibwa. The Ojibwa delighted in telling the stories of Nanabozho, tales of his trickery, strength, wisdom and foolishness.

The Native people of Canada have a vivid energy in their living stories. Included in the collection are twenty-one tales telling of the adventures and exploits of Nanabozho. There are stories of "Nanabozho and the Wild Geese", "How Nanabozho Brought Fire". The author has retained the rich humor, intensity, and adventure of the Nanabozho stories.

In the preface, the author gives credit to the white men for writing down the stories on paper. She says: "…had they not done so, some of these stories might be lost by this time, for the Indian people have turned away from the old patterns of living." That thinking was the norm for decades. What a shame that these words were included in what is generally a very well done book. The book is a faithful retelling of the Nanabozho stories.

The book was awarded the Book-of-the-Year Medal in 1965 by the Canadian Association of Children's Librarians. The Medal is presented for the best children's book by a Canadian author.

→✢←

Reid, William; *Out of the Silence;* Photographs by Adelaide de Menil; New Press; 1971; Grades 3 - 6

The sea-faring Indians of the Pacific Northwest were devoted to art. They erected forests of sculptured columns and maintained one of the most art centered cultures in the world. The book is a tribute to the spirit of the coastal people of long ago.

Black and white photographs reflect the totem pole art in a beautiful, thought-provoking book. It is useful for elementary classes as well as secondary. Highly recommended. Appropriate for all ages.

Bill Reid, a descendant of the last great Haida chief, says he turned to art because "his spirit demanded it".

>·<

Reinhard, Johan; ***Discovering the Inca Ice Maiden, My Adventures on Ampato;*** Photographs by John Reinhard except those by Stephen L. Alvarez on pages 6 – 7 and 36; National Geographic Society; 1998; Grades 4 and up

Nevado Sabancaya, a volcanic peak in the Andean Mountains, began erupting in 1990. The erupting volcano spewed dark ash over nearby Nevada Ampato blackening the snow, "which slowly began absorbing the sun's rays, causing the snow to melt." A section of Ampato's highest summit collapsed. "Within this mix of falling ice and rock was a cloth-wrapped bundle." *The Ice Maiden* is a first person account of the discovery of a Peruvian ice mummy on Mount Ampato on September 8, 1995.

In masterful prose and remarkable pictures, Reinhard guides his readers through his adventures as he and his Peruvian assistant, Miguel Zarate, work to preserve and protect their incredible discovery. Reinhard writes: "Even from 40 feet away, it was possible to see reddish feathers sticking out near the top of the ridge. We had both seen feathers like this on Inca statues at other sites, and so we knew instantly they would most likely be from a feathered headdress." When they discover the mummy, Reinhard made a decision to transport the Ice Maiden down the mountainside before she melted. It was a perilous descent, but the beginning of an astounding scientific journey.

Scientists from all over the world came to study the Inca girl and in "May 1996, a police motorcade accomapanied the ice maiden to the Arequipa airport....she was being transported to Washington D. C. On May 13, 1996, she was taken in a van to the Department of Radiology at Johns Hopkins University Hospital. There some of the world's most advanced technology awaited her."

Combining scientific discovery, Inca society, archeology, and gripping adventure, the first person account soars with energy and excitement. Children experienced a sense of mystery and scientific discovery when reading the text. The photos add immeasureably to a child's understanding of the Ice Maiden and her history. A timeline and glossary at the end of the book is very helpful.

Dr. Johan Reinhard is a National Geographic Explorer-in-Residence, a recipient of the Rolex Award for Enterprise in the field of exploration, and is noted in the **Guinness Book of World Records** for the discovery of the Inca Ice Maiden. He has received many other awards and has written many books and articles.

His book is a delight. It is written with the utmost respect for Native people and culture. Children thought it was "awesome."

→✦←

Reit, Seymour; *Child of the Navajos;* Photographs by Paul Conklin; Dodd, Mead; 1971; Grades 3 - 6

Jerry Begay is a nine year old Navajo boy living on an Arizona reservation. Through text and photographs, the reader follows Jerry as he goes to school and participates with his family at home. Jerry's Indian heritage is still a vital part of his daily life.

The pictures are excellent and the text informative, but limited.

→←

Reynolds, Quentin; ***Custer's Last Stand;*** illustrated by Frederick T. Chapman; Random House; 1951; Grades 3 - 6

General Custer lives vividly in the pages of this book. Custer's life is reconstructed - on his father's farm, as a cadet at West Point, as an officer in the civil war and as an Indian fighter in the West. Custer wanted two things in life, to be a general in the U.S. Army and to be an Indian fighter.

The book is a typical romanticized version of Custer, the hero. Many young readers will be influenced by the hero image of Custer and negative stereotypes of Native people will be reinforced.

→←

Rockpoint Community School; ***Between Sacred Mountains: Navajo Stories and Lessons from the Land;*** Sun Tracks and the University of Arizona Press; 1982; Grades 6 - Up

The adults who read this book had one collective response - WOW! It is a book rich in history, culture, pictures, maps, stories, poetry, essays and much more.

It was "written for the young people of Rock Point Community School on the Navajo Reservation. It was commissioned by the Navajo parents and grandparents on the Rock Point School Board because they wanted their children to be aware of their own unique history and to understand its relevance to the problems and challenges of today."

The students who read the book found it to be a little overwhelming. There is so much material that it can seem formidable to some children. Don't let that stop them from using this informative material. The book should be available to be used by students.

It is an absolutely extraordinary book; honest, pure, and rich.

→←

Rockwell, Anne; *The Dancing Stars: An Iroquios Legend;* illustrated by the author; Crowell; 1972; Grades K - 3

The book is a retelling of the Iroquois story about the creation of the constellation, the Pleiades. It is a story of seven young Indian brothers who loved to dance and play in the forest. The moon decided to trick the boys into dancing in the sky forever. It is also the story of the deep love the brothers have for one another.

Written in simple language, the book could be utilized for reading aloud to children. The colorful, stylized illustrations fold earth and sky into an imaginative oneness.

>+<

Rockwell, Anne; ***The Good Llama;*** illustrated by the author; World; 1968; Grades K - 3

According to the ancient Incas, a great flood once covered the earth long ago. The book is based on this ageless tale of the good llama who led the animals to safety when the flood covered the earth and nearly drowned the sun. The story tells how the powerful sun had to learn to share the heavens with the moon.

Bright, bold illustrations in full color are based on figures from Incan pottery and textiles. It is a lively tale suitable for reading aloud.

>+<

Rockwood, Joyce; ***Groundhog's Horse;*** illustrated by Victor Kalin; Holt, Rinehart and Winston; 1978; Grades 4 - 6

Set in 1750, the story is about Groundhog, a young Cherokee boy, and his horse, Midnight. Groundhog is especially proud of his horse and tells everyone what a remarkable animal it is. But no one else sees anything special about the horse and the people in the village laugh at him.

When Midnight is stolen by the Creeks in a raid on the village, no one will go to get Midnight back since none of the warriors feel the horse is worth the effort. Groundhog sets out on his own adventure to free his horse from the enemy and makes the acquaintance of a new friend named Duck.

The story is a well written, amusing tale about the Cherokees and treats the people in a sensitive manner. Grandfather is portrayed as rather grumpy, but the author is drawing a genuine character, not someone in a romanticized manner. Children will enjoy the action and daring of the story.

※

Rockwood, Joyce; **To Spoil the Sun;** Holt, Rinehart & Winston; 1976; Grades 6 - Up

Rain Dove is a young Cherokee girl of nine years when the story begins. It is her personal story and spans two generations. The reader follows Rain Dove through her family relationships, her marriage to the spiritually powerful Mink and then her marriage to Trotting Wolf. Rain Dove becomes a mother herself and maintains the traditional Cherokee life. Rain Dove's story is the story of the Cherokee. It is a story of dreaded omens, of Spanish ships and strangers whose skin is light but whose souls are evil and foul. We hear the stories of invisible fire and finally Rain Dove and her family are part of the devastation the invisible fire brings. We watch horror struck as the Cherokee are stilled by the flaming torture of smallpox.

A beautifully written story that evokes the first in a long series of tragic events that strike the Cherokee. Excellent book. Highly recommended.

⇸⇷

Rodanas, Kristina (adapted by); ***Dance of the Sacred Circle, A Native American Tale;*** illustrated by the author; Little, Brown & Company, 1994; Grades 3 – 6

A young orphan boy is cared for by the people of the tribe, but there is a lack of food. The hunters came home empty-handed and the people "began to go hungry". The boy listened to the stories told by the "old ones" who "spoke of the Great Chief in the Sky, whose breath gave life to all the world." The young boy sets out alone to find the Great Chief. When the boy finds him, he learns that a special gift will be created to take back to the tribe. A sacred council is called to help the Great Chief create a new animal, the horse, that will bring help and hope to the people.

"For many years to come they would live in happiness, and the boy would have an important place in the tribe as keeper of the Great Chief's precious gift."

The author has done extensive research into the forming of this story. In the credits, the people are called Blackfoot, Blackfeet, and Sihasapa Indians. Blackfoot people usually refer to themselves as Blackfoot; U. S. and tribal governments officially use Blackfeet as in Blackfeet Indian Reservation. Siksika is a derivation of Siksikaikwan meaning Blackfoot person.

With simple text and authentic illustrations, Rodanas tells the tale of the importance of the horse to tribal life. The storytelling and art are expressed fluently and respectfully.

※

Rogers, Jean; ***King Island Christmas;*** illustrated by Rie Munoz; Greenwillow Books; 1985; Grades K - 3

For months, the people of King Island had been waiting for the arrival of their new priest, and now, just before Christmas, the priest was stranded on a freighter. The ship was anchored in the turbulent Bering Sea with waves so fierce that no one could safely venture forth to bring the priest to the island. In an astonishing collective effort, the King Islanders found a way to bring the priest ashore - "Christmas had come to King Island".

It is a delightful book that children will enjoy, not only at Christmas. The bright, colorful illustrations add to the spirit of a lovely story. The Eskimo people are portrayed with sensitivity and warmth, but the child reader needs to be aware that the story is fiction.

※

Rohmer, Harriet, Octavio Chow and Morris Viadure; ***The Invisible Hunters/Los Cazadores Invisibles;*** illustrated by Joe Sam; Children's Book Press; 1987; All grades

The bilingual text is from a legend of the Miskito Indians of Nicaragua. Set in the seventeenth-century, it illustrates the "crucial first moments of contact between an indigenous culture and the outside world".

Three Miskito hunters receive the power of invisibility when they make a pact with the sacred Dar vine. The power enables them to be great hunters and in return, they promise "never to sell the wari meat...never to hunt with guns...only with the traditional hunting sticks." They become famous hunters, but soon the British traders arrive and the hunters break their vow. The climax is chilling as the hunters learn that in breaking the promise, they will always be invisible and must leave their village forever.

The story is from the oral tradition of Nicaragua. The illustrations are vibrant collages which add to the overall beauty of the tale.

⇥⇤

Roop, Peter and Connie Roop; *Ahyoka and the Talking Leaves;* illustrated by Yoshi Miyaki; A Beechtree Paperback Book; 1992; Grades 3 – 5

Ahyoka, daughter of Sequoyah, helped her father develop a system for writing the Cherokee language. The book examines the process that Ahyoka and Sequoyah took in order to develop the Cherokee syllabary.

Ahyoka and Sequoyah had spent "two summers and two winters" drawing pictures of the words in their language. Frustration mounted when they realized they could not draw a picture for every word in the language. How would they draw "anger, sorrow, dusk, autumn"? Frustration also comes in the form of Mother's anger. Mother, worried about the family farm and livelihood, does not want Sequoyah and Ahyoka to continue work on the language.

Ostracized by the community and accused of magic, Sequoyah leaves home and Ahyoka follows him. When Ahyoka holds a book, she asks her father how the marks in the book talk. "That is the secret," Sequoyah answered. "They speak English. We must make them speakTsalagi."

It is Ahyoka who makes the discovery that letters related to sounds and there was no need to have a picture of every word. After twelve years of work the syllabary was finished. Proof of the success of the "talking leaves" came in 1825 when the New Testament was printed in Cherokee and "in 1828 *Tsalagi Tsulehisanuinhi, The Cherokee Phoenix* newspaper, was first published."

Sequoyah and Ahyoka are the only people in history to make up a complete written language.

The book is a well-written historical fiction. An epilogue of historical facts and a bibliography are included that will give the reader information on what happened after the syllabary was completed.

The illustrations add meaning to the text with sensitivity and warmth.

Historical note: The Cherokees, Chocktaws, Chickasaws, Creeks, and Seminoles, known as "The Five Civilized Tribes", asked missionaries to open schools for them with the hopes of proving they were peaceful, progressive, and hard-working. It was the missionaries who felt that Indian languages could never be written.

Peter Roop and Connie Roop are both teachers. They have traveled extensively.

><

Roop, Peter; *The Buffalo Jump;* illustrated by Bill Farnsworth; Northland Publishing; 1996; Grades 1 – 4

In an author's note, Mr. Roop explains that the "site that inspired this story is the Madison Buffalo Jump in Montana. Standing on the cliff, looking down at the ledge where the *ahwa waki* landed as a thundering herd of buffalo plunged over the cliff, made me wonder what would happen if…?

The answer is *The Buffalo Jump.*"

Little Blaze is a fast runner, faster than his older brother, Curly Bear, so he is disappointed when his father chooses the brother to be the decoy that leads the buffalo to their death as they plunge over the cliff. The buffalo jump meant food for the people; it meant skins for lodges and robes. During the run toward the *piksun,* "the buffalo jump cliff", Curly Bear tires, and tumbles in a heap. Little Blaze rescues his brother and the buffalo jump is a success. Both boys are recognized for their bravery and Little Blaze receives a new name, Charging Bull.

Along with *piksun,* other words from the Blackfoot people are used: "*Omuk-may-sto*", Raven and "*Ahwa waki*", the buffalo jumper. Children will enjoy the inclusion of these words.

Illustrations represent the culture, landscape, and lifestyle of the people. The pictures are rich in color and filled with energy. Dramatic scenes of stampeding buffalo add to the suspense of the story.

Peter Roop was the Wisconsin Teacher of the Year in 1986.

Blackfoot people usually refer to themselves as Blackfoot, whereas U.S. and tribal governments officially use Blackfeet as in Blackfeet Indian Reservation. Siksika is a derivation of Siksikaikwan meaning a Blackfoot person.

➤✦➤

Roop, Peter and Connie Roop; *If You Lived With the Cherokee;* illustrated by Kevin Smith; Scholastic Inc.; 1998; Grades 3 – 6

The book is a question and answer format. Questions range from "Who are the Cherokee?" to "What is it like to be a Cherokee today?" Other questions cover homes, clothes, hunting ceremonies, celebrations, schooling, and other topics. Twenty-nine questions are discussed in the text.

"Who are the Cherokee?" They call themselves Aniyunwiga, (Ani Yunwiya) "meaning the Principal People."

"Did the Cherokee scalp their enemies?" gives an indication of how the material is covered. The authors have this to say about the practice of scalping: "Yes, but they did not do this before the Europeans came. They learned to scalp from the Europeans. Even then they rarely scalped an enemy." Most authors avoid reporting that it was the Europeans who brought the practice of scalping to the North American continent. Peter and Connie Roop handle it simply, accurately, but without sensationalizing the issue.

In sensitive prose, the authors discuss Sequoya, (also spelled Sequoyah – Sik-wa-yi)) The Trail of Tears, schooling, worship, and the treatment of those who became sick. History and culture are joined at the end with a section on how the Cherokee live today. "In 1984, there was the first reunion of the Eastern and Western Cherokee since 1838." Traditions and culture were celebrated. "Coals from the sacred fire carried west along the Trail of Tears were mixed with the coals from Qualla Boundary. A new sacred fire was lit from these coals, a fire that will burn as long as the Principal People walk the earth." The Cherokee Syllabary is on the last page of the book.

Overall, the impression is that the authors are respectful and factual in presenting the heritage of the Cherokee. Peter Roop was the Wisconsin Teacher of the Year in 1986.

Full-color illustrations add immeasureably to the text, giving clarity to the games, homes, medicine, and celebrations. The artist is Cherokee. This is a great book.

→⋇←

Roth, Susan L.; **Kanahena, A Cherokee Story;** illustrated by the author; St. Martin's Press; 1988; Grades 2 - 3

As the story begins, we are introduced to an old woman "stirring a hanging pot on an open fire, stirring something yellow, grainy, soupy". There is also a young child - "What are you making?"

she asks. "Kanahena. Real Kanahena..." All this dialogue spurs the old woman into remembering an "old Cherokee story".

The tale is a Cherokee legend about a Terrapin who gets into trouble over the Kanahena and has to use his own ingenuity to save himself.

The illustrations are collages "using natural materials, including leaves, grasses, cotton, and real cornmeal, along with colored paper". It appears to be an attempt to be "artsy", but it fails miserably. Instead we have illustrations of an elderly woman and child that are damaging to Native people. The collages are a mockery, the cover picture is derogatory and the overall tone lacks sensitivity. And hominy is not the same as corn meal mush.

The old woman has hair that is long, fuzzy cotton; her clothes are various "natural materials" that are outrageous and she's wearing a headband of sorts; the overall look is demeaning to Native people as well as the elderly.

After the story is told, the little girl wants to eat some of the Kanahena, and says: "But I want to eat it with a regular spoon." A regular spoon? What will children think she usually eats with?

There's a recipe at the end of the book - it's really corn meal mush (Kanahena), but the woman says: "No one makes it now, no one but me." Really?

Pass this book up.

Roth, Susan L.; ***The Story of Light;*** illustrated by the author; William Morrow and Co., Inc.; 1990; Grades K - 3

> A retelling of a Cherokee tale, ***The Story of Light*** is a pourquoi story that tells of the time when the animals lived in darkness and couldn't see. The animals met and decided that Possum should get the sun, but in his quest he scorched his eyes. Buzzard is next to reach the sun and burns the top of his head so there were no feathers left. Finally, small spider "brought the sun to her animal people. It's The Story of Light..."
>
> Bright, dramatic collages in black, white and yellow illustrate the text.

Russell, Francis; ***The French and Indian Wars;*** American Heritage Publishing, Co., Inc.; 1962; Grades 5 - 6

> The book is part of the American Heritage Junior Library designed to give middle grade children a sense of history. Filled with historic documents, photographs, drawings, rare prints, reproductions of color paintings and maps, the text gives a thorough account of the "French and Indian Wars".
>
> Before a child even begins reading the narrative, a scene of "Indians" ambushing Braddock's army is shown on the cover. The front endsheet is a reproduction of a painting of Count Frontenac watching as "his Indian allies torture a captive." Chapter One opens with another color painting of a "bloody

nighttime raid". It talks about the French, but it is only "Indians" that are drawn with the caption stating: "Men, women, and children were killed and scalped; even dogs and cattle were butchered."

What sense of history will children have when they read the narrative - "...several hundred Abenaki Indians eager for scalps and plunder"? When planning an attack on a nearby garrison they "...might have taken it by surprise if the Abenaki had not spotted a Scotsman about a mile from the fort. His red hair was too much of a temptation, and with a whoop, they were on him. The echoing scalping cries roused the garrison..." - "...the rest were hacked to death and scalped." - "...the blood-lusting Abenaki..."

When the settlers are confronted, the "Indians" would "...taunt the white women..." who were their captives. In reference to a woman with her child it states: "Another snatched up the baby and killed it in front of her." Regarding an old man who was captured: "Then the war whoop echoed, and the knives flashed briefly as they took the old man's scalp."

One of the captives married the "brave" who captured her and later would visit her white relatives "bringing her dusky children with her." Eunace, the captive, "dressed as a squaw...returned to the older, savage life..." The Native people are "savages" who struck down the captives as is repeated endlessly - "An Indian killed her with one blow of his axe."

More derogatory images are seen throughout the text: "The Indians were unpredictable. At one moment a warrior might savagely murder a baby; at another moment carry an ailing child for weeks along the captives' trail. An Indian might turn gentle, but as with a tame wolf, it was a gentleness never to be trusted." "So heedless were the red men of human suffering that the word cruelty seems inadequate to describe their ingenious tortures. Even the gentle Roger Williams called them "wolves with the brains of men." Another passage tells of a crying baby - "...one of the braves, angered by its thin crying, tossed it in a river."

Regarding the captives: "Escape was perilous. Any captive caught trying it was brought back and slowly and publicly roasted to death." There are "...yowling Indians removing the scalps of the dead." - Mohawks who are "...annoyed at not being allowed to torture prisoners..." and "Indians" who snatch children away from their white mothers.

The illustrations are appalling - stereotypical, ominous and extremely degrading. There is a painting showing a "...ferocious Iroquois warrior...He carries an enemy scalp draped over his musket." There are "historical" paintings of "Indians" killing babies, scalping women and torturing their captives.

History has been manipulated in this book to the disadvantage of Native people. War is not an easy subject to write about, but the constant negative depiction of tribal people is insulting. Children need to know that the attitudes expressed in the narrative as well as in the selection of illustrations are demeaning and one-sided. This book can cause a lot of damage to children's sense of history and of their attitudes toward Native people.

Even though the copyright date is 1962, it is still on library shelves. I checked it out on June 29, 2007. Why do we allow the toxins to flow to our children?

Sandoz, Mari; ***The Horsecatcher;*** Westminster; 1957; Grades 6 - Up

>Young Elk pursues his dream of catching and taming horses rather than following the traditions of his tribe, the Cheyennes, and become a warrior. He learns that being a horsecatcher is dangerous and requires great courage. Young Elk learns that if he is not going to be a warrior, he must still assume his basic responsibility to his family and tribe.

>Ms. Sandoz has written a novel with adventure and realism. It is sensitively written and skillfully portrays the life of the Cheyenne Indians. She is also the author of the popular novel ***Cheyenne Autumn.***

>Mari Sandoz is the recipient of numerus awards, including an honorary Doctorate of Literature from the University of Nebraska and she was inducted into the Nebraska Hall of Fame. In 1969, the Mari Sandoz Award was established by the Nebraska Library Association.

Scheer, George F.; ***Cherokee Animal Tales;*** illustrated by Roberts Frankenberg; Holiday House; 1968; Grades 3 - 6

>A retelling of the oral traditions of the Cherokee. The stories relate the Cherokee tales of why various animals acquired certain physical characteristics. An introductory chapter gives a

glimpse of Cherokee history. It is a good example of a pourquoi story.

Black and white drawings are imaginative and give vitality to the text.

→←

Schweitzer, Byrd Baylor; *Amigo;* illustrated by Garth Williams; Macmillan; 1963; Grades K - 3

Francisco, a young Mexican boy, wants a pet. It must be a wild pet, because his family is too poor to feed another animal. Francisco discovered Amigo, a funny, furry prairie dog who wants a boy for a pet. Through patience, love and understanding, Amigo and Francisco come to know each other.

Illustrations are in soft, desert colors bringing the story to life.

→←

Schweitzer, Byrd Baylor; **One Small Blue Bead;** illustrated by Symeon Shimin; Macmillan; 1965; Grades 3 - 6

In rhymed verse, the author captures the mood of wonderment as an old man and young boy speak their dream of a world beyond their own. Move backward in time to a prehistoric campfire as the old man says, "There must be caves just like our own - Somewhere --- And other men like me." Only the young boy believes the dream as the old man sets forth on a journey to learn more about the world. When he returns, he brings with him a new boy. Around his neck, the new boy wears "one small blue bead."

It is a book of unusual power - more than a picture book. The concepts reach into the imagination and compel the reader to grasp thoughts beyond the known. The incredible shapes and scenes of Symeon Shimin's exquisite illustrations fold earth and people together into a oneness of beauty.

Scott, Ann Herbert; ***On Mother's Lap;*** illustrated by Glo Coalson; McGraw, Hill; 1972; Grades K - 3

An enchanting story of a young child being rocked on mother's lap. The young child, Michael, brings toys and puppy to join him. When baby sister awakes, Michael finds there's room for her too, all on mother's lap and wrapped in a reindeer blanket.

Although not stated in the text, this simply told tale is of an Inuit family. The strength of the illustrations convey the feeling of Inuit family life, culture and dwellings. Beautifully illustrated, a pleasure to read.

Seton, Julia; ***Indian Creation Stories;*** illustrated by Marceil Taylor; Seton Village Press; 1952; Grades 3 - 6

The book is a collection of creation stories from North American Indian Tribes. The author has condensed the stories to make them more "readable" and educate children to the "romance" of American history.

The tribal groups from which the stories were derived are not identified. The dialogue is stilted and contains shifting viewpoints, at times speaking of "we, the Indian" and "the Indian." The corruption of the material is inappropriate. At one point, "Nona-bo-jou"quotes the Anglo-Saxon "nothing ventured, nothing gained."

The book is not recommended. Native people do not need their stories changed, adapted or romanticized. Making stories readable for students does not mean over-simplification and manipulation.

Shannon, Terry; *A Dog Team for Ongluk;* illustrated by Charles Payzant; Melmont; 1962; Grades K - 3

Ongluk, a young Eskimo boy, wishes to have a dog team of his own. When he asks about his team, he is told "you will see." The mystery is explained when his father's sled dog has three puppies and Ongluk finds himself the owner and keeper of a dog team.

A delightful picture-story book that will be enjoyed by the primary reader. A great book for reading aloud.

Shannon, Terry; ***A Playmate for Puna;*** illustrated by Charles Payzant; Melmont; 1963; Grades K - 3

Puna is an Indian boy who lives in the Andes Mountains. Puna wins the friendship of a baby llama, Michu. The time came when Michu's mother was taken away to graze with the rest of the herd. Puna helps Michu until she gains independence.

The illustrations are in red, black and white. It is a simple story that will be enjoyed by primary age children.

→←

Shannon, Terry; ***Stones, Bones and Arrowheads;*** illustrated by Charles Payzant; Whitman; 1962; Grades 3 - 6

The book is an introduction to geology and archeology for young readers. Information, which will deepen a child's understanding of the significance of prehistoric finds, is presented in a well written text. It will stimulate interest in pre-history and an appreciation for the scientists who work in this area.

The illustrations are accurate and add clarity and interest to the text. However, the contempory people working on the exhibits are white as are the children watching and looking at the displays. It's too bad the author and illustrator didn't include Native people as active participants and observers.

It's important to make children aware that some of these archeological digs are offensive to some Native people.

→←

Shapp, Charles and Martha; ***Let's Find Out About Indians;*** illustrated by Peter Costanza; Watts; 1962; Grades K - 3

The book is a generalized account of Indians of long ago. It tells about Indian hunting, farming and fishing.

It is a very superficial book with no in-depth study of any tribal group. The content is vague and generic.

―――

Shearer, Tony; ***Lord of the Dawn: Quetzalcoatl;*** illustrated by the author; Naturegraph; 1971; Grades 6 - Up

Quetzalcoatl is the Lord of the Dawn. His name means "the Plumed Serpent." The author studied archeology in Mexico as well as the culture and civilization of the Indians of ancient Mexico. The book is a song, a poetic evocation of a great and wonderful people and their mysterious dreams. A powerful book, it sings to us from the depths of the jungle, from rock carvings and hills, and the beautiful Native people who have accepted the spiritual responsibility for Earth Mother.

Imaginative yet meaningful drawings enhance the mood of the text.

Mr. Shearer is Lakota.

―――

Shearer, Tony; ***The Praying Flute;*** illustrated by the author; Sun Pub.; 1975; Grades 6 - Up

The book is an Indian fantasy which leads us downward into the realms of the Earth Guardians. Old Quanab recites this enchanting tale as he lights his pipe beneath his Memory Tree and waits for the listeners to get comfortable. The reader enters the world of Quill and Altim Elut and experiences a new view of man's relationship with the earth. Little Girl, with her praying flute, becomes the mirror image of our Earth Mother. The serious theme is on destruction of the environment.

Special care has been given to the designs on each page. All illustrations are black and white.

Tony Shearer is Lakota.

→←

Shemie, Bonnie; *Houses of Bark: Tipi, Wigwam and Longhouse;* illustrated by the author; Tundra Books; 1990; Grades 4 - 6

Bonnie Shemie has written a book that combines meticulous research and accuracy of detail into a text that demonstrates the ingenuity of Native people. Bark was indispensable for shelters and the author focuses on three main types of dwellings: the tipi, the wigwam and the longhouse. Detailed drawings show the construction of these houses and the simple text informs about the daily life of the people.

Double-page colored illustrations along with the black and white drawings add a clarity and interest to the text that is a testimony to the inventiveness, skill and resourcefulness of the people who lived in these "houses of bark". Though the text is simple, it is a distilled type of narrative that is informative and accurate. The author treats the material with understanding and intelligence.

Shemie, Bonnie; ***Houses of Hide and Earth;*** illustrated by the author; Tundra Books; 1991; Grades 4 - 6

Young readers are given practical and interesting information from an author/illustrator who has done extensive research, condensed the information and presented it in an accessible and appealing volume. It is profusely illustrated with black and white explanatory drawings as well as with full color pictures.

The narrative tells how the people adapted and improved the houses in which they lived; how they were built, decorated and lived in. Included in the text is information about the earthlodge which dates from AD 700. Larger than the tipi, the earthlodge extended up to 90 feet and formed a village of as many as 100 dwellings.

Shemie discusses how the tipi and earthlodge were laid out according to religious beliefs. She presents facts on burial platforms, sweat lodges and the amazing structure used to celebrate the sun dance. All of this is meticulously explained as a careful means of understanding the structures and the land on the western Plains. She treats the people with respect and admiration; stressing the success of the Native people in achieving a continuum in their life.

"Inside, every family member had a special place, just as each person had a special role on earth."

Shemie, Bonnie; ***Houses of Snow, Skin and Bones;*** illustrated by the author; Tundra Books; 1989; Grades 4 - 6

In the introduction, the author talks about the "severest climate on earth" and says: "The dwellings of northern peoples have always impressed travelers with how much was done with so little, and with how clever the simple can be."

The snow houses were typical of the Inuit people in northern Canada and are routinely called igloo, but "the Inuit call all houses igloos and call the snow house igluvigak." Bonnie Shemie has made detailed drawings to show the construction of the igluvigak as well as other shelters used in the far north. Included in the book are examples of the quarmang with it's stone foundations "that have lasted a thousand years", sod houses, and the skin tents of summer. A simple text also tells how the people lived.

Five color paintings and end maps show daily life and twenty-four drawings illustrate the tools, structures, and basic construction of the shelters. It is an informational book that is accurate and well produced showing the inventiveness and ingenuity of the Inuit.

Shippen, Katherine B.; ***Lightfoot;*** illustrated by Tom Two-Arrows; Viking; 1955; Grades 3 - 6

The story of Lightfoot provides a look at the customs, life, sports and history of the Iroquois. Woven into the story are the legends of the Iroquois, which is part of Lightfoot's education. Lightfoot is growing up at the time of the great League of the Iroquois. It is a story of a boy becoming a man in a setting of maple syrup making and lacrosse.

Tom Two-Arrows, who illustrates the text, is an Iroquois who grew up on the Onondaga Reservation in New York State. Included in the black and white drawings are Indian symbols whose meanings are explained at the beginning of the book.

→><←

Showers, Paul; *Your Skin and Mine;* illustrated by Paul Galdone; Crowell; 1965; Grades K - 3

Although this book is not specifically about Indians, it can be helpful in introducing young children to physical differences of people. In a direct yet simple manner, the book discusses the reasons for varying skin color and other physical characteristics that make each of us unique individuals.

Accompanying illustrations add clarity and interest to the text.

Don't expect this book to change a child's preconceived notion about different people. It may help them understand a basic scientific concept, but will not correct attitudes. It is a genuine attempt to improve a child's outlook, however.

Siberell, Anne; ***Whale in the Sky;*** illustrated by the author; Dutton; 1982; Grades K - 2

In this very simple retelling of a "Northwest coast story," the reader is introduced to Thunderbird, who "watched over the sea and all its creatures". Thunderbird sees Whale chasing all the salmon while frog trembles on the riverbank. Frog tells Raven who tells Thunderbird. At this point, Thunderbird "grabbed Whale in his terrible talons and flew high into the sky...Then he dropped Whale on the highest mountain". Whale "promised to stay out of the river if he could return to the sea". In the end, "The chief of the people told this tale to the carver. The carver made the story into a totem pole". End of story.

The illustrations, in color, are from woodcuts.

Some flaws in the story line are clearly not minor. For instance - the Thunderbird as depicted in this story is not a Thunderbird at all, but a bald eagle. The Native people are not identified, it is just a "Northwest coast story". The "chief" is standing next to the carver with a mask on top of his head. The tale is overly simple and superficial.

Sleator, William; ***The Angry Moon;*** Little, Brown; 1970; Grades K - 3

The text is a retelling of a Tlingit Indian legend. In this imaginative tale, the Moon is the villian. When a young Indian girl laughs at the Moon's face, she is carried off to the sky and made a prisoner. Lupan, her friend, shoots arrows into the sky all that night. The arrows link into a ladder which Lupan climbs and with the help of an old woman's magic, he frees the girl. They are pursued across the sky country by the angry Moon. They triumph by escaping back to their village on earth.

The bold, colorful paintings are beautifully stylized. The artist has adapted original Tlingit Indian designs into the paintings. The book touches both earth and sky with vitality and imagination. It's a great read-aloud book.

→←

Smith, E. Brooks and Robert Meredith (adapted by); ***Pilgrim Courage;*** illustrated by Leonard Everett Fisher; Little, Brown and Co.; 1962; Grades 4 - 6

There is a title and two sub-titles of this account of the Plymouth colony adapted for children. ***Pilgrim Courage:*** "Being Governor Bradford's Firsthand Account of the Escape, Voyage, Explorations and Indian Encounters of the First Settlers of Plymouth" and also "Episodes from the Original History of Plimoth Plantation with passages from the journals of William Bradford and Edward Winslow."

As the book jacket claims, it is also a story of the "troubles with Indians". For instance: "And if they should overcome these difficulties, then there was the continual danger of the savage people, who were cruel, barbarous and most treacherous in their rage and merciless when they captured. The savages were not only content to kill and take away life, but they delighted in tormenting men in the most bloody manner. They would skin alive some with the shells of fishes and cut off the arms and legs of others by piecemeal. Then they would broil these limbs on the hot coals and eat pieces of their flesh in their sight while they still lived."

When they are marching on the seaside, "...they spied five or six men with a dog coming toward them. They were Indians! The savages fled from them up into the woods..."

Interestingly, the Pilgrims are called the "defenders". Such as: "The cry of the Indians was dreadful, especially when they saw the defenders run out toward the shallop to recover arms...Yet there was a lusty and valiant savage who stood behind a tree..." An accompanying illustration matches the text.

"...the men came out and chased the Indians about a quarter of a mile, shouted once or twice, shot off two or three of their pieces and returned. This they did so the Indians might know that they were not afraid of them or discouraged in any way. Thus it pleased God to vanquish their enemies..."

A chapter on the "Friendly Relations with the Indians" isn't any better. "All this while the Indians came skulking about. Sometimes they showed themselves at a distance, but ran away when approached. Once the Indians stole some tools..." There is never a mention of the corn, provisions, and land that the Pilgrims were taking from the Native people, but the text refers to the stealing done by the "Indians".

Later in the book it says: "But on Friday the sixteenth there was cause for alarm. A savage came boldly all alone, walked past the houses, and straight to the meeting house. He would have walked in had he not been stopped at the door…The Indian's name was Samoset…As he was the first savage they could talk to, they questioned him about many things."

There are illustrations interspersed with text that conform to an unwavering pattern of oversimplification and formula that is so common in drawings of "Indians". Though the book professes to present the true Pilgrims, it in no way reflects any authenticity concerning Native people. Men who had preconceived notions of the "savagery" of the people wrote these original journals. Native people possessed the land the Pilgrims wanted. It is understandable that the Pilgrims wanted to make the Native people appear subhuman; it was a way of justifying the conquest of the continent.

Professor Smith is noted for "revitalizing and reaffirming American History for young readers by making original sources available to them". This is a one-sided history; a reaffirmation of negative feelings toward Native people. These journals should have been left for mature historians; not for young people who lack the insight into how history can be manipulated, altered, and dramatized.

→←

Smucker, Barbara C.; ***Wigwam in the City;*** illustrated by Gil Miret; E.P. Dutton & Co.; 1966; Grades 6 - Up

Susan Bearskin's family leaves their home on the Lac du Flambeau reservation and move to Chicago. Susan had been among friends, relatives and familiar places on the reservation. Chicago is strange and unfriendly. Susan's brother has run away from home. Uncle John had told her to "Be brave enough to be someone in that world, then come back and help your tribe."

The story is realistic, reflecting the feelings and adjustments many Indians face as they make the transition from reservation life to urban living. It is the story of Susan Bearskin gently interwoven into the plight of a family showing courage and dignity in difficult circumstances. Simple black and white woodcuts illustrate the text.

The feel of the story shows it's sixties style.

⇸⇷

Sneve, Virginia Driving Hawk; **Betrayed;** Holiday House; 1974; Grades 3 - 6

The story is based on events and documents of the 1862 Sioux uprising in Minnesota. It is the story of the starving Santee Sioux who lashed out at the settlers because of the treachery and broken promises of the United States government. Many of the settlers are taken captive and must travel with the hunted Indians as they try to escape in the cold and snow. It is also the story of Waanatan, a member of the Teton tribe, who received a vision directing him to rescue the captives. Waanaton and a small group of young men track down the fugitives and barter for the white women and children.

The story is historically correct. However, unless the reader is especially sensitive to the story of the Santee, some negative stereotypes could be reinforced. One chapter is called "Slaughter

Slough." The book talks of the "murderous howls of the Indians" or "a bloody scalp dangled from its belt."

Make sure children are aware of the implications involved.

Virgina Driving Hawk Sneve is from the Rosebud Sioux Reservation.

→><←

Sneve, Virginia Driving Hawk; ***The Chichi Hoohoo Bogeyman;*** illustrated by Nadema Agard; Holiday House; 1975; Grades 3 - 6

This is the story of three young girls, cousins, visiting their Lakota grandparents in South Dakota. When a strange man frightens them while on an expedition one day, they are sure they've found a real bogeyman. They nickname the stranger "the chichi hoohoo bogeyman" for three spirits in Lakota, Hopi and white society. The cousins are also alarmed by the mysterious story their Uncle George tells. On another day they again encounter the strange man and that night one of the cousins disappears. As the mystery is unraveled, the girls learn a lesson about kindness. The "strange" man turns out to be deaf.

Black and white drawings reflect the substance of the story. Both the author and artist are Native American.

Virgina Driving Hawk Sneve is from the Rosebud Sioux Reservation.

Sneve, Virginia Driving Hawk; *High Elk's Treasure;* illustrated by Oren Lyons; Holiday; 1972; Grades 3 - 6

High Elk was a Lakota who lived long ago. He had become well known because he had bred an exceptional strain of palaminos. Young Joe, High Elk's great grandson, hoped to once again build a magnificent herd of palaminos. One day Joe and his sister must take shelter from a storm and enter the cave where High Elk once lived. Discovering a treasure in a parfleche in the cave, Joe brings it home where it is kept until an anthropologist and the band chief unlock its secret and value.

By the conclusion of the book, a lost horse is rescued, the family is reunited with a relative, the treasure found in the parfleche is explained, and a colt is born that will continue the line begun by High Elk. Grandmother is a strong presence in the novel, linking old traditions to her grandson's future.

It is a well-written novel of life on a Lakota reservation. Virginia Driving Hawk Sneve is from the Rosebud Sioux Reservation.

Illustrator Oren Lyons is a chief on the Onondaga Reserve. He is a traditional Faithkeeper, a member of the Onondaga Nation Council of Chiefs, and has received the Elder and Wiser Award of the Rosa Parks Institute for Human Rights. Other honors include the Ellis Island Congressional Medal of Honor and the First Annual Earth Day International Award of the United Nations.

Sneve, Virginia Driving Hawk; *Jimmy Yellow Hawk;* illustrated by Oren Lyons; Holiday; 1972; Grades 3 - 6

> The story centers on a young Lakota boy, Little Jim. Interwoven into the story is the fun of growing up on a ranch, along with the beautiful and meaningful tales that Little Jim hears from his family. One area of conflict is the name "Little Jim." How "Little Jim" gets his name changed according to the Lakota custom of merit is the main theme of the story.
>
> It is a book of adventure and excitement that will appeal to children. Reservation life is blended with the drama of the rodeo, the excitement of a dance contest, and the search for a lost mare.
>
> Virginia Driving Hawk Sneve is from the Rosebud Sioux Reservation.
>
> Oren Lyons is a chief on the Onondaga Reserve. Chief Lyons has received many awards including the National Audubon Award and the Elder and Wiser Award of the Rosa Parks Institute for Human Rights.

Sneve, Virginia Driving Hawk; *When Thunders Spoke;* illustrated by Oren Lyons; Holiday House; 1974; Grades 3 - 6

> Norman Two Bull is a fifteen year old Lakota. He considers himself too smart to accept the beliefs of his ancestors.

Collecting agates to trade at the trading post sets him on a perilous climb to the top of the butte where young Lakota men once sought visions. While on the climb he discovers a coup stick and brings it home. Strange and unusual things begin to happen when the coup stick is hung on the wall.

Black and white drawings set the mood of the story. Virginia Driving Hawk Sneve is from the Rosebud Sioux Reservation.

A traditional Faithkeeper, Mr. Lyons is a chief of the Turtle Clan of the Onondaga Nation. He is a member of the Onondaga Nation Council of Chiefs and has received many honors, including the Elder and Wiser Award of the Rosa Parks Institute for Human Rights, the Ellis Island Congressional Medal of Honor and the National Audubon Award. He has an honorary Doctor of Law degree from Syracuse University.

➜✦

Speare, Elizabeth George; *The Sign of the Beaver;* Dell; 1983; Grades 4 - 6

Thirteen-year-old Matt must stay alone in the new Maine cabin while his father returns to Massachusetts for the rest of the family. It is 1768 and Matt, encountering a number of unfortunate circumstances, must learn to depend on the help of a resourceful "Indian boy". The boy, Attean, and his grandfather, Saknis, help Matt acquire the knowledge necessary to survive in the forest.

The author has succumbed to the formula for fiction about Native people. They speak in broken English, appear to be barbarous, and the women are squaws and do most of the work.

Some examples: "With an ugly chill against his backbone, Matt stared at the hideously painted face. Then he recognized Attean...'What's the war paint for?' he demanded. 'Not war paint...Squaws make feast with bear. My grandfather say you come.'"

At the village, there are "savage rites". "Then he was aware of the Indians. They sat silently on either side of the fire, their painted faces ghastly in the flickering light." "Then began a sound that sent a tingle, half dread and half pleasure down Matt's spine. A lone Indian leaped to the head of the line...He strutted and pranced in ridiculous contortions, for all the world like a clown in a village fair."

Throughout the text, the Native people speak in sub-standard English. Attean's sister: "Me Marie, sister of Attean...Me go with." "Attean think squaw girl not good for much..."

Matt wants to teach Attean to read, but: "What for I read? My Grandfather mighty hunter. My father mighty hunter. They not read." When Matt gives Attean the silver watch that belonged to his grandfather: "Probably, Matt thought, Attean would never learn to use it."

In the end, the "Indians" sort of disappear into the forest never to be seen again. Convenient device. Not correct, but conventional.

The book is a Newberry Honor Book. The critical acclaim should have just been critical.

Stan, Susan; ***The Ojibwe;*** illustrated by Luciano Lazzarino; Rourke Publications, Inc.; 1989; Grades 4 - 6

> ***The Ojibwe*** examines the history, values, teaching, traditional life and treaties of the Ojibwe people. It explains the meaning of Ojibwe, Chippewa and Anishinabe. Preparation for the book included help from Sally Hunter, a member of the White Earth Band of Chippewa, and Ona Whitebird, a member of the Red Lake Band of Chippewa.
>
> The book is filled with colorful drawings of Anishinabe life, both historical and contemporary, as well as photographs in both color and black and white. A concluding page gives "Important Dates in Ojibwe History". An index is included. Cover design was created by Ojibwe artist Jeffrey Chapman.
>
> Though slim in content, the narrative and illustrations do an admirable job of introducing the child to the life of the Ojibwe.

Steiner, Stan; ***The Last Horse;*** illustrated by Beatien Yazz; Macmillian; 1961; Grades 3 - 6

> Little No Feather is a nine year old Navajo boy, son of Broken Feathers. At school, his teacher changes his name to Johnny Yazzie. Johnny has an old horse, Old White Star, who can do marvelous things. Johnny must battle to save his old horse from being sold so their owners could buy trucks instead. In an

exciting climax, Johnny successfully wins the battle to keep his horse and shows the importance of preserving traditions.

The book is written in episodes that make it ideal for reading aloud. Colorful paintings provide an atmosphere of beauty and capture the essence of the text.

Steltzer, Ulli; ***Building an Igloo;*** photographs by the author; Douglas & McIntyre; 1981; Grades K - 3

Children are fascinated with igloos and the severe climate of the Northern Arctic. Ulli Steltzer does an impressive job of taking the "igloo" out of the usual alphabet book format and carefully instructs about this ecologically friendly structure. She has given us a distilled text that is informative yet simple, with superb black and white photographs to further demonstrate and explain.

Tookillkee and his son, Jopee, are the builders. As a young child, Tookillkee lived in an igloo, but "like all Inuit of today he lives in a house." He learned to build an igloo when he was a young boy and "Ever since, when he goes hunting far away... he has built an igloo for shelter."

Sensitively produced, it is a narrative picture book that will serve as a corrective for the "I is for igloo" theme of other books.

Steltzer, Ulli; *A Haida Potlatch;* University of Washington Press; 1984; All Grades

In the introduction, Marjorie Halpin has this to say about the potlatch: "In the old days the Haida potlatched to each other - and danced - when a new house was built and when a man raised a totem pole in honour of his uncle, whose noble name he inherited and pledged his life to uphold. Today, not only has the occasion for the event changed but so have the witnesses. The Haida are now potlatching as a people to the world. Through Ulli's camera, you and I are invited to be their witnesses."

She also says, "The faces you will see in Ulli Steltzer's fine photographs are, as Joe David says, shining 'like the light around the sun.' Look closely at these faces and you will see what dancing is about."

Because of the widespread misconceptions about the potlatch, this lovely book is able to teach with sensitivity and authentic documentation the meaning and nature of the potlatch. The text, taken from speeches made at the potlatch and interviews with the participants, offers some profound and meaningful insights.

Because of the format of the book - large black and white photographs with captions and brief interviews - the book is appropriate for all ages. Teachers could use the book in the classroom to read aloud and discuss. Children need to experience what Robert Davidson describes at the end of the text: "You open a door and there are ten more doors, and you open them and there are new ideas for new directions."

Steptoe, John; ***The Story of Jumping Mouse;*** illustrated by the author; Lothrop; 1984; Grades 1 - 3

A young mouse lives as other mice do "in the brush near a great river." Their day is spent hunting for food, but at night "they gathered to hear the old ones tell stories...his favorite was the tale of the far-off land".

The young mouse, "warned that the journey would be long and perilous", begins his travels to the "far-off land". Searching for the mysteries that lie beyond the customs of home, he finds a number of creatures in need and gives a part of himself. This is a story of compassion and fear that turns into joy when the young mouse finds he has metamorphosed into an eagle.

John Steptoe is an amazing and gifted storyteller. The story of ***Jumping Mouse*** is one he heard many years ago. He says: "...and it has always haunted me. It spoke to me about things that I would like to say to children...I know that I've included many things that are my own in this retelling, but that is what a storyteller does in the oral tradition. I owe a debt of gratitude to the original storytellers. I think they would have understood me..."

The illustrations, in black and white, are poignant and luminous. It is a beautiful, sensitive and powerful book. ***Jumping Mouse*** would be a good start for non-Native children to learn about the storytelling of Native people.

Strete, Craig Kee; ***When Grandfather Journeys into Winter;*** illustrated by Hal Frenck; Greenwillow Books; 1979; Grades 4 - 6

This book is filled with the love of Tayhua and his young grandson, Little Thunder. At the Horsebreaking, Tayhua rides a horse that has thrown all other riders and in doing so, wins the valuable stallion for his beloved grandson. It is to be Tayhua's final ride and Little Thunder must face the inevitable death of his grandfather. The relationship between the two is a strong bond with Tayhua teaching Little Thunder how to love and finally, how to face death.

It is a book that children will find appealing, but it does have a couple of places that should be discussed. The description of Tayhua's house is stereotypical. It "badly needed paint, and some of the windows were cracked and broken. There were more weeds than grass in the front yard, and the battered wreck of an old Ford pickup truck with all the windows and doors gone stood in the center." Yes, there are houses like that, but children need to know that it is not typical; that there are many types of houses. Also, Little Thunder's mother, Elk Woman, is given some bad press. Tayhua calls her "my two-legged screech owl of a daughter...and her yelling will make the whole house fall on her head."

The plus side of this book is that it stands up well as a whole and relates to Native people as they were living in the 1970s. A discussion of 1979 life in relation to the present day could provide lively discussion.

Surany, Anico; *The Golden Frog;* illustrated by Leonard Everett Fisher; Putnam; 1963; Grades K - 3

> Aurelio is a young boy who lives in a coastal village in Panama. His greatest desire is to help raise money for a village trading boat. He helps his father in the fields but gains little to give of his own. Eventually he stumbles on a fabulous find which has a dramatic effect on his family and the villagers.
>
> The colorful illustrations are based on a ceremonial applique textile made by the San Blas Indian women of Panama. The book is great for sharing in oral story time. Older children would also enjoy it.

Surany, Anico; *Ride the Cold Wind;* illustrated by Leonard Everett Fisher; G.P. Putnam's Sons; 1964; Grades K - 3

> Paco is a young Peruvian Indian boy who lives in the Andes Mountains with his family. Paco must tend the llamas, a job he does not like. He wants to go fishing with the men of the village. Most of all, he wants to catch the great golden trout who lives at the bottom of Lake Titicaca. One morning Paco and his sister, Pepita, take the boat unto the lake to go fishing. Paco learns a valuable lesson that day.
>
> Delightful illustrations capture the mood of this well told tale.

Surpee, Burton and Ross, Ann; ***Bear's Heart;*** Lippincott; 1977; Grades 3 - 6

Bear's Heart was a Cheyenne Indian who was arrested by the United States Army during the winter of 1874-75. As a member of a war party, he had fled from hunger on the reservation after the game was decimated. The government had not kept the terms of the treaty. Bear's Heart was from the Great Plains but was sent to a prison in Florida. While a prisoner, he recorded events of his life in a series of colored pictures. His captors had given him the materials - a school notebook, colored pencils and inks.

The book is carefully researched and follows Bear's Heart from the Plains to prison and back again. All illustrations are those done by Bear's Heart as he recorded a graphic documentation of a part of American History.

Sutton, Felix; ***The How and Why Book of North American Indians;*** illustrated by Leonard Vosburgh; Grosset & Dunlap; 1965; Grades 4 - 6

Though the original copyright is 1965, Price, Stern and Sloan reissued the book in 1985. The format of the book is a question and answer style. The first chapter is entitled: "The First Indians" with questions such as "Where did they come from?", "How can we trace the Indian migration?" and "How did the Indians get their name?" Native people are then categorized by geographic group. "The Northeastern Forest Dweller", "The Southeastern Farmer Tribes", and so on.

Some sample narrative excerpts:

"Work on the farms was done by the women and older children. The men were the hunters and fighters, and they considered manual labor beneath their dignity."

"Perhaps the cruelest Indian competiton of all was self-torture inflicted during sun dance ceremonies of some Plains Indian tribes." The caption under a picture states: "According to Indian superstition, Tlingit medicine man shakes his rattle to drive away the evil spirits which cause the illness of a fellow tribesman." "Most of the chiefs were extremely wealthy, and they took a childish delight in displaying their wealth."

The Eskimos are called "The Raw Fish Eaters" and have this written about them: "Eskimos are shorter than Indians. For the most part, they have sturdy heavy-set bodies, round chubby faces, and are generally fat as a natural protection against the severe Arctic cold."

There are stereotypes, distortions and generalizations. The book is still available on the Internet

→←

Sutton, Felix; ***Indian Chiefs of the West;*** illustrated by Russell Hoover; Julian Messner; 1970; Grades 3 - 6

The book is an account of five great Indian Leaders. It is also the story of the Indians in their struggle to survive and the U.S.

government's shameful treatment of Native Americans. The chiefs which are presented are Sequoyah, Crazy Horse, Chief Joseph, Sitting Bull and Geronimo.

Black and white drawings illustrate the text. The text moves from accuracy to stereotypes and back again. Be wary of some of the wording.

Tannahill, Reay; ***Food in History;*** Stein and Day; 1973; Grades 6 - Up

The book tells the extraordinary tale of how eating habits have influenced human development. Food made history. It was the horizon-expanding quest for spices that opened up the "New World" and food that opened trade routes to the Americas.

The book is lengthy, over 400 pages, but valuable for research. It discusses the American contributions of maize, manioc, potatoes, beans, tomatoes, and other foods to the total dietary delights of the modern world. The foods indigenous to the Americas present a substantial list to the diet of the rest of the world. The book deals with a panoramic view of food on a world scale, so it takes some detective work to find information on foods used by Native people of the Western Hemisphere. However, one chapter is devoted entirely to the Americas with more information throughout the book.

Tapahonso, Luci; ***A Breeze Swept Through;*** illustrated by Jaune Quick-to-see Smith; West End Press; 1987; Grades 5 - 6

Luci Tapahonso has given us a powerful collection of poems that sing with energy and life. Her poems speak of seasons, Hill's Brothers Coffee, secrets of the land, Grandmother, starting school, Pepsi, the birth of a daughter at Christmas, and much more. She is an assistant professor of English, Women's Studies, and American Indian Studies at the University of New Mexico in Albuquerque.

The poems are truly a gift to the reader. They speak eloquently to all people and would be a valuable resource for anyone working with children.

Luci Tapahonso is a Navajo and Jaune Quick-to-See Smith is a member of the Flathead tribe. Together, they have given us a splendid and remarkable book.

→✦←

Tehanetorens; ***Tales of the Iroquois;*** illustrated by Kahionhes; pictographs by Techanetorens; Akwesasne Notes; 1976; All Grades

Tehanetorens is an Elder of the Mohawk Nation. He shares the power of traditional Iroquois stories in this book which is illustrated with black on brown drawings and authentic pictographs. These "teaching tales" were originally published by the Six Nations Museum in pamphlet form.

Some of the stories included are "The Creation", "The Rabbit Dance", "The Wampum Bird", "Thunder Boy", "The Hermit

Thrush", "The Discovery of Fire", "Why We Have Mosquitoes", "The Seven Dancers", and "The Fierce Beast".

This is one of the finest collections of stories available for children. The foreword explains a little about traditional storytelling. "Ideally, the best way for a story to be communicated is in the Old Way - elders gathered with their younger relatives, during the colder months, educating each other within the family circle…However, since stories are not told so often in these days, this book is presented as a stepping-stone, with the hope that those who hear and read these Tales of the Iroquois will have them fixed in their memories…"

John Kahionhes Fadden is a member of the Turtle Clan of the Mohawk Nation. He has illustrated more than twenty books about Native people.

It is a truly wonderful book that is appropriate for all ages.

>|<

Thompson, Hildegard; ***Getting to Know American Indians Today;*** illustrated by Shannon Stirnweis; Coward, McCann; 1965; Grades 3 - 6

The author spent several years with the Bureau of Indian Affairs in Washington D. C. The tone of the book espouses the Bureau's philosophy.

A few introductory pages give a general overview of Indians in a historical perspective. It also discusses BIA boarding schools. Through the activities of the Yazzie family the reader learns about the Navajos. Concluding pages give glimpses of other tribes and noted Indian personalities, but the rapidity in which the information is presented may be confusing to some children. An index plus a pronunciation chart of Indian words is included at the conclusion of the text.

→←

Thompson, Ruth; ***Indians of the Plains;*** Artwork by Chris Price; Photography by Chris Fairclough; Franklin Watts; 1991; Grades 4 - 6

Beginning the text is "The Story of Indians". This takes one page of narrative which includes four pictures and also includes a full page map. "Hunting the Buffalo" is given two pages with lots of space given to illustrations. "Using the Buffalo" is given two pages also, again with drawings taking up many of the pages. The book continues in this style through "Living in a Tepee", "Picture Writing", and so on.

Once you have all this information on "Indians", you can make moccasins, beadwork, and war bonnets. Don't expect any help from the pages explaining these projects, however, because the directions are vague and inadequate.

The pages devoted to making a war bonnet show a white child with painted face and paper war bonnet. The idea is to cut feather shapes out of stiff paper, make "diagonal snips all the way around..." and paint the top part of each feather black "to look like an eagle feather". To make the bonnet itself, you need corrugated cardboard, felt and embroidery thread.

Because of the need for multicultural materials, publishers are cranking books out with little regard for content. The bottom line seems to be dollar signs. People responsible for selecting and buying children's books must be held accountable for the resources they are collecting.

※

Tobias, Tobi; ***Maria Tallchief;*** illustrated by Michael Hampshire; Crowell; 1970; Grades 3 - 6

Maria Tallchief, an Osage Indian, was born in 1925 in Oklahoma. At the age of fifteen, she chose between her two loves, music and dance. She soon became one of the most exciting performers in the ballet world. In 1966, she "hung up her shoes" to devote time to her family.

It is an informative and well-written book which presents a genuine biographical sketch of a famous Osage woman. Delicate black and white drawings add sensitivity and warmth to the narrative.

※

Tolbloom, Wanda; ***People of the Snow; Eskimos of Arctic Canada;*** Coward-McCann; 1956; Grades 3 - 6

Eskimos have managed to survive in one of the coldest, bitterest, most barren lands in the world. Many facets of Eskimo life are explained: How an igloo is made, the task of preparing a skin into a useable hide, hunting tactics and many more. The book deals with the changes brought by a technological society.

The book could be utilized as a social studies supplement. Appropriate for older students as well. Illustrated with maps and photographs.

If a child finds this book, be sure he or she is familiar with the books by Bonnie Shemie, Ulli Steltzer, and David and Charlotte Yue. It would also be important to introduce the word Inuit into a child's vocabulary.

→←

Toye, William; ***The Fire Stealer;*** illustrated by Elizabeth Cleaver; Oxford University Press; 1979; Grades K - 3

The Fire Stealer is a retelling of the Anishinabe story designed to tell how fire came to the people. The hero of the story is Nanabozho, the creator-magician of the Anishinabe. Nanabozho had the ability to turn himself into many things and, in this case, he turns himself into a rabbit who is befriended by a young girl. In the story, Nanabozho teaches the people how to use fire to warm themselves, cook their food and shows them fire's reflection in nature.

The illustrations are variations of collage done in dramatic color. The Anishinabe children who read the book enjoyed the simplicity of the pictures and especially liked the pictographs on the opening pages as well as the natural materials.

It's too bad the author did not avoid the common pitfall of referring to Nanabozho as "an Indian boy", but while it is disappointing, it does not detract from the story. It is only on the back of the book that the reader learns the origin of the tale is from the "Ojibwa" - also known as Chippewa. Children need to know that the people refer to themselves as the Anishinabe.

Elizabeth Cleaver and William Toye have collaborated on other books dealing with "Canadian Indian Legends". Each of them has received numerous awards for their books.

⇥⇤

Toye, William; ***How Summer Came to Canada;*** illustrated by Elizabeth Cleaver; Oxford; 1969; Grades K - 3

This is a legend of the Micmac Indians of eastern Canada. The tale tells how Winter came down from his home in the far north to live and the once green land became frozen. Glooskap, the mythical creator, brought Summer to Canada. Summer persuades Winter to share the land with her. Each reigns for half the year.

Mr. Toye presents this beautiful Micmac tale with simplicity yet with a story line strong enough to stand on its own for storytelling. The illustrations are boldly colored and add to the imaginative images of the text. The pictures feature scenes of icy desolation and colorful tapestries of flowering landscapes. The book would also be effective and worthwhile for older children.

Mr. Toye has received two awards from the Canadian Association of Children's Librarians and the Howard-Gibbon Medal.

Elizabeth Cleaver has received numerous awards including the Howard-Gibbon Award, the Book-of-the-Year Medal from the

Canadian Association of Children's Librarians, and the Hans Christian Andersen Certificate of Honour.

Toye, William; ***The Loon's Necklace;*** illustrated by Elizabeth Cleaver; Oxford University Press; 1977; 1990; Grades K - 3

Back in the 1950s, the story of the Loon's necklace was made into a short film which was very well done and was extremely popular as well. Shown throughout Canada and some parts of the United States, the film was used by teachers and other groups as a means of sharing the culture of Native people.

The tale is a Tsimshian legend about an old man whose sight is restored by a loon. As a reward, the man gives the loon his precious shell necklace "and tossed it to the bird. It fell on the Loon's neck, while a sprinkling of loose shells covered his back. Where the shells touched his black feathers, beautiful white markings appeared."

Elizabeth Cleaver's unique illustrations - collages of torn and cut paper - add to the richness of the story.

Both the author and illustrator have won numerous awards in Canada for their work. The book was awarded the Howard-Gibbon Medal for author and illustrator.

Toye, William; ***The Mountain Goats of Temlaham;*** illustrated by Elizabeth Cleaver; Walck; 1969; Grades K - 3

This tale comes from the oral tradition of the Tsimshian Indians of British Columbia. Set against the background of high, mountainous country, the story tells of the great hunting ability of the men of Temlaham. According to the law of the hunt, they killed only what was needed for their own living needs. Eventually, they became greedy and wasteful. The children began tormenting and abusing the mountain goats. Raven Feather, a young boy, rescued a young goat which was being tormented. When the goats took their revenge, Raven Feather alone survived to tell the story.

Bold, colorful pictures illustrate the book. It is an excellent book for sharing with a whole class for storytelling. The content of the story line makes it appealing for older children as well and creates good discussion.

Elizabeth Cleaver received the Howard-Gibbon Award, the Book-of –the-Year Medal from the Canadian Association of Children's Librarians in 1974 for ***The Miraculous Hind***, and the Hans Christian Andersen Certificate of Honour.

William Toye has received the Howard-Gibbon Award. He received two awards from the Canadian Association of Children's Librarians: In 1961, he received the award for ***The St. Lawrence;*** the other was in 1971 for ***Cartier Discovers the St. Lawrence.***

※

Traveller Bird; ***The Path to Snowbird Mountain: Cherokee Legends;*** illustrated by the author; Farrar, Straus & Giroux; 1972; Grades 3 - 6

Sixteen legends of the Cherokee are retold in this book. The tales tell about the beginnings of the earth and how it was populated only by animals. The animals are able to talk and yet maintain their distinct animal nature. Each tale is prefaced with a brief commentary by the author. A brief history of the Cherokee is discussed in an introductory chapter. The legend of how the Seven-Clan Scribe society obtained a written syllabary is written in a concluding chapter.

Traveller Bird is a full-blood Cherokee-Shawnee-Comanche. Black and white drawings accompany the text.

Traven, B.; ***The Creation of the Sun and Moon;*** illustrated by Alberto Beltran; Hill & Wang; 1968; Grades 3 - 6

Chicovaneg, a young man, is the hero in this beautiful Mexican legend. He rekindles the Sun after it has been extinguished by evil spirits and thus saves mankind. Chicovaneg's son, with the help of the rabbit Tul, creates a moon to provide man with night time light.

The stunning illustrations kindle the imagination as well as reflecting the rich culture of Mexico. It is a fine retelling of an ancient Indian legend.

Turner, Bonnie; ***The Haunted Igloo;*** Houghton Mifflin Co.; 1991; Grades 4 - 6

Set in the 1930s, the story revolves around a young Canadian boy named Jean-Paul Ardoin. Because he is small in stature and has a limp caused by a birth defect, he is the brunt of ridicule and exclusion on the part of a group of "tough" Inuit boys. At one point, the Inuit boys force him into a deserted igloo that they say is haunted, but for Jean-Paul it becomes a life-threatening experience in the face of the brutal environment of the Arctic.

In the beginning, Jean-Paul's family attempts to learn the language of the Native people: "So, how could I speak with Eskimo women? Like this? Kapik kapik...nakomik kapik nakomiki! I would sound like a woodpecker!"

Jean-Paul tells his mother he can teach her one word, because it's what the boys at school call him: "Okalerk...It means hare...It's because I walk like a rabbit." When his mother exclaims that he does not walk that way, Jean-Paul says, "Well, I limp..."

Before the Inuit boys force him into the igloo, he is made to eat raw fish: "Jean-Paul knew he didn't have a choice...He brought the fish to his mouth once, then brought it down again...Waves of sickness rose inside his chest. A bitter, acid taste came into his throat...he sat for a moment with the mouthful of raw fish."

When it comes time to enter the igloo, Jean-Paul has second thoughts. He is very frightened, but the Inuit boys continue taunting and teasing him, eventually leaving him alone inside the igloo with no lights and apparently no way out. A blizzard begins raging outside and Jean-Paul, understandably, feels terrorized.

The three Inuit boys return to town to warm up and they enter the Hudson Bay Trading Post. "There was no heat in the building, for Eskimos and Indians were used to doing without. But compared with the raging storm outdoors, this room was quite comfortable."

Since the Inuit boys neglect to return in time to rescue him, Jean-Paul almost dies as a result of the incident in the igloo and later in the blizzard.

Everything turns out all right in the end, thanks to the intelligence and forgiving nature of Jean-Paul and his family. When he and his mother visit the home of one of his tormentors, the woman, Chinook's mother, is fascinated by the hair of Jean-Paul's mother. "Anana says she wants hair that color of mush. She says how do you make yellow hair?"

The concluding paragraph has Chinook, one of the Inuit boys, still calling Jean-Paul by the name of Okalerk - hare. When Jean-Paul says perhaps they should name his new baby brother Chinook after his new friend, "Chinook stopped what he was doing and grabbed his throat. 'Ukk!' he cried, sticking out his tongue. 'That's no good name for a French baby...'"

"Readers will sympathize immediately with young Jean-Paul..." gushes the book jacket. And why not? All throughout the story he is terrorized, called names, ridiculed for being "lame", almost dies, and is clearly the victim of cruelty. Yet in spite of all his trials, Jean-Paul remains lovable, smart, inventive, and in the end, forgiving. Who are the bad guys in this whole scenario? The Inuit.

Lest you think the reviewer has erred, here's a direct quote from the synopsis on the books' jacket: "But like the runt of a litter, Jean-Paul is taunted and excluded from activities by a group of tough Inuit boys because of his small size and a limp caused by a birth defect." The original copyright date is 1991; it isn't a reprint of an old novel. The book is filled with derision of Inuit people. It is insensitive and unfair.

Houghton Mifflin should know better.

><

Udry, Janice May; ***The Sunflower Garden;*** illustrated by Beatrice Darwin; Harvey House; 1969; Grades K - 3

Pipsa, a young Algonkian, was the only girl in a family of five brothers. All the boys were older than Pipsa except one. Pipsa often cared for her baby brother. Pipsa's father was very proud of his sons' abilities but he never thought of praising a little girl. Pipsa introduced the sunflower seed to her village. All the work of the sunflower garden was left to her. One day, as she was chopping weeds away from the large sunflowers that had grown, she heard something frightening. Pipsa's quick actions that day plus the marvelous sunflower garden changed her father's attitude toward little girls. Drawings in subdued colors illustrate the text.

With publishers rushing to include multi-cultural stories in their basic reading series and other collections, this story has become a popular inclusion.

Some stereotypes flow through the pages, but the most disturbing part of the story is that Pipsa's father does not praise her. Native people cherished their children.

※

Voight, Virginia; *The Adventures of Hiawatha;* Garrard; 1969; Grades 3 - 6

Hiawatha was an Ojibway Indian youth who is a child of the West Wind and the Moon. His abilities come from many spirits. Hiawatha's father tells him he is to help the Ojibway with their struggles against extinction.

Accompanying illustrations are imaginative.

※

Voight, Virginia; *Close to the Rising Sun: Algonkian Indian Legends;* Garrard; 1972; Grades 3 - 6

A collection of Algonkian stories that explain how people came to be and their struggle for survival. The tales are well written and provide background into the lives and customs of the Algonkian Indians.

The illustrations add to the enjoyment of the stories.

※

Voight, Virginia; ***Massasoit, Friend of the Pilgrims;*** Garrard; 1971; Grades 3 - 6

> Yellow Feather was the son of the high chief of the Wampanoag tribe. Later his name was changed to Massasoit, which means "The Brave One," or "The Great One." Massasoit became Chief of the Wampanoags and united neighboring tribes. When the first Europeans arrived, Massasoit offered friendship and taught the Pilgrims to hunt, how to plant and survive in their new land.
>
> The book is written with simplicity and understanding and contains enough adventure to keep reluctant readers interested.
>
> Some of the real issues surrounding Native people and the Pilgrims are avoided. Quite usual.

→←

Voight, Virginia; ***Sacajawea;*** illustrated by Erica Merkling; G.P. Putnam; 1967; Grades 3 – 6.

> The book relates Sacajawea's birth and childhood in the "Shining Mountains," (Rocky Mountains), her capture by the Minneataree (Hidatsa), and her eventual marriage to a French trader named Charboneau. It tells the story of her role as guide for Lewis and Clark in their search for the Pacific Ocean. Sacajawea makes the journey with her infant son, Pompe.
>
> The book is standard fare in relation to Sacajawea and Native people.

>＜

Waltrip, Lela and Rufus; *Indian Women;* David McKay, 1964; Grades 6 and Up

The contributions made to America by Indian women are important. Long before most European women were granted a voice and vote in their affairs, Indian women were accorded the privilege of participating in Tribal decisions. Thirteen biographies are included in the book. Some are well known women like Sacajawea and Pocahontas; others are not so well known. There are women such as Winema, Big Eyes of the Wichitas, Tomassa, and Pablita Velarde. Maria Martinez and Annie Dodge Wauneka also have chapters devoted to them. Also included are Sarah Winnemucca, Neosho, Cynthia Ann Parker, Indian Emily, and Dat-So-La-Lee.

Written with warmth and sympathy, the authors have written an important book. It is informative yet interesting and entertaining. There are no illustrations.

>＜

Warren, Mary Phraner; *Walk in My Moccasins;* illustrated by Victor Mays; Westminster Press; 1966; Grades 4 - 6

The author has set down a story of a white family's adoption of "Indian" children after the parent's were killed in a car accident. Partly autobiographical, the narrative tells of the adjustments everyone makes in the adoption process. There are the neighbors and friends who share various views and attitudes to the newly formed family.

Mrs. Warren's own family started with a "year-old Iranian baby...And only eleven months after that, through the welfare department, they started the adoption procedure for a family of five Sioux Indian children. In June they took the two 'older' girls who were five and a half and seven years of age. The other three children, four, two, and one years old, were picked up as the Warrens moved to a different part of Montana."

An afterword says that Mrs. Warren wrote the book for the enjoyment of "her own instant family, and for the enjoyment of all other adopted families too."

Much of the book is predictable "Sixties" style about the white family adopting minority kids.

One disturbing aspect appears at the beginning of the text. "'You know what I wish?' Mary Beth tried not to cringe when Melody's fingers combed quickly through her hair. 'I wish we could have another Indian mother. Why do you s'pose Indian people, don't adopt all the Indian children like us who need homes?'

"'You know perfectly well why not,' retorted Melody. 'They're too poor, and they have no nice place to live, and not enough food.' She listed all the reasons Miss Perry, the social worker, had mentioned when they had asked."

The implication here is that Native people were not able to care for the children; that it took the goodness of the white people to take the children and give them a home. A couple of adopted minority teen-agers read the book and thought the author did an okay job, but the prevailing attitude toward adopting minority children still prevails. The "Aren't you wonderful for adopting these children because their own people can't take of them" mentality. The author is being honest, that was the attitude taken by social workers. Deplorable.

><

White, Anne Terry, (adapted by); *The American Indian;* Random House; 1963; Grades 5 - 6

The text is heralded as a "fast-moving narrative, which tells the wonder-filled story of the American Indians from prehistoric times to the present". It is an adaptation of *The American Heritage Book of Indians* by William Brandon and has an introduction by President John F. Kennedy. It is supposedly written in an even-handed manner.

This is what the book has to say about the "Indians" of New Amsterdam: "The Indians hung around New Amsterdam, as the colony on Manhattan Island was called, and made themselves a nuisance. They were lazy, insolent, and thievish as monkeys".

The Iroquois are described thusly: "Far and wide the Iroquois were held to be a cruel people. Their torture of captives was notorious. It is quite true that Iroquois women took greatest delight in inventing tortures. While screaming women and children burned the victim with torches and gouged out bits of his flesh with jagged pieces of seashell, the captive would be encouraged to keep singing his defiant death song...it is the Iroquois who first come to mind when we think of torture and death song."

Apparently, everything that happened to "Indians" was their own fault. The book states: "Living, not getting...was also his weakness. It was this that spelled his doom. This was the thing that destroyed the Indian nations. For living, not getting, made a gulf separating whites and Indians". That attitude merely reinforces the notion that the land was here for the taking; that the Native people were too naive to keep the land and use it. What about the European invasion of the Western Hemisphere? It becomes a rather convenient exclusion in the text.

In describing the potlatch: "Such behavior in our society would be called abnormal, but on the Northwest Coast it was the usual thing." One of the initiation ceremonies is discussed as a "dreaded ordeal". "Then, wasted and hysterical, he came out. A dancing woman went out to meet him. In her out-stretched arms she carried a corpse...In the house he was seized with wildness. He bit flesh from the arms of those who were taking part in the ceremony...He didn't really eat the corpse. The ceremony ended with a feast of dog."

In describing the Eskimo people: "...they went through a terrible time. The one good thing the Russians had done was to control the liquor." In discussing when the Russians left, it is said: "...what the liquor did was more spectacular...It had become, instead, the time to swap furs and ivory for whiskey. The Eskimos would go on a mighty celebration and wake up to find winter at hand and nothing in the meat pit. They would then starve to death."

The illustrations tend to reinforce negative stereotypes. One engraving that is reproduced shows "Indians" attacking a family in their home. There are pictures showing "colorful Ottawa", a "resolute Indian", the "fury of a Seminole attack" and a dance described as a "wild ceremony".

The book serves to perpetuate negative stereotypes. Children do not have the necessary experience, knowledge and psychological sophistication to counteract the derogatory images portrayed. There are such broad generalizations made that the child reader will not come to an understanding of the family, culture and belief system of the Native people.

Reading this book page by page, you may be surprised at the kind of information we are putting into kid's heads. Too many adults feel that if it's "An American Heritage" book it must be all right. It's not. Definitely not.

❖

Wilde, Arthur L.; ***Apache Boy;*** photographs by Don Christie and others; Grosset & Dunlap; 1968; Grades 3 - 6

The book relates the story of Noland Clay, a ten year old Apache boy who plays a leading role in the motion picture, ***The Stalking Moon.*** A brief introductory chapter gives a glimpse of Apache history. Fine black and white photography with accompanying text looks at Noland's life on the reservation, in Hollywood and back on the reservation.

The stamp of Hollywood permeates the book. Even some of the photographs, which are excellent, appear to be staged.

The book glamorizes "Indian" life and does not deal realistically with the world Native children live in.

Wilder, Laura Ingalls; ***Little House on the Prairie;*** illustrated by Garth Williams; Harper & Row; 1953; (first published in 1935); Grades 4 - 6

Laura Ingalls Wilder has written a popular series of books about the life of her family in the 1800s. It is a first hand account of pioneer life and the "opening of the American West". For the most part, the "Little House" books are warm-hearted family adventure; some of them don't deal with Native people at all. ***Little House on the Prairie*** is not one of those. Instead, it is a book with glaring stereotypes about "Indians".

It is understandable that Laura and her family were frightened during that time period in United States history. Fear is an accurate portrayal of how the settlers felt. That same element of fear must have been familiar to every Native child on that same prairie; children who were being uprooted from their ancestral homes by hostile settlers and United States military forces. The fear and mistrust felt by Native people is not presented in the text of this book which results in errors by omission.

Six chapters of the book contain the word "Indian" - "Indians in the House", "Indian Camp", "The Tall Indian", "Indian Jamboree", "Indian War-Cry" and "Indians Ride Away". There are also references to "Indians" elsewhere in the narrative.

At one point, Indians come into the house. "She" refers to Laura. "...she looked over her shoulder...and saw two naked, wild men coming...They were tall, thin, fierce-looking men. Their skin was brownish red...Their eyes were black and still and glittering, like snake's eyes..." She describes them as "wild men" and "Laura wrinkled her nose and said, 'They smell awful.'" When Ma gave them food, "They ate every morsel of it, and even picked up the crumbs from the hearth."

Even the dog, Jack, was brought into the scene: "Jack hated Indians", and Ma said she didn't blame him. She said, "I declare, Indians are getting so thick around here that I can't look up without seeing one.'" Pa defends the "Indians" to his family, but one day he was hunting and two Indians came to the house. "Those Indians were dirty and scowling and mean. They acted as if the house belonged to them. One of them looked through Ma's cupboard and took all the cornbread. The other took Pa's tobacco-pouch...They made harsh sounds at each other in their throats."

Pa explains to Laura that the government is making the Indians move and says: "That's why we're here, Laura. White people are going to settle all this country, and we get the best land because we get here first and take our pick..."

In describing the sounds she hears, Laura writes that she heard again the "...wild, shrill, fast-beating sound from the Indian camps." Also, she says: "...the Indians were wildly yelling...that terrible sound came again...They don't need guns. That yell's enough to scare anybody to death..." "...fast, shrill, yapping yells...The terrible war cry came again and again...the war-cries were more terrible than the most dreadful nightmare..."

Laura describes the Native people from the perspective of a child who is overwhelmed by the events around her. "One by one on the path, more and more savage warriors were riding behind Du Chene. Brown face after brown face went by." - "...Little naked brown Indians...and the little Indians did not have to wear clothes...Laura looked and looked at the Indian children...She had a naughty wish to be a little Indian girl. Of course she did not really mean it..." When Laura sees an Indian baby, she wants it for her own. "Laura looked straight into the bright eyes of the little baby nearer her...It's hair was as black as a crow and its eyes were black as a night when no stars shine."

The tone of the book is marked by the negative images presented of Native people. Because children throughout the world read these books, it is important that the child reader is aware of the distortions and the reasons for such negative concepts on the part of a favored author. This "Little House" book perpetuates negative images and stereotypes. It's not going to go away. It needs to be dealt with.

→←

Wilson, Hazel; ***His Indian Brother;*** illustrated by Robert Henneberger; E.M. Hale & Co.; 1955; Grades 3 - 6

Brad Porter was alone in the Maine wilderness of 1809. He waited for the return of his father who was bringing the family to the cabin they had built. When his father didn't return, Brad would have starved to death had it not been for friendly Penobscot Indians. Brad learns the ways of the forest from his Indian brother, Sabattis. It is a story of courage and adventure in a cross cultural setting.

Though fictionalized, the story is based on a real incident. Brad's parents show the settlers stereotyped view of the Indian and are quite vocal about their perceptions. As with many such stories, the child is saved by "friendly" Indians.

Wolfson, Evelyn; *American Indian Utensils;* illustrated by Nancy Poydar; David McKay Co., Inc.; 1979; Grades 4 - 6

A well-documented description of how to construct various utensils used by Native people, the sub-title of the book gives it's intent - "Make Your Own Basketry, Woodenware, and Pottery with Natural Materials".

The author also tells how to identify, gather and prepare six common plants that can be used in the actual construction of a specific project. Step-by-step instructions are given which are accompanied by photos, drawings and diagrams to further aid the reader in actually producing a finished product.

Three main categories are the subject of the text - "Basketry", "Pottery" and "Woodenware". A brief introduction gives some background information for the reader, but the main focus is clearly the "make your own" project. Though most children will use the book for reading rather than for doing, it is a well-organized text that will be helpful for students wanting to learn more about Native people.

The book makes no pretenses to be a know all or be all kind of text. The approach is simple, direct and honest. There is nothing that will cause harm to a child's self-concept or to a child's attitude toward Native people.

Wolfson, Evelyn; *From Abenaki to Zuni: A Dictionary of Native American Tribes;* illustrated by William Sauts Bock; Walker and Co.; 1988; Grades 4 - 6

Included in this dictionary are sixty-eight North American Indian tribes with information on each group. The format of the book is to provide a short description of each group followed by a narrative of two or three pages giving further information. The beginning of each segment includes: "Meaning of Name", "Culture Area", "Location", "Dwelling Types", "Clothing Material", "Transportation" and "Food".

Profusely illustrated with over 250 pictures and maps, the book can be a tool for children in research studies or for the child doing recreational reading. The information is concise and accurate.

Included in the text is an appendix of major tribes of North America, a glossary, a suggested bibliography, a suggested reading list, and an index. All of these aids makes an accessible volume for the child interested in research.

The illustrator, William Sauts Bock, is a descendant of the Lenne Lenape tribe and a leader of the Lenape Indian Wolf Clan.

→≍←

Wood, Douglas; *Northwoods Cradle Song, From a Menominee Lullaby;* illustrated by Lisa Desimini; Simon and Schuster Books for Young Readers; 1996; Grades K – 2

An adaptation of a Menominee lullaby, the story flows with restful poetry. The soothing cradle song of the drowsy marsh hen, the weary sun, and the calling loon is combined with a number of peaceful images to lull a child to sleep. Ne pa Ko means sleepyhead.

"Ne pa Ko, my sleepy head, / Weary sun has gone to bed. / Silver star begins to shine, / Cradled in the tallest pine." "Sleep, little warrior, sleep. / Go to sleep. / Go to sleep." Some parents may question the use of the word warrior. The word "warrior" is part of the original Menominee lullaby.

In the Author's Note, Douglas Wood explains that he has researched the history of the lullaby and then "adapted and expanded the words". Wood explains that he found the original poem in **Runes of the North** by Sigurd Olson. The Menominee Lullaby is part of Chapter One, "The Dream Net", in Olson's book. The dream net is also known as a dream catcher. Olson says that it "was with the Menominees of Wisonsin that I found a translation of an ancient cradle song which to me embodies all of the beauty and poetry of the legend itself."

Douglas Wood is a composer and performer as well as the author of the award-winning book **Old Turtle.** His songs focus on the environment.

Lisa Desimini explains in the Illustrator's Note that her "sources for illustrations were taken from the Historical Society of Wisconsin and The Native American Museum library."

The text is rhythmic, simple, and soothing, making it a restful bedtime story. Lovely paintings filled with color, warmth, and spirit add a soothing dimension to the phrasing.

Wood, Douglas; ***Rabbit and the Moon;*** illustrated by Leslie Baker; Simon and Schuster Books for Young Readers; 1998; Grades K – 3

"Once, long ago-in the morning of the world-there was a rabbit." Rabbit knew the Earth from very near, but he had a dream "of riding upon the moon at night, far above the Earth." Rabbit asked Eagle to fly him to the moon, but Eagle was too busy. Not wanting to give up, Rabbit asked Red-tailed Hawk and Owl and Snow Goose. Rabbit continued asking the birds of the forest for help, but no one would fly him to the moon.

With ears drooping, Rabbit sat all alone. He was ready to give up when Crane said: "I will carry you to the moon, Rabbit." It was a difficult journey, but they finally made it. Crane's legs had changed, "… now Crane's legs were long and thin, stretched out from carrying Rabbit to the moon." With gratitude Rabbit gave Crane a gift, a bright red headdress.

In this enchanting pourquoi story, we learn why Crane's legs are so long, how he came by the red on his head, and why we still see Rabbit on the moon.

Delightful watercolors capture the mood of the story, engaging the reader in Rabbit's dilemma. Leslie Baker has illustrated many picture books. In 1988 she received the International Reading Association Children's Book Award.

Douglas Wood has skillfully adapted the Cree legend that nourishes dreams and respects friendship. Mr. Wood has received numerous awards, including the 1993 American

Bookseller's Association ABBY Award for **Old Turtle**. Mr. Wood is a musician, storyteller, Northwoods wilderness guide and a recording artist.

>‹-

Wood, Douglas; *The Windigo's Return; A North Woods Story;* illustrated by Greg Couch; Simon and Schuster Books for Young Readers; 1996; Grades 3 – 4

Everything was fine in the land of the Ojibwe, "until one day, when something strange happened." One by one people begin disappearing into the forest. "Now a dark fear crept through the village, like smoke from a dying campfire." One man, Waboose, remembered a story he had heard long before. "He knew that there was a Windigo in the forest and that the Windigo was eating the People!"

A young girl has a scheme to trap the Windigo and destroy the spirit being. The Windigo threatens to "come back again and again and again and I'll eat you, and you, and you, and your grandchildren, forever and ever." At night the people sprinkle the ashes of Windigo to prevent his return. The following summer, the ashes metamorphose into mosquitoes, eating the people as the Windigo had said.

Illustrations by Greg Couch are full of the atmosphere of the Windigo. The pictures glow with the colors of a campfire, whirling shapes, and dark tones. Matching the text, the paintings, in acrylic and colored pencil, take the reader into the dreaded world of the Windigo.

One caveat - the illustrations show the Ojibwe with large, stereotypical noses. What a shame.

Douglas Wood has captured the essence of a Windigo story. He is the author of **Old Turtle**, the winner of the 1993 American Booksellers' Association ABBY Award and the International Reading Association's Book of the Year Award.

The Tlingit have a similar story about a wicked giant who must be killed by fire and whose ashes become mosquitoes. Other tribes have comparable pourquoi stories about mosquitoes. John E. Smelcer shares a similar story from the Tlingit in his book, **The Raven and the Totem.**

→←

Worthylake, Mary M.; **Children of the Seed Gatherers;** illustrated by Henry Luhrs; Melmont; 1964; Grades 3 - 6

Kiho and Lema are Poma Indians. The Poma were among the Native people living in California and Oregon who were known as seed gatherers. The adventures of Kiho and Lema give an informative look at the seasonal activities of the Pomo.

It is a well-written book that provides an insight into one of the unique cultures of our country. The illustrations add clarity and interest to the text.

→←

Wright, Wendell; **Naha, Boy of the Seminoles;** illustrated by James Black; Coronet; 1957; Grades K - 3

A very simple text tells the story of a young Seminole boy living in the Florida Everglades. It is primarily a picture book with full color illustrations on every page. At the end of the book there are some questions concerning the content.

※

Yellow Robe, Rosebud (Ruth); *An Album of the American Indian;* Watts; 1969; Grades 3 - 6

The author has organized the book into five general categories: Indian Cultures of long ago, Coming of the White Man, The Indian Wars, Reservation Life and The Indian in the Modern Age. The section on cultures is divided into geographical locations. A glossary of Indian words is included at the end of the book.

The book comes alive through the effective use of black and white photographs. The photographs come from many sources and include photos of historical interest, cultural items and 1960s activities.

The author is Lakota.

※

Yellow Robe, Rosebud; *Tonweya and the Eagles and Other Lakota Indian Tales;* illustrated by Jerry Pinkney; Dial Press; 1979; Grades 4 - 6

For this notable collection of stories, Rosebud Yellow Robe has written down the stories she was told as a child. Her father,

Chief Chauncey Yellow Robe, was an hereditary chief of the Lakota-oyate tribe and the storyteller to whom she listened. He is the boy Chano who in turn had heard these stories from his father and from his grandparents.

Chano said: "People all over the world have their own way of life, but through their stories we find we can understand them and live with them."

Included are some of the favorite stories of the Lakota people: delightful tales of the red-winged eagles of Tonweya: a wonderful Iktomi story; Brave Bear's narrow escape from death; the account of Wastewin and the Beaver; plus many more. The foreword gives background information on Chano's family and an Epilogue as well as a glossary and pronunciation guide are helpful to the reader.

Rosebud Yellow Robe is an important storyteller.

Yolen, Jane; ***Rainbow Rider:*** illustrated by Michael Foreman; Thomas J. Crowell; 1974; Grades K - 3

In a brand new world, Rainbow Rider is the only living person, alone with no friends. He tried to make a friend out of sand, but when that didn't work, he decided to make a friend out of a tumbleweed. He continues trying until he finally succeeds.

The book jacket gushes that the author "has written an original modern creation myth." For the basis of her story she "evokes the beautiful creation myths of the Indians of North and South America." Stories from the people on two continents condensed into one easy-to-read, simplified tale. In reality, the narrative is a mishmash resulting in a book that dishonors Native people and their own powerful stories.

The author has made a career of creating new stories from traditional folktales. The illustrator lives in London.

⸺

Yolen, Jane; ***Sky Dogs;*** illustrated by Barry Moser; Harcourt Brace Jovanovich, Publishers; 1990; Grades 3 - 4

With the arrival of horses on the North American continent, the lives of Native people were dramatically changed and stories were told about the first sightings of these exciting creatures. ***Sky Dogs*** is the story of horses first appearing to the Blackfeet people. A small boy, later called He-who-loves-horses, reminisces about the reaction of the people when they encounter horses for the first time.

The story is simply told, but there are some complications with the tale. When seeing the horses, the men "muttered" for "they were afraid" and children hid behind their mother's skirts or the nearest tipi. The suggestion throughout the book is of a people who were naively afraid of these new animals rather than a people who were curious and who successfully lived their lives encountering the complexities of nature on a daily basis. These were not fearful people; these were people who were creative, ingenious, resourceful and brave.

The author's note says: "I have drawn from parts of these stories as well as parts of tales about the Blackfeet creator, Old

Man, to make a new story..." The resulting book is one that is a distortion and not one of the true stories told by Native people. The original stories are marvelous traditions.

An especially good book dealing with the arrival of the horse to North America is ***The Gift of the Sacred Dog*** by Paul Goble.

Yue, Charlotte and David Yue; ***The Pueblo;*** Houghton Mifflin Co.; 1986; Grades 4 - 6

In this well-illustrated book, Charlotte and David Yue introduce the reader to the world of the Pueblo. They describe the structure of Pueblo dwellings and the relationship of the people to the land. Life in a Pueblo and other structures is discussed. Text and illustrations combine to provide an honest and realistic account of the Pueblo people.

The author's respect for Native people is evident in the content and spirit of the material. The Yues write with accuracy and intelligence, which is all too rare in books published for and about Native people. And - they make it clear that the Pueblo life continues. "The old way of life goes on. They may change unimportant things like the clothing they wear and the kinds of houses they live in, but they continue to live their lives as part of the spiritual community of the Pueblo."

Yue, David and Charlotte Yue; *The Igloo;* Houghton Mifflin; 1988; Grades 4 - 6

The text and illustrations of this absorbing book are filled with precise detail as the reader is introduced to the world of the Eskimo. The material is well organized, concise and intelligently presented. Though the book is just over a hundred pages, it contains a wealth of information that will be useful to both children and adults. The book begins with a brief history of the groups of people that are referred to as Eskimos. Poetic descriptions of the seasons and their relationship with the life of the people are powerful.

The Yues describe the construction of an igloo and tell what it is like to live in one. They discuss clothing, food, families, games, travel in the Arctic and community life. A good bibliography is included at the end of the text. The illustrations are filled with fascinating detail and demonstrate an appreciation for the life of the Native people. Beyond an enjoyable read, the book is an excellent resource for reference and curriculum support.

The Yues received the Parents' Choice Award for ***The Wigwam and the Longhouse.***

→✢←

Yue, David and Charlotte Yue; *The Tipi: A Center of Native American Life;* Knopf; 1984; Grades 4 – 6

"An encampment of tipis on the Great Plains must have been an awesome sight - a large circle of cone-shaped tents standing majestically against the flat landscape." The Yues present an informative and intelligent book on a "sophisticated dwelling designed and built with enormous skill to meet the demands of life on the Great Plains".

The text is a straightforward account of the structure of the tipi, furnishings, elements of design, tipi manners, the spiritual importance of the tipi and much more. It deals with a broad look at the life of the Native people - the legends, social life, the abiding spirituality, the constant search for food as well as a chapter on comforts and luxuries. An afterword is included on "What Happened to Tipis".

David Yue has a Master of Architecture degree and his excellent black and white line drawings are handled with clarity and accuracy. The exceptional prose by Charlotte Yue is able to teach about the traditions and life of a complex society. The book deserves a superior rating.

→←

Zitkala-Sa; ***Old Indian Legends;*** illustrated by Angel De Cora; University of Nebraska Press; 1985; Grades 4 - 6

Originally published in 1902, the writing reflects the time period when, according to the introduction, "She was being formed into a cultured, Christian lady". Agnes M. Picotte continues in the foreword: "Zitkala-Sa impressed me as a great role model for American Indians interested in music, oratory, and writing. A master of language, she also became a violinist of some note, played other instruments, and sang solo and in choral groups". The foreword gives an insight into the life of this Yankton-Nakota woman who told stories in "an easy, engaging style with a certain dramatic power".

Most of the fourteen stories are about Iktomi, the Spider, who is always in trouble of some kind. Iktomi is the trickster - sneaky, selfish, lazy and vain.

"Iktomi is a wily fellow. His hands are always kept in mischief. He prefers to spread a snare rather than to earn the smallest thing with honest hunting...Poor Iktomi cannot help being a little imp. And so long as he is a naughty fairy, he cannot find a single friend."

Part of the 1902 phraseology is the author's use of the word "fairy". That was a term used for her white audience and not part of the original stories. She also used the term "Indian Princess" which was an expected terminology of the time period.

As is noted on the book's cover: "Until her death in 1938, Zitala-Sa stood between two cultures as preserver and translator." This is a valuable book and truly a gift to the reader.

Index

A

Abisch, Roz 1
Adopted by Eagles 123, 124
Ahyoka and the Talking Leaves 275
Akavak, An Eskimo Journey 160
Alaska; Pioneer Stories of a Twentieth-Century Frontier 236
Alice Yazzie's Year 212
Aliki 2
All of You Was Singing 205
All Our Relatives, Traditional Native American Thoughts about Nature 124
American Indian Beadwork 171
American Indian Mythology 212
American Indian Utensils 335
Amigo 285
Amon, Aline 2
Anderson, Jean 187
And it is Still That Way 20
Annie and the Old One 235
Anpao, An American Indian Odyssey 150
An Album of the American Indian 341
Apaches 174, 196
Apache Boy 331
Archambault, John xx, 214
Arctic Memories 105, 106
Arctic Son 118
Armer, Laura 3
Arrow to the Sun 222, 224
Aseban 201
Ashabranner, Brent 3, 5
Awiakta, Marilou 6, 7, 70
A Boy of Tache 39
A Breeze Swept Through 313
A Child's Alaska 243
A Day in Oraibi: A Hopi Indian Village 177
A Dog Team for Ongluk 287
A God on Every Mountain Top 19
A Haida Potlatch 306
A Legend from Crazy Horse Clan 38
A Long Time Ago is Just Like Today 216
A Pictorial History of the American Indian 196
A Playmate for Puna 288
A Promise is a Promise 242
A Thousand Years of American Indian Storytelling 149
A Time to be Brave 192

B

Badger, The Mischief Maker 151
Bailey, Ralph Edgar xx, 7
Baker, Betty xx, xxii, 8, 10
Baker, Laura Nelson 11
Baker, Olaf 12
Bales, Carol Ann 12
Bamman, Henry 13
Banks, Lynne Reid ix, xx, 14, 15, 16
Bannon, Laura 16
Barnouw, Victor xxi, 17
Barth, Edna 18
Baylor, Byrd 19, 20, 21, 22, 23, 24, 256, 285
Bealer, Alex W. 24
Beals, Frank Lee 25, 26
Bear's Heart 310
Beck, Barbara L. xxi, 27, 28
Before You Came This Way 21
Behn, Harry 28
Belting, Natalia 29, 30
Benchley, Nathaniel 30, 31
Benny's Flag 193
Benton-Benai, Edward 32
Bernstein, Margery 33
Betrayed 298
Between Sacred Mountains: Navajo Stories and Lessons from the Land 269
Beyond the Ridge 125
Bierhorst, John 34, 35, 36, 37
Big Crow, Moses Nelson (Eyo Hiktepi) 38

Andie Peterson

Black Hills: Sacred Hills 76
Black Star, Bright Dawn 249
Blades, Ann 39
Blassingame, Wyatt 39
Bleeker, Sonia xxv, 40, 41, 42, 43, 44, 45, 46, 47, 48
Blood, Charles 48
Blue Canyon Horse 77
Blue Jay and the Monster 72
Brave Eagle's Account of the Fetterman Fight 126
Brewer, Linda Skinner 49
Brewster, Benjamin (pseud. - Mary Elting) 49
Brink, Carol Ryrie 50, 53
Brother Eagle, Sister Sky; A Message from Chief Seattle 177
Brown, Dee 53, 105
Bruchac, Joseph ix, xxii, 54, 55, 56, 57, 58, 59, 60, 67, 68, 69, 70, 71, 207
Bryant, Kathleen 60, 61
Buckskin Brigade 187
Buff, Conrad 62
Buff, Mary 62, 63
Buffalo Bill 98, 99
Buffalo Boy 74
Buffalo Days 166
Buffalo Woman 127, 132, 133
Building an Igloo 305
Bulla, Clyde Robert 64, 65, 66
Burshears, J.F. 171

C

Caddie Woodlawn 50, 53
Caduto, Michael 67, 69, 70
Campbell, Camilla 72
Campbell, Karel 72
Cedar, Georgiana Dorcas 73
Chandler, Edna 74, 75, 76
Charging Eagle, Tom 76
Cheer Up Old Man 216
Cherokees 175
Cherokee Animal Tales 284

Chi-Wee 240
Chief Black Hawk 25
Chief Joseph 7, 77, 312
Chief Joseph's Own Story 77
Chief Seattle, Great Statesman 240
Children of the Seed Gatherers 340
Child of the Navajos 268
Chipmunk in the Forest 87
Chow, Octavio 274
Circle of Seasons 78
Clamshell Boy: A Makah Legend 90
Clark, Ann Nolan 77, 78, 79, 80, 82, 83, 84, 85
Clark, Ian Christie 86
Close to the Rising Sun: Algonkian Indian Legends 325
Clutesi, George C. 86, 87
Clymer, Eleanor 87, 88
Clymer, Theodore 89
Coatsworth, Elizabeth 89, 90
Cochise of Arizona 196
Cohlene, Terri 90
Coleman, Sister Bernard 91
Collura, Mary-Ellen Lang 91
Cooper, Amy Jo 92
Corn is Maize 2
Costo, Rupert 149
Coyote, A Trickster Tale from the American Southwest 223
Coyote Cry 21
Coyote Tales 181
Crazy Horse, Sioux Warrior 231
Creekmore, Raymond 94
Custer's Last Stand 269

D

D'Amato, Alex 97
D'Amato, Janet 97
d'Aulaire, Edgar Parin 98, 99
d'Aulaire, Ingri 98, 99
Dakotas 175
Dalgliesh, Alice 94, 95
Dancing Cloud 62
Dancing Feathers 191

Dan Frontier with the Indians 174
Death of the Iron Horse 128
dePaola, Tomie 100
Discovering the Inca Ice Maiden, My Adventures on Ampato 267
Doctor Coyote 35
Dog Story 209
Dolch, Edward 101, 102, 103
Dolch, Marguerite 101, 102, 103
Dorian, Edith 103
Do Not Annoy the Indians xx, 8
Dream of the Blue Heron xxi, 17
Dream Quest 92, 93
Dream Wolf 129, 130
Drift 221

E

Eagle Feather 64
Eagle Mask: A West Coast Indian Tale 161
Eagle Wing 91
Eastman, Charles 104
Edge of Two Worlds 183
Ehrlich, Amy 105
Ekoomiak, Normee 105
Ellis, Mel 106
Elston, Georgia 107
Elting, Mary 108
Erdoes, Richard 108
Esbensen, Barbara Juster 109, 110, 111
Estep, Irene 112

F

Farguhar, Margaret C. 112
Feague, Mildred 113
Foods the Indians Gave Us 146
Food in History 312
Forbidden Frontier 142
Four Corners of the Sky 89
Friskey, Margaret 114, 115
Fritz, Jean 115, 116
From Abenaki to Zuni: A Dictionary of Native American Tribes 336
Frozen Fire 161

G

Gebhard, Wilfried 117
George, Jean Craighead 118, 119, 120, 121
George Morrison, The Story of an American Indian 193
Getting to Know American Indians Today 314
Giving: Ojibwa Stories and Legends from the Children of Curve Lake 107
Glooscap and his Magic 152
Glubok, Shirley 122, 123
Goble, Dorothy 126, 130, 138
Goble, Paul 123, 124, 125, 126, 127, 128, 129, 130, 131, 132, 133, 134, 135, 136, 137, 138, 139
God is in the Mountain 186
Good Hunting, Little Indian 252
Granny and the Indians 252
Grossman, Virginia 140
Groundhog's Horse 271

H

Hader, Berta 141
Hader, Elmer 141
Hah-Nee of the Cliff Dwellers 62
Half-Breed 198
Happily May I Walk, American Indian and Alaskan Natives Today 153
Harris, Christie 142, 143, 144
Haseley, Dennis 145
Hays, Vernon 146
Hays, Wilma 146, 147, 148
Henry, Edna 149
Henry, Jeannette 149
Hiawatha and Megissogwon 207
Highwater, Jamake 150, 151
High Elk's Treasure 300
Hill, Kay 151, 152
Hirschfelder, Arlene 153
His Indian Brother 334
Hodgers, Margaret 154
Hofsinde, Robert 155, 156, 157
Hokahey! American Indians Then and

Now 103
Holberg, Ruth Langland 158
Holling, Holling C. 159
Hood, Flora 159
Horsemen of the Western Plateaus: The Nez Perce Indians 44
Houses of Bark: Tipi, Wigwam and Longhouse 290
Houses of Hide and Earth 291
Houses of Snow, Skin and Bones 292
Houston, James 160, 161, 162, 163, 164, 165
How Summer Came to Canada 318
How the Birds Got Their Colours 180
Hoyt-Goldsmith, Diane 166, 167, 168
Hudson, Jan 169
Hunt, W. Ben 171, 172, 173
Hurley, William 174

I

If You Lived With the Cherokee 278
If You Lived With the Sioux Indians 227
Iktomi and the Berries 134
Iktomi and the Boulder 135
Iktomi and the Buffalo Skull 136
Iktomi and the Buzzard 136
Iktomi and the Ducks 137
Inatuk's Friend 241
Indians, The First Americans 215
Indians at Home 155
Indians of the Longhouse: The Story of the Iroquois 45
Indians of the Plains (Rachlis) 263
Indians of the Plains (Thompson) 315
Indians on the Move 157
Indian and Eskimo Art of Canada 86
Indian Boyhood 104
Indian Campfire Tales 259
Indian Captive: The Story of Mary Jemison 201
Indian Chiefs of the West 311
Indian Children of America 112
Indian Crafts 97
Indian Creation Stories 286

Indian Fighter: The Story of Nelson A. Miles xx, 7
Indian Fishing and Camping 155
Indian Hunting 156
Indian Legacy: Native American Influences on World Life and Cultures 262
Indian Tales 254, 265, 341
Indian Two Feet and His Eagle Feather 115
Indian Two Feet and the Grizzly Bear 114
Indian Warriors and their Weapons 157
Indian Women 327
In My Mother's House 79, 80, 81
Iroquois 112
Iroquois Stories: Heroes and Heroines, Monsters and Magic 56
Israel, Marion 174
I Breathe a New Song: Poems of the Eskimo 206
I Sing for the Animals 134

J

Jackson, Garnet 176
James, Harry C. 177
Jeffers, Susan xxix, 177, 178, 240
Jimmy Yellow Hawk 301
Johnny Stands 251
Johnston, Basil 180
Johnston, Johanna 180
Johnston, Patronella 181
John Billington, Friend of Squanto 65
Jones, Hettie 181, 182
Jones, Weyman 183, 184
Josefina and the Hanging Tree 218
Julie of the Wolves 120, 121, 122

K

Kalak of the Ice 190
Kanahena, A Cherokee Story 279
Katz, Jane B. 185
Katz, Ruth J. 185
Keats, Ezra Jack 186

Keepers of Life: Discovering Plants Through Native American Stories and Earth Activities for Children 70
Keepers of the Animals: Native American Stories and Wildlife Activities for Children 67
Keepers of the Earth: Native American Stories and Environmental Activities for Children 69
Kemi-An Indian Boy: Before the White Man Came 63
Kennedy, Leonard 13
Kevin Cloud: A Chippewa Boy in the City 12
Kimball, Yeffe 187
King Island Christmas 274
Kjelgaard, Jim 187, 190
Kleitsch, Christel 191, 192
Knots on a Counting Rope xx, 214, 215
Kobrin, Janet 33
Kohn, Bernice 192
Kokopelli's Gift 60
Kostich, Dragos 193
Krasilovsky, Phyllis 193
Kusugak, Michael 242, 243

L

Lacapa, Michael 194
Lacy, Dan 194
Ladder to the Sky 110, 111
LaFarge, Oliver 196
Lampman, Evelyn Sibley 198, 199
Lavine, Sigmund 200
LeGarde, Amelia 201
Lenski, Lois 201, 202
Leonard, Jonathan Norton 203
Lerner, Marguerite Rush 204
LeSueur, Meridel 204
Let's Be Indians xxvi, 253
Let's Find Out About Indians 289
Levine, Joseph 260
Lewis, Richard 205, 206
Lightfoot 292, 293

Link, Martin 48
Little Elk Hunts Buffalo: As Little Elk Tells it in Picture Writing 225
Little House on the Prairie 332
Little Indian 254
Little Sioux Girl 202
Little Sky Eagle and the Pumpkin Drum 113
Little Thunder 73
Little Wolf 228
Little Wolf and the Thunder Stick 74
Lodge Stories in Basic Vocabulary 101
Lokoshi Learns to Hunt Seals 94
London, Jonathan 59
Long, Sylvia ix, xxvii, 140
Longfellow, Henry Wadsworth 207, 208
Lord of the Dawn: Quetzalcoatl 289
Luenn, Nancy 208
Luke and the Indians 158
Lyons, Grant 209
Lyons, Oren 209

M

Maestro, Betsy 210
Magic Maize 63
Maher, Ramona 212
Manabozho and the Bullrushes 217
Many Smokes; Many Moons, A Chronology of American Indian History Through Indian Art 151
Maria Tallchief 316
Marriott, Alice 213
Marriott, Alice Lee 212, 214
Martin, Bill, Jr. 214
Martin, Patricia Miles 215
Martinson, David 216, 217, 218
Marvin, Isabel Ridout 218
Massasoit, Friend of the Pilgrims 326
Mathers, Sharon 219
Max, Jill 220
Mayne, William 221
McDermott, Beverly Brodsky 222
McDermott, Gerald 222, 223, 224,

225
McGaw, Jessie 225, 226
McGaw, Jessie Brewer 226
McGovern, Ann 227, 228
McGraw, Eloise Jarvis 228
McNeer, May 230
Meadowcroft, Enid LaMonte 231
Medicine Man's Daughter 82
Meigs, Cornelia 233
Meredith, Robert 295
Miles, Miska 235
Miller, Luree 236
Miller, Scott 236
Mission Indians of California 45
Mitchell, Barbara 237
Moccasin Trail 228
Momaday, Natachee Scott 239
Montgomery, Elizabeth Rider 240
Moon, Carl 240
Moon, Grace 240, 241
Morrow, Suzanne Stark 241
Munsch, Robert 242
Murphy, Claire Rudolf 243
Musicians of the Sun 224
Mystery Adventure of the Indian Burial Ground 13

N

Nabokov, Peter 244
Naha, Boy of the Seminoles 340
Nannabah's Friend 258
National Museum of the American Indian xxv, 245
Native American Cookbook 149
Native American Testimony, An Anthology of Indian and White Relations: First Encounter to Dispossession 244
Navaho Sister 199
Naylor, Phyllis Reynolds 246
Nessa's Fish 208
Noko, Captive of Columbus 147
Northwoods Cradle Song, From a Menominee Lullaby 336

Nutik, the Wolf Pup 120

O

O'Dell, Scott 249
Ojibway 175
Ojibwa Summer 163
Old Indian Legends 346
Once More Upon a Totem 143
Once Upon a Totem 143
One Little Indian 241
One Small Blue Bead 285
Only the Names Remain: The Cherokees and the Trail of Tears 24
On Mother's Lap 286
Ortiz, Simon J. 250
Out of the Earth I Sing: Poetry and Songs of Primitive Peoples of the World 206
Out of the Silence 266
Owl in the Cedar Tree 239
O Children of the Wind and Pines 11
O Wakaga: Activities for Learning About the Plains Indians 49

P

Pacific Coast Indians of North America 209
Paige, Harry W. 251
Painted Pony Runs Away: As Little Elk Tells it in Picture Writing 226
Parish, Peggy 252, 253, 254
Parker, Arthur C. 254
Parnall, Peter 255
Penner, Lucille Recht 256
People of the Snow; Eskimos of Arctic Canada 316
Perrine, Mary 258
Phillips, W.S. 259
Pilgrim Courage 295
Pilgrim Thanksgiving 147
Pine, Tillie S. 260, 261
Poatgieter, Hermina 262
Pocahontas and the Strangers 65
Pontiac, Lion in the Forest 148

Pueblo Storyteller 167
Pumpkin Personalities 185

R

Rabbit and the Moon 338
Rachlin, Carol K. 212
Rachlis, Eugene 263
Radford, Ruby L. 264
Rainbow Rider 342
Raskin, Edith 265
Raskin, Joseph 265
Raven, A Trickster Tale from the Pacific Northwest 225
Raven's Cry 144, 145
Real Wild Rice 217
Red Fox and his Canoe 30
Red Hawk's Account of Custer's Last Battle 138
Red Man, White Man, African Chief: The Story of Skin Color 204
Reid, Dorothy M. 265
Reindeer Trail 141, 142
Reinhard, Johan 267
Reit, Seymour 268
Reynolds, Quentin 269
Ride the Cold Wind 309
Rising Fawn and the Fire Mystery 6
Rising Voices, Writings of Young Native Americans 153
Rockpoint Community School 269
Rockwell, Anne 270, 271
Rockwood, Joyce 271, 272
Rogers, Jean 274
Rohmer, Harriet 274
Roop, Connie 275, 277, 278, 279
Roop, Peter 275, 277, 278, 279
Ross, Ann 310
Roth, Susan L. 279, 281
Russell, Francis 281

S

Sacajawea 326
Sacajawea, Indian Guide 39
Salt Boy 258, 259

Sandoz, Mari 284
Scheer, George F. 284
Schweitzer, Byrd Baylor 285
Scott, Ann Herbert 286
Secret of the Andes 82, 83
Sedna: An Eskimo Myth 222
Seeing the Circle 57
Sequoya 264
Sequoyah, Leader of the Cherokees 213
Seton, Julia 286
Shannon, Terry 287, 288
Shapp, Charles 289
Shapp, Martha 289
Shearer, Tony 289
Shemay, The Bird in the Sugarbush 218
Shemie, Bonnie 290, 291, 292
Shippen, Katherine 292
Showers, Paul 293
Siberell, Anne 294
Sidewalk Indian 106
Singer, Beverly R. 153, 154
Skinner, Linda 49
Skunny Wundy, Seneca Indian Tales 254
Sky Dogs 343
Sleator, William 294
Small Wolf 31
Smith, E. Brooks 295
Smucker, Barbara C. 297
Sneve, Virginia Driving Hawk 298, 299, 300, 301
Snow Bear 121, 122
Songs from this Earth on Turtle's Back: Contemporary American Indian Poetry 58
Songs of the Chippewa 37
Songs of the Dream People: Chants and Images from the Indians and Eskimos of North America 163
Son of Raven, Son of Deer 86
Sparrow Hawk 204
Speare, Elizabeth George 302
Spider Spins a Story: Fourteen Legends from Native America 220
Squanto, Friend of the Pilgrims 66
Squaw Man's Son 199

Stan, Susan 304
Star Boy 139, 140
Star Mountain and Other Legends of Mexico 72
Steiner, Stan 304
Steltzer, Ulli 305, 306
Stephens, Paul 191, 192
Steptoe, John 307
Stones, Bones and Arrowheads 288
Strete, Craig Kee 308
Surany, Anico 309
Surpee, Burton 310
Sutton, Felix 310, 311
Sweetgrass 169, 170, 171

T

Tafoya, Terry 219
Taka and his Dog 75
Tales of Nanabozho 265
Tales of Nokomis 181
Tales of the Iroquois 226, 313, 314
Talking Hands 2
Talking Leaves: The Story of Sequoyah 192
Tall Boy and the Coyote 75
Tannahill, Reay 312
Tapahonso, Luci 313
Teepee Stories in Basic Vocabulary 102
Tehanetorens 226, 313
Ten Little Rabbits x, xxvii, 140
Tepee Tales of the American Indian: Retold for Our Times 53
They Put on Masks 23
The Adventures of Hiawatha 325
The American Indian 329
The Angry Moon 294
The Apache Indian: Raiders of the Southwest 40
The Art of American Indian Cooking 187
The Art of the Eskimo 122
The Art of the North American Indian 123
The Aztec: Indians of Mexico 41
The Book of Indians 159

The Buffalo Jump 277
The Cave 89
The Cherokee: Indians of the Mountains 42
The Chichi Hoohoo Bogeyman 299
The Chippewa Indians: Rice Gatherers of the Great Lakes 42
The Complete Book of Indian Crafts and Lore 172
The Complete How-to Book of Indian Craft 173
The Courage of Sarah Noble 94
The Creation of the Sun and Moon 321
The Crow Indians: Hunters of the Northern Plains 43
The Dancing Fox, Arctic Folktales 34
The Dancing Stars: An Iroquios Legend 270
The Delaware Indians: Eastern Fishermen and Farmers 43
The Desert is Theirs 20, 22, 235, 256
The Desert People 79
The Discovery of the Americas 210
The Double Life of Pocahontas xxiv, 115
The Earth is on a Fish's Back: Tales of Beginnings 29
The Earth Under Sky Bear's Feet: Native American Poems of the Land 54
The Eskimo: Arctic Hunters and Trappers 44
The Eskimos Knew 260
The Fire Bringer: A Paiute Indian Legend 154
The Fire Plume: Legends of the American Indian 36
The Fire Stealer 317
The First Book of Indians 49
The First Book of the Aztecs 27
The First Book of the Maya 28
The First Farmers 203
The First Strawberries, A Cherokee Story 55
The First Thanksgiving (George) 119
The First Thanksgiving (Jackson) 176
The First Year xxiv, 231

The Flute Player, An Apache Folktale 194
The French and Indian Wars 281
The Friendly Wolf 130
The Games the Indians Played 200
The Gift of the Sacred Dog 131, 344
The Girl Who Loved Wild Horses 133
The Girl Who Married a Ghost and Other Tales from the North American Indians 36
The Goat in the Rug 48
The Golden Book of Crafts and Hobbies 173
The Golden Frog 309
The Good Giants and the Bad Pukwudgies 116
The Good Llama 271
The Great Buffalo Race 109
The Great Fish 255, 256
The Haunted Igloo 321
The Hopi Way 108
The Horsecatcher 284
The How and Why Book of North American Indians 310
The Igloo 345
The Inca: Indians of the Andes 45
The Incas Knew 260
The Indians and the Strangers 180
The Indians Knew 261
The Indian in the Cupboard xx, 14
The Invisible Hunters/Los Cazadores Invisibles 274
The Last Horse 304
The Legend of the Bluebonnet 100
The Legend of the White Buffalo Woman 132
The Little Indian and the Angel 113
The Little Indian Basket Maker 83
The Little Indian Pottery Maker 84
The Loon's Necklace 319
The Lost Colony 194
The Mamook Book: Activities for Learning About the Northwest Coast Indians 219
The Mishomis Book: The Voice of the Ojibway 32

The Mountain Goats of Temlaham 319
The Navajo: Herders, Weavers and Silversmiths 46
The Ojibwe 304
The Painted Cave 28
The Path to Snowbird Mountain: Cherokee Legends 320
The People Shall Continue xxii, 32, 250
The Praying Flute 289
The Pueblo 46, 344
The Pueblo Indians: Farmers of the Rio Grande 46
The Return of the Buffaloes 133, 139
The Return of the Indian 15
The Ring in the Prairie 37
The Scared One 145
The Sea Hunters: Indians of the Northwestern Coast 47
The Secret of the Indian 16
The Seminole Indians 47
The Sign of the Beaver 302
The Sioux Indians: Hunters and Warriors of the Plains 48
The Sound of Flutes 108
The Spider, The Cave and The Pottery Bowl 88
The Stars are Silver Reindeer 30
The Star Maiden 111
The Story of Jumping Mouse 307
The Story of Light 281
The Summer Maker: An Ojibway Indian Myth 33
The Sunflower Garden 324
The Talking Leaf 184
The Thanksgiving Story 95
The Tipi: A Center of Native American Life 345
The Trees Stand Shining: Poetry of the North American Indian 182
The True Story of Pocahontas 256
The Turquoise Horse 159
The White Archer: an Eskimo Legend 165
The Willow Whistle 233
The Windigo's Return; A North Woods

Story 339
The Wind Eagle and Other Abenaki Stories 60
Thirteen Moons on Turtles Back: A Native American Year of Moons 59
This for That 85
This Song Remembers: Self-Portraits of Native Americans in the Arts 185
Thompson, Hildegard 314
Thompson, Ruth 315
Three Fools and a Horse 10
Tikta' Liktak: An Eskimo Legend 164
Tobias, Tobi 316
Tolbloom, Wanda 316
Tomahawks and Trombones 237
Tonweya and the Eagles and Other Lakota Indian Tales 341
Totem Pole 168
Toye, William 317, 318, 319
To Live in Two Worlds 5
To Spoil the Sun 272
To Walk the Sky Path 246
Traveller Bird 320, 321
Traven, B. 321
Turkeys, Pilgrims, and Indian Corn: The Story of the Thanksgiving Symbols 18
Turner, Bonnie 321
'Twas in the Moon of Wintertime 1

U

Udry, Janice May 324

V

Viadure, Morris 274
Voight, Virginia 325, 326

W

Walk in My Moccasins 327
Waltrip, Lela 327
Waltrip, Rufus 327
Warren, Mary Phraner 327
War Chief of the Seminoles 230

Waterless Mountain 3
Whale in the Sky 294
What Eddie Can Do xxvi, 117
When Clay Sings 24
When Grandfather Journeys into Winter 308
When the Moon is New 16
When the Rain Sings, Poems by Young Native Americans 245
When Thunders Spoke 301
Where the Buffaloes Begin 12
White, Anne Terry 329
Whitehead, Robert 13
Wigwam in the City 297
Wigwam Stories in Basic Vocabulary 103
Wilde, Arthur L. 331
Wilder, Laura Ingalls 332
Wilson, Hazel 334
Wilson, W.N. 103
Winners 91
Winter Telling Stories 214
Wolfson, Evelyn 335, 336
Wolf Brother 190
Wolf Run: A Caribou Eskimo Tale 165
Wood, Douglas 336, 338, 339
Worthylake, Mary M. 340
Wounded Knee 105
Wright, Wendell 340

Y

Yellow Robe, Rosebud 341
Yolen, Jane 342, 343
Young Hawk 76
Your Skin and Mine 293
Yue, Charlotte 344, 345
Yue, David 344, 345

Z

Zeilinger, Ron 76
Zitkala-Sa 346

About the Author

Andie Peterson holds the distinction of being one of the few women who has been honored with an Eagle Feather. The award came from the Grand Portage Band of Lake Superior Chippewa and the Minnesota Chippewa Tribe. At the same honoring ceremony, she was given an Anishinabe name: Gigizheb Anang Ikwe which means Morning Star Woman.

Andie was a Minnesota Teacher of the Year, a finalist for the National Teacher of the Year Award, and received the Leo Reano Award from the National Education Association. She was the recipient of special awards from two Minnesota governors, received three Minnesota School Bell Awards for editorial writing, was a Knight Ridder/Duluth News Tribune Teacher of the Year, and the Northland Foundation Teacher of the Year. She also received the WCCO Good Neighbor Award.

She served on numerous boards including a Minnesota Department of Education committee and a Minnesota Board of Teaching committee on gifted education licensure. Andie has published over two-hundred columns and articles and has been a featured speaker at workshops, colleges, churches, and school districts. She has served on many local, state, and national boards and committees.

Andie served four terms as Mayor of the City of Grand Marais, Minnesota. Her teaching career was in Minnesota where she taught school at Grand Portage and Grand Marais. She is married and has four children.

Northern Explosion, A Laura Kjelstad Mystery, is Andie's first novel and is available through local bookstores and Internet sources.

A Second Look, Native Americans in Children's Books
By Andie Peterson